HISTORY OF WORLD ARCHITECTURE

Pier Luigi Nervi, General Editor

ROMAN ARCHITECTURE

John B. Ward-Perkins

Harry N. Abrams, Inc., Publishers, New York

Series Coordinator: Giuseppe Positano de Vincentiis

Produced under the supervision of Carlo Pirovano,
editorial director of Electa Editrice

Design: Diego Birelli, art director of Electa Editrice
Photographs: Bruno Balestrini
Drawings: Sheila E. Gibson

Library of Congress Cataloging in Publication Data

Ward-Perkins, John Bryan, 1912–
  Roman architecture.
  (History of world architecture)
  Bibliography: p.
  Includes index.
  1. Architecture, Roman. I. Title.
NA310.W32   722'.7   75–29475
ISBN 0–8109–1022–5

PREFACE

Architectural criticism has nearly always been concerned with the visible aspect of individual buildings, taking this to be the decisive factor in the formulation of value judgments and in the classification of those "styles" which appear in textbooks, and which have thus become common knowledge. But once it is recognized that every building is, by definition, a work subject to the limitations imposed by the materials and building techniques at hand, and that every building must prove its stability, as well as its capacity to endure and serve the needs it was built for, it becomes clear that the aesthetic aspect alone is inadequate when we come to appraise a creative activity, difficult enough to judge in the past, rapidly becoming more complex in our own day, and destined to become more so in the foreseeable future.

Nevertheless, what has struck me most, on studying the architecture of the past and present, is the fact that the works which are generally regarded by the critics and the general public as examples of pure beauty are also the fruit of exemplary building techniques, once one has taken into account the quality of the materials and the technical knowledge available. And it is natural to suspect that such a coincidence is not entirely casual.

Building in the past was wholly a matter of following static intuitions, which were, in turn, the result of meditation, experience, and above all of an understanding of the capacity of certain structures and materials to resist external forces. Meditation upon structural patterns and the characteristics of various materials, together with the appraisal of one's own experiences and those of others, is an act of love toward the process of construction for its own sake, both on the part of the architect and his collaborators and assistants. Indeed, we may wonder whether this is not the hidden bond which unites the appearance and substance of the finest buildings of the past, distant though that past may be, into a single "thing of beauty."

One might even think that the quality of the materials available not only determined architectural patterns but also the decorative detail with which the first simple construction was gradually enriched.

One might find a justification for the difference in refinement and elegance between Greek architecture, with its basic use of marble—a highly resistant material, upon which the most delicate carvings can be carried out—and the majestic concrete structures of Roman architecture, built out of a mixture of lime and pozzolana, and supported by massive walls, to compensate for their intrinsic weaknesses.

Would it be too rash to connect these objective architectural characteristics with the different artistic sensibilities of the two peoples?

One must recognize, therefore, the importance of completing the description of the examples illustrated with an interpretation of their constructional and aesthetic characteristics, so that the connection between the twin aspects of building emerges as a natural, logical consequence.

This consequence, if understood and accepted in good faith by certain avant-garde circles, could put an end to the disastrous haste with which our architecture is rushing toward an empty, costly, and at times impractical formalism. It might also recall architects and men of culture to a more serene appraisal of the objective elements of building and to the respect that is due to a morality of architecture. For this is just as important for the future of our cities as is morality, understood as a rule of life, for an orderly civil existence.

PIER LUIGI NERVI

TABLE OF CONTENTS

Of all the arts, architecture is that in which the Roman claim to originality is strongest. Westerners are still living in the afterglow of an age that was brought up to regard the Parthenon as the supreme surviving architectural creation of classical antiquity. To our ancestors it would have seemed heresy to assert that, despite the manifest perfections of the Parthenon, the Pantheon in Rome is unquestionably the more important monument in terms both of the creative architectural thinking of its time and of its significance for the future of European architecture. And yet the heresy of yesterday is well on the way to becoming the orthodoxy of today. For that reason alone the history of Roman architecture would be worth investigation, and one of the principal aims of this book will in fact be to document and to explain the emergence of the "new" Roman architecture—of which the Pantheon is at once a symbol and one of the outstanding achievements.

If that were the sole purpose of this volume, the task would be a quite simple one. But architecture is also an expression of the culture of a particular time and place, and few subjects have been more hotly and inconclusively debated than the nature of the cultural relationship between the two successive centers of power in the classical world, Greece and Rome. In the case of architecture the problem is less complex than in some of the other arts—sculpture, for example—since the distinctive architectural personality of Rome is too clear, too explicit to brook denial. Nevertheless, so much of its formal vocabulary was borrowed directly from Greece, and so many previous discussions of the subject have focused upon this relationship, that a brief statement of the nature of the problem is a necessary preliminary here.

Greek architecture had been the product of a self-confident civilization which throughout its great creative period, from the seventh to the fourth centuries B.C., managed to maintain an extraordinary unity of artistic purpose. Confronted by a building or a statue produced by Greece, or under Greek influence, the layman today has no problem in recognizing, or the art historian in defining, the qualities that distinguish it as Greek. The credit for this must of course go first to the rare creative genius of the Greeks themselves. It is important, however, to recognize that this genius was fostered and its impact greatly enhanced by historical circumstance: in matters of art the cultures with which Greece was in direct contact prior to the conquests of Alexander the Great were receivers, not givers (the only major exception was Egypt, from which Archaic Greece did indeed learn much). The Persian genius lay emphatically in other fields; the Semitic peoples of the Levant had little to offer beyond a fund of borrowed motifs and a superb tradition of technical craftsmanship;

and everywhere else the classical Greeks found themselves dealing with peoples whose levels of material culture made them eager recipients of Greek artifacts and ideas, with at first very little to offer in exchange. Small wonder, then, that from Sicily to the Black Sea—and after Alexander far out into the ancient East—the products of Greek art struck deep, leaving a mark which today can still almost unerringly be recognized.

Rome had a very different effect. Roman art and architecture were born and took shape in a world that was already dominated both by the substance and by the idea of Greek achievement, first through the Greek colonies in the West, at second hand through Etruria, and then—after Rome's eastward expansion—directly from metropolitan Greece itself. The relationship was a highly complex one, involving other cultures as well; and although today we implicitly hold Greece and Rome jointly responsible for the civilization of classical antiquity, art is one of the fields in which the precise nature of the Roman contribution is hard to define and remains the subject of much controversy. At one extreme are those scholars who have sought for some specifically and intrinsically "Roman" ingredient which could be regarded as responsible for the innate "Roman-ness" (romanità) of its products. At the other extreme are those who have been prepared to dismiss all Roman art as merely a late, and by the standards of Greek classicism a decadent, extension of Greek art. Few scholars today would question that the reality lies somewhere between those two extreme views. It is generally accepted that the art and architecture of Rome were the products of a complex and continually developing historical situation within which political, social, and economic factors all played an important part. Such a situation by its very nature precludes simplistic interpretations of the art to which it gives rise. Granted that the leading roles were played by Greece and Rome, the relationship between the two could rarely be that of a simple dialogue. In musical terms one might express it rather as a *duo concertante,* of which the two leading instruments play out their parts within the framework of a full orchestral score; or, to vary the musical analogy, as a symphonic movement, one of the two principal themes of which is clearly stated at the outset, the other only taking shape as the movement progresses, emerging finally as a logical product of the whole preceding development. Whereas Greek architecture had been very largely free to grow to maturity in accordance with the inner logic of its own social and aesthetic premises, Roman architecture through much of its history was denied that artistic luxury. We must therefore study it as a manifestation of the complex, shifting, and often exasperatingly elusive historical phenomenon which was Rome and its Empire.

The earliest history of Roman building falls within the domain of the anthropologist and the historian of religion rather than that of the architecturla historian. The oval huts of timber, wattle, and thatch, as we see them in the earliest levels of settlement on the Palatine *(Plate 1),* the ditched and palisaded enclosures which separated the village from its surrounding fields, the holy places associated with the seasonal magic of a primitive rustic people—all of these were pregnant with significance for the taboos and ritual observances of later Rome. But it is not until the sixth century B.C., under direct Etruscan influence, that we encounter buildings which themselves can be said to have left a significant mark on subsequent architectural history.

The first, and for centuries to come the most prestigious, of these was the Temple of Jupiter Optimus Maximus, Juno, and Minerva on the Capitoline, traditionally said to have been dedicated in 509 B.C. *(Plates 3, 4).* For Rome this state temple was in many respects an epoch-making building: in its sheer size (204 × 174 ft., or 62.25 × 53.30 m., in plan); in the materials of its platform and cellas (dressed stone) and of the rest of its superstructure (timber faced with elaborately shaped and gaily painted terracotta plaques); in the wealth of its lifesize terracotta statuary, of which we can form a good idea from that of the so-called Portonaccio, an Etruscan temple at Veii *(Plate 2),* which was almost certainly the product of the same workshop; and above all in its Greek-inspired conception of the temple as a monumental building rather than as the ritually sanctified enclosure *(templum)* of primitive Italian usage. These were all relatively recent innovations in Etruria itself, stimulated by its close contacts with the Greek colonies of South Italy and by the activities of Greek craftsmen working in Central Italy. But the result was far from being a slavish imitation of the Greek model. The low, spreading proportions, the triplication of the cella (a common but by no means universal feature), the continuation of the rear wall across the full width of the building—these were all substantial modifications of Greek practice to suit Etruscan requirements. As late as the second century B.C. the typical Etrusco-Italic temple was still a low, spreading building with deep overhanging eaves *(Plate 2),* the proportions of which would have seemed quaintly outlandish to any Greek *(cf. Plate 5).* We are immediately and forcibly reminded that the relationship of Greece and Rome was rarely to be so straightforward as that of master and pupil.

The following centuries saw the gradual establishment of Roman political ascendency over Central Italy and with it the slow, steady emergence of a specifically Roman architecture. The materials were those available locally: dressed stone for monumental work; timber both as a framework and for roofing; terracotta revetments and roofing

1. *Rome, model of the archaic settlement on the Palatine*

tiles; and for secondary walls a variety of materials which might be used either independently or with a reinforcement of timber or stone. One which was in widespread use, although for obvious reasons it has left little trace in archaeological records, was sun-dried brick; another was the mortared rubble which, from its humble beginnings as an inert fill for terraces and platforms, gradually (as the quality of the mortar improved) emerged in late Republican times as an autonomous building material of great flexibility and promise.

In Rome itself and generally throughout the volcanic areas of Latium there were abundant supplies of fine clay and of a soft volcanic rock, tufa *(Plate 7),* which lent itself readily to quarrying in the rectangular dressed blocks which we find already in the Temple of Jupiter Optimus Maximus on the Capitoline. In the hills to the north and east of Rome the stone was very different, a limestone which splits naturally into boulders of irregular shape. Here the natural tendency was to use the stone as it was, dressing it only so far as was needed to create the magnificent polygonal walls and terraces of sites such as Alatri, Ameria *(Plate 37),* Cori, Ferentinum *(Plate 40),* Norba, and Signia *(Plate 38).* There was, it is true, a steady trend toward the regularity of coursing without which one cannot envisage many of the more sophisticated forms of classical architecture. But for some five hundred years the two types of masonry, squared ashlar and polygonal walling, existed side by side largely on the basis of local supply and convenience.

2. *Veii (Etruria), model of the Portonaccio Etruscan temple, late sixth century* B.C.

3. *Rome, restored plan of the Temple of Jupiter Optimus Maximus, Juno, and Minerva on the Capitoline, dedicated in 509* B.C.

4. *Rome, coin showing the Temple of Jupiter Optimus Maximus on the Capitoline, as restored in traditional form c. 76* B.C.

5. *Poseidonia (Paestum), elevation and plan of the Temple of Hera, a typical Greek temple*

6. *Poseidonia (Paestum), elevation and plan of the temple beside the forum, a typical Hellenized Italic temple, as reconstructed c. 100* B.C.

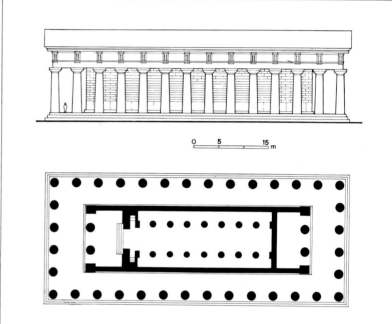

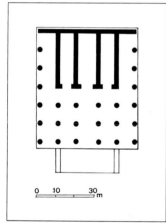

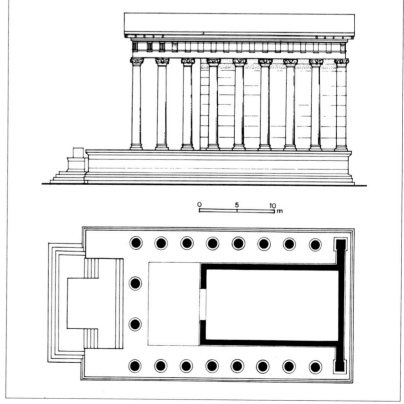

Much the same considerations apply to the various facings that were used with the mortared rubblework *(opus caementicium)* of the late Republic and of the Empire. By this time the pace of building was more rapid and the impact of contemporary fashion correspondingly stronger: in Rome itself the development from the earliest, irregular patchwork *(opus incertum; Plate 157)*, through the tidy checkerboard of reticulate work *(opus reticulatum; Plate 159)*, to the neatly coursed brick facings of the Imperial age *(opus testaceum; Plate 164)* was a matter of generations, not of centuries. Even so, the materials available locally played an important part. The fine *opus incertum* of the Sanctuary of Fortuna Primigenia at Praeneste (Palestrina) is a logical expression of the qualities of the local stone; and as Roman building methods spread to North Italy and beyond we find an extraordinary variety of usage (small coursed blocks, irregular splinters, even rounded river pebbles), of which the common denominator in each case is that this was the material most readily available locally.

To the observer today it calls for a conscious effort of will to believe that the masonry of a wall like that illustrated in Plate 162 was not built to be seen. With certain obvious exceptions, however (such as city walls), the external masonry of the Republican period was normally concealed beneath a layer of stucco as a protection against weathering. The first stone near Rome to be regularly used as a monumental material in its own right was the calcarious travertine *(lapis tiburtinus)* quarried in the plain below Tibur (Tivoli). Like other lesser stones before it, travertine continued to be used internally for its sheer constructional strength, as in the substructures of the Temple of Castor and Pollux in the Forum Romanum *(Plate 8)*. But its capacity to resist weathering and its attractive silvery-gray, lightly pitted surface also made it an ideal facing material for such monumental buildings as the Colosseum *(Plate 108)*, the Stadium of Domitian (today the Piazza Navona), or the emperor Hadrian's Pons Aelius *(Plate 43)*. Marble was another material that was regularly meant to be seen for what it was. On the other hand, the vast expanses of brick-surfaced concrete which are visible in the Forum Romanum or the Baths of Caracalla convey an utterly false impression of the architect's original visual intention. Indeed, one of the problems facing the student of Roman architecture is that what he sees now and what the Romans themselves once saw are often two different things.

What were the factors which gave formal shape to the architecture of Rome? Early writers were unanimous in attributing an important role to the influence of Etruria. The last kings of Rome, the Tarquins, were Etruscan *condottieri*; and even after their expulsion in

8. *Rome, Temple of Castor and Pollux in the Forum Romanum, showing remains of the marble facing and substructures of the Augustan temple constructed of travertine, tufa, and concrete*

509 B.C. the monuments of rich Etruscan cities such as Veii and Caere lay at Rome's doorstep. The Temple of Jupiter Optimus Maximus on the Capitoline remained for centuries a proud symbol of the heritage of Etruscan ritual which pervaded every aspect of Roman religion. At a more prosaic level we may say that in matters of engineering, hydraulics, and sanitation, in the techniques and handling of materials, and in all other practical aspects of the builder's craft, the Romans built on the solid foundations laid by their Etruscan predecessors.

Another, and in the long run, even more important factor in the development of a Roman architectural vocabulary was the emergence of political and social institutions that were specifically Roman and called for specifically Roman settings. Central to these was the Forum Romanum, a multi-purpose open public space around which were grouped some of the city's most venerable monuments: the Regia, the residence of the Pontifex Maximus, who inherited the religious duties of the kings; the small Temple of Vesta, which contained the sacred hearth, symbol of the life spirit of the city; the Temple of Saturn (501–493 B.C.); the Temple of Castor and Pollux (484 B.C.); and, at the northwest end, a ritually sanctified precinct to serve as the place of public assembly (the *comitium*) and, overlooking it, the Curia, or Senate, where the city fathers met. Archaeological investigations have furnished a clear picture of the earliest stages of only one of these monuments—the Regia. Here, overlying the remains of a large Early Iron Age timber hut, are the remains of a fifth-century hall with a central hearth, preceded by two antechambers, and adjoining it a walled courtyard with a well, all built (the lower courses, at any rate) of squared stone blocks. Thus in microcosm we may glimpse the birth of the architecture that was to become Roman.

At first the city of Rome was a modest provincial island, quite removed from the mainstream of contemporary Mediterranean culture. It was not until after the successful conclusion of the Latin War in 338 B.C. that Rome found herself mistress of substantial areas of western and central Italy. One immediate result was a widening of her horizons to include direct contact with the Greek cities of Campania and the South. Another was to give a new dimension and significance to the military colonies which were one of Rome's most effective answers to the problem of controlling and assimilating the ever-widening circle of territory under her domination. Whereas the establishment of the earliest colonies had probably involved little more than the dispossession and subsequent replacement of some of the population of existing towns, after 338 B.C. many of them were newly founded on previously uninhabited sites.

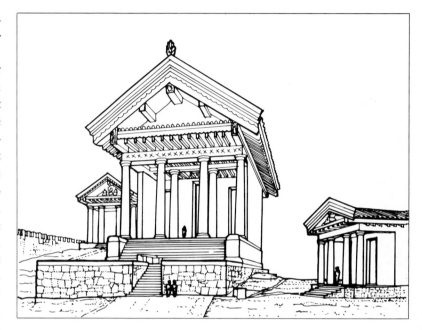

This in itself was bound to stimulate fresh thinking about what a town should be and about the sort of buildings that would be required to house its institutions.

It is in fact from some of these newly founded colonies rather than from Rome itself that we can best learn something of Roman architecture at this crucial stage of its formal development. Almost without exception the early buildings of Rome are merely venerable names, for their substance was either buried or swept away in antiquity by later builders. It is only in the colonies—and notably at Ostia (settled at the end of the fourth century B.C.), Alba Fucens (303), and Cosa (273)—that excavation has been able to reveal something of the actual buildings which were modeled upon them. Cosa is particularly valuable in this respect, not only because of the scale and quality of its excavations, but also because, its original function fulfilled, the town quietly dwindled away, with very little of the urban renewal which all too often virtually obliterated the architecture of the Republic. The formal layout of its streets, though very far from being a slavish copy, derives ultimately from the Greek colonies of South Italy; the fine polygonal masonry walls are in the established Central Italian tradition; and the buildings are already clearly and specifically Roman. There are the citadel *(arx)* with its two temples, the larger one dedicated to the Capitoline triad *(Plate 9)*; the elongated, rectangular forum *(Plate 10)* with, opening off it, the circular *comitium* and the Curia, a pair of temples, several public offices, a basilica, and a monumental arch at the entrance; a large number of cisterns (the town was entirely dependent on the collection and storage of rainwater); and the houses of the citizens. By no means all of these buildings were contemporary with Cosa's initial foundation, but they were the sort of buildings which the founders had in mind. We shall be returning to some of them in a later chapter.

From the complex political history of the later Republic we may single out two series of events which were to have a determining effect upon the subsequent development of Roman architecture. One of these was Rome's advance northward across the Apennines, with the foundation of military colonies at Sena Gallica (Senigallia, 289–283 B.C.), Ariminum (Rimini, 268), Placentia (Piacenza, 218), and Cremona (218). The formal incorporation into Italy of the Po Valley in the mid-first century B.C. was its logical conclusion. It was in North Italy that Rome first seriously had to deal with the problem of establishing the urban forms of a Mediterranean-type civilization in an area where previously they had only a precarious hold. Here in the colonies and municipalities of the second and first centuries B.C. was the breeding ground where Rome evolved the urban patterns and the standardized models of civic architecture which under Augustus and

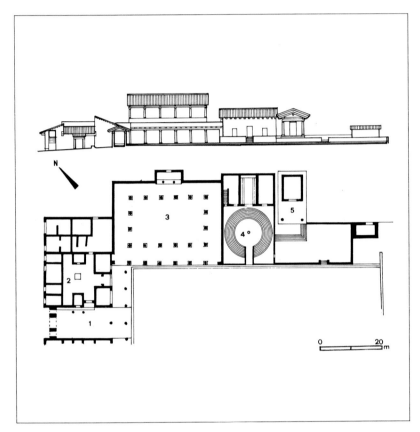

his successors were to be so effectively employed in the urbanization of the Roman West. But all this still lay in the future, and will be discussed in a later chapter. Furthermore, the creative impulses behind these developments, whatever their remoter origins, were channeled almost exclusively through Rome itself and through the political and social mechanisms of the system of which it was by then the undisputed center.

Of more immediate significance was Rome's inexorable advance southward within Italy, punctuated by the defeat of Tarentum (Taranto) in 272 B.C. and the annexation of Sicily in 241. This was followed in the first half of the second century by her steadily increasing military involvement in Greece and Asia Minor, beginning with the war against Philip V of Macedonia (199–197 B.C.) and culminating in the sack of Corinth and the annexation of Macedonia and Achaea (146 B.C.) and the establishment of the province of Asia a few years later.

Campania, Sicily, and the South were quite different from North Italy. These were an integral, albeit geographically outlying, part of the contemporary Hellenistic world. It is true that in many parts of it—notably in Campania—the Greek settlers had long ago been forced to come to terms, politically and socially, with their native Italic neighbors, but culturally these areas remained provincial Greek territory. When in 273 B.C.—the year of Cosa's foundation in Etruria—Rome also established a military colony at Paestum (the former Greek colony of Poseidonia, which for the last hundred and fifty years had been under native Lucanian domination), the new settlers found themselves faced at every turn by Greek monuments and Greek traditions of craftsmanship. Among these were the magnificent Doric temples which, rather by the happy accident of their conservation than because they were in any way exceptional, are today among the outstanding surviving buildings of classical antiquity. This did not mean that the new settlers lost their own cultural identity: they were an outpost of Rome, and in addition to the forum at Paestum there are two monuments which vividly attest the continuing vitality of many of their Roman institutions and habits. One of these is a circular *comitium* of the same unmistakably Roman type as that at Cosa; the other is a temple whose podium was accessible only from the front by steps, and whose superstructure comprised a deep porch and a cella of which the back wall extended across the podium—all characteristically Etrusco-Roman features. Nevertheless, the direct confrontation with the living substance of Greek culture could not fail to be a stimulating experience for Greeks, Romans, and Lucanians alike. Quite irrespective of its repercussions on the architecture of Rome itself and of Latium, Campania emerged as one of the main creative architectural centers of the late Republic, responsible for such typically Roman building types as the amphitheater, the theater (in its Roman form), the atrium-peristyle house, and almost certainly the Roman bath, the market building *(macellum)*, and the basilica.

If the conquest of South Italy was unsettling, how much more so was that of metropolitan Greece. The capture and sack of Syracuse in 212 B.C. offered a taste of what was to come. Syracuse had been one of the wealthiest cities of the Greek world, and the paintings and sculptures carried off to grace the triumph of its conqueror, Marcellus, were Rome's first massive exposure to the sophistication of Classical and Hellenistic art. Less than twenty years later, in 194 B.C., came the magnificent triumph of Flamininus at the conclusion of the war against Philip V of Macedonia; this was followed successively by the conquest of large parts of Asia Minor and (as mentioned above) by the sack of Corinth in 146 B.C. and the establishment of Roman suzerainty over the whole of mainland Greece. The flood of gold and silver, of statues and of paintings which poured into Rome was a fact to which no Roman could remain indifferent. Right down to the end of the Republic puritanical traditionalists such as Cato were numerous and vocal enough to exercise a powerful restraining influence on public opinion, while at the other extreme there were the enthusiastic philhellenes—men such as Scipio Aemilianus, friend and patron of the Greek historian Polybius, men to whom the literature, philosophy, and art of Greece opened up a new universe of experience. Between the two lay the mass of the more or less educated public which found itself forcibly confronted at every turn by the products of an older, richer, more sophisticated culture.

The story of this first dramatic exposure of Rome to the art of Greece goes a long way toward explaining not only the subsequent development of Roman art but also (and hardly less important to our own understanding) the extraordinarily biased vision of it held both by contemporary Roman and by many later critics. Many post-Renaissance attitudes to Roman art are inevitably rooted in the judgment of such writers as Vitruvius and Pliny, who in turn were prisoners of their own inherited prejudices and preconceptions. It was in the second century B.C. that the latter took shape. On the one hand there was the dazzling revelation of the quality and intrinsic wealth of Greek artistic achievement; and yet this was all the work of a people over whom the Romans had resoundingly proved their own military and political superiority. Was it not perhaps the part of wisdom to steer clear of so seemingly treacherous a talent? A hundred years later even so knowledgeable and sensitive a connoisseur of Greek art as Cicero still found it convenient to pay lip service to the notion that art was somehow inconsistent with the accepted Roman scale of virtues. And yet it was quite impossible to ignore the fact that in the temples of Rome the old wooden or terracotta statues were everywhere being replaced by pieces brought from Greece; that victorious generals were starting to build monuments (such as the Porticus Metelli, 146 B.C.) in which to display their artistic loot; or that the houses of wealthy Romans boasted an ever-increasing profusion of paintings, hangings, sculpture, and exquisite dinner services in gold and silver, all of Greek origin. Moreover, such objects were outstandingly valuable—as any Roman could understand. Aesthetic appreciation, fashion, familiarity, commercial good sense, even the hostility of the puritanical reaction, all met on the common ground that considered art a typically Greek creation.

Roman art never fully recovered from the resulting state of cultural shock. As we shall see, architects were in a better position than painters or sculptors to react positively to the new situation, but even they found it hard to abandon certain basic assumptions of Greek artistic authority. Right down to late antiquity the traditional Greek orders remained a virtual *sine qua non* of certain aspects of Roman monumental building. Or again, when in 13 B.C. work was begun on the Ara Pacis *(Plates 89–92),* the first of a long line of monuments designed to display politically oriented architectural reliefs, the content and the symbolism might be as Roman as the message they were designed to convey, but the artistic forms were borrowed directly from Greece and were carved by Greek workmen brought from Athens. Two centuries later the sculptors of the state reliefs which now adorn the attic of the Arch of Constantine (which were taken from a monument erected in honor of Marcus Aurelius) were still working within the framework of the same tradition—accomplished and in terms of the accepted conventions effective, but artistically as meaningless as the reliefs on London's Albert Memorial. The first major Roman monument of official relief sculpture to escape the dead hand of conservative Greek taste was the Column of Trajan, dedicated in A.D. 112.

Within certain fields (and monumental sculpture was emphatically one of these) the results of this attitude were little short of disastrous. There was wealth in Rome as never before, and there was a growing circle of artistic patronage; but what the wealthy patron wanted for the adornment of his villa was Greek art (the career of Verres, governor of Sicily from 73 to 71 B.C., shows to what lengths one man was prepared to go to obtain it). Since the supply of genuine Greek sculpture was not unlimited, there soon developed a flourishing commerce, based principally in Athens, in more or less exact copies of the Greek masterpieces. The fact that these Neo-Attic pieces

reverted to long-outmoded styles and models would not in itself have mattered so much, since such evocations of the past are by no means necessarily a sterile artistic phenomenon (it was, after all, the descendants of these same craftsmen who in the second and third centuries A.D. produced the series of Attic sarcophagi which were among the most attractive works of minor sculpture produced in the Roman world). What did matter was that the output of the Neo-Attic workshops, which came into being simply to satisfy the demands of a generation of newly moneyed middle-class collectors, comprised a mélange of styles that was as devoid of aesthetic unity as the furniture and *objets d'art* of the average cluttered Victorian drawing room. The public which they served so faithfully seems to have been totally without a sense of style. Archaic, Classical, and Hellenistic copies competed for attention alongside adaptations and classicizing pastiches in the appalling profusion that still mocks us from the walls of the antique sculpture galleries of Europe and America. To rediscover the springs of creative spontaneity the native Italic artist had to fight his way through the dead weight of an alien tradition which had mastered every resource of technical skill but which had long ago lost its own artistic soul.

Architecture resisted such pressures better than sculpture or painting, yet with certain exceptions: Caius Cestius, a Roman who had served in Egypt, had built for himself in Rome a tomb in the form of an Egyptian pyramid *(Plate 11)*; the slightly earlier Monument of the Julii *(Plate 12)* at Saint-Rémy-de-Provence (ancient Glanum) is a free adaptation of the Hellenized tower-tombs of the Semitic East. One might even bring workmen and materials to Rome to build a near-authentic replica of a Greek building, as did the founder of the Round Temple in the Forum Boarium in the first half of the first century B.C. *(Plates 13, 14)*. But such direct copying was not usual. The majority of the "academies," the *mouseia,* and the *stadia* which figure so largely in the accounts of the villas of the late Republican philhellenes (and which were designed to house their owners' collections of Greek sculpture) were architectural conceits, free fantasias on literary ideas of building types rather than close copies of actual Greek buildings *(Plates 172–174)*. This was a mode to which we find Hadrian returning in his villa at Tivoli (ancient Tibur). The Canopus, for example, with its formal lake and its Egyptianizing sculpture (side by side with replicas of the caryatids of the Erechtheum in Athens) was a suggestive evocation, not a direct copy, of the famous sanctuary near Alexandria after which it was named.

Even more important for the integrity of the Italian architectural tradition was the fact that, whereas models and styles may reflect foreign trends, building practices as a general rule do not. Roman

13, 14. Rome, Round Temple in the Forum Boarium (so-called Temple of Vesta), first half of the first century B.C.

architecture was founded on a long tradition of laboriously acquired practical craftsmanship, a tradition which was always ready to assimilate and even to copy new architectural forms, but which in matters of methods and materials was fundamentally resistant to the sort of wholesale artistic take-over by Greece to which Roman sculptors and painters had submitted.

In such circumstances the Roman advance into South Italy may be held to have been an event of greater importance for the development of late Republican architecture than the conquest of Greece itself. It was in Campania that a number of the familiar building types of later Roman architecture first took monumental shape—theaters and amphitheaters, for example. In Rome itself the defenders of the old Roman morality were long able to prevent the construction in permanent materials of buildings for public entertainment. The first permanent theater in Rome was that of Pompey *(Plate 54),* built in 55 B.C., at least twenty years after the conversion to Roman form of the theater at Pompeii and the building of its smaller companion, the Covered Theater *(Plate 15).* The amphitheater at Pompeii *(Plates 16–18),* a building of the same date, was another stone-built monument. And yet, despite the fact that these models were from Central Italy, where there was a long tradition of amphitheaters constructed in timber, Rome itself as late as 29 B.C. with the construction of the amphitheater of Statilius Taurus had still to be content with a building whose superstructure was of timber, resting on stone footings. Not until the Colosseum (A.D. 71–80) did Rome have a permanent amphitheater of its own.

The story of the evolution of the Roman theater and amphitheater is admittedly a somewhat special case. But there are several other very familiar Roman building types that seem to have developed first in Campania: the Roman bath building, the idea of which may well have taken shape from the use of the volcanic springs abounding in the Pozzuoli-Baia area; the market building *(macellum),* with a circular pavilion in the middle of a porticoed enclosure; and very possibly the basilica. This last is a particularly instructive example. Whatever the precise significance of the term *basilica* (from the Greek βασιλική), it certainly implies a measure of Greek-speaking parentage; and the architectural form to which the name was applied—a lofty central nave framed on two or more sides by colonnaded aisles—could well have taken shape in Campania, where the earliest surviving example, at Pompeii, is little if at all later than what were certainly the earliest examples in Rome, those built alongside the Forum Romanum between 184 and 170 B.C. But although the basic idea for the basilica was probably taken over from Greek-speaking South Italy, it was not adopted uncritically. The long axis

15. *Pompeii, plan of the theaters. 1) large open theater; 2) small covered theater; 3) adjoining portico (later barracks of the gladiators)*

16. *Pompeii, amphitheater, aerial view*

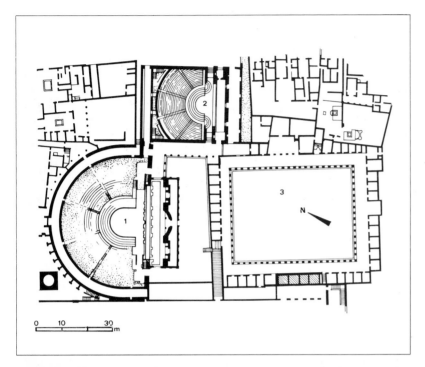

of the building was turned ninety degrees and the whole frontage was opened up with columns, so that the building became, in effect, a covered extension of that long-established Italic institution, the forum. It was in this modified metropolitan Roman version that the basilica spread rapidly through Central and North Italy (Cosa, Ardea, Alba Fucens, Saepinum, Herdoniae, Velleia), becoming one of the standard building types of Imperial Rome—both in Italy and throughout the western provinces.

It was this capacity to assimilate, and where necessary to modify, the creations of others which was the saving strength of the Roman builders of the last two centuries of the Republic. Some innovations could be accepted with little or no superficial change. Examples of this are the peristyle, as a feature of the well-to-do Roman villa, or the evolved Ionic capital characteristic of Samnite Pompeii, which turns up with remarkably little variation from Taranto to Aquileia. In most cases, however, there was a necessary process of mutual assimilation. Formally a building such as the Doric temple of Hercules at Cori *(Plates 22, 23)* is still essentially of the old Italic type, raised on a molded podium and accessible only from the front, up steps (now lost) and through a pedimented columnar porch. But the wooden construction and the low, spreading profile of the Italic models have given way to the local limestone (formerly faced with stucco) and to an elegance of proportion that would have been unthinkable a few generations earlier. In the Rectangular Temple in Rome's Forum Boarium *(Plate 60)*, of the same or slightly later date, we can see the same processes at work in the capital, the principal difference being that in this case the order is Ionic and the materials (travertine and tufa faced with stucco) those of contemporary building in Rome. The fusion of Italic and Greek elements is complete. A contemporary Greek would have thought the result quaint and provincial, but this was because it also expressed local needs in terms of local building practice.

Like the historical situation of which it was a product, this new Romano-Hellenistic architecture was a complex phenomenon; and before turning in detail to a few of the principal monuments of late Republican Rome and its environs, it will be helpful to single out some of the individual threads that made up the larger pattern. One of these was the new life that was given to such traditionally Italic types of building as the forward-facing, podium-based temple. We have already glanced at a couple of examples, and we shall be seeing many more. It was the reinterpretation of such buildings in terms of the outward forms and proportions of the Greek orders which enabled them to survive the competition of more sophisticated but alien models, thereby ensuring an enduring Italic contribution to the formal vocabulary of later Roman architecture.

17. *Pompeii, amphitheater, exterior showing access ramps to seating area*
18. *Pompeii, amphitheater, view of the arena and seating area*

19. *Pompeii, view of the forum, looking northwest toward the Capitolium*

20. *Pompeii, plan of the forum. 1) Capitolium; 2) macellum (meat market); 3) lararium; 4) Temple of Vespasian; 5) Eumachia building (center of the fullers' guild); 6) voting precinct; 7) city offices; 8) basilica; 9) Temple of Apollo; 10) forum holitorium (vegetable market)*

21. *Pompeii, detail of the forum and (right) entrance to the basilica*

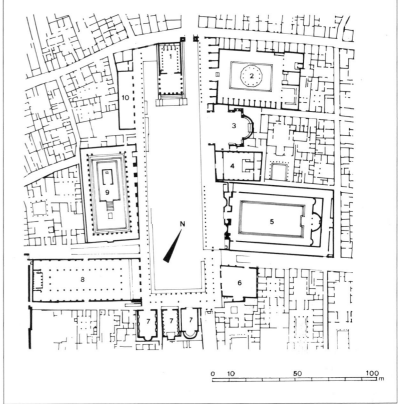

Another important characteristic of the period was the emergence of new types of buildings to meet the increasingly complex requirements of a society in a stage of rapid evolution. This touched on almost every aspect of life, both public and private. The forum is a good example: as we have already remarked, it first took shape—like the Greek agora before it—as an all-purpose open space which might be called on to serve in turn as a setting for the community's most venerable sanctuaries, as a place of political or military assembly, as an open-air court of law, or as a market place. It could even be used as a place of public entertainment, as was the Forum Romanum, where gladiatorial displays were staged down to the end of Republican times. There might, of course, be public buildings and open spaces situated elsewhere from a very early date: the citadel *(arx),* for example, and some of the temples, or the cattle market, which was regularly situated near one of the city gates. But it was in the second century B.C. that the processes of specialization and decentralization took on a fresh momentum as a result of Rome's new political and economic standing within the Hellenistic world. This was when the basilica, the senate house *(curia),* and the place of public assembly *(comitium)* took architectural shape as independent buildings grouped around the open space of the forum, followed in due course by such other specialized public buildings as record offices *(tabularia)* and voting precincts *(saepta).* Around the forum or elsewhere there began to spring up market buildings *(macella),* porticoes with shops and offices, and warehouses *(horrea).* Where Rome led, the planners and architects of the military colonies and municipalities of provincial Italy soon followed suit. This was the moment when many of the familiar building types of later Roman architecture acquired the authority of established practice, an authority that was subsequently to transport them over large parts of the Mediterranean world.

No less important in the long run was the fact that these buildings were the proving ground of what was to become a revolutionary new building material, *opus caementicium*—Roman concrete. This is a topic which will be discussed in greater detail in a later chapter. At this point we need only remark that Roman concrete first took shape, almost by accident, in the yards of everyday working builders, who found it an increasingly effective and economical substitute for the building materials of the established Central Italian tradition. Among other things, they found that it could be used to replace the old-fashioned flat wooden ceilings by various simple forms of vaulting, for which dressed stone was a cumbrous and rather costly medium. As we shall see, much of the later history of Roman architecture was to stem from this basic discovery. At this early stage, however, all the evidence suggests that it was the convenience and relative cheapness of

the new material which interested architects rather than its possible use in the creation of new architectural forms. Nevertheless, side by side with these new constructional practices there were also certain formal innovations, two of which may be singled out as of outstanding significance for the future. One was the steadily increasing use of the arch as a substitute for the flat architrave or lintel of canonical Greek usage. The other was the growing tendency to treat the Greek orders as elements of a decorative facade which might or might not express the constructional logic of the underlying structure.

The Romans did not invent either the arch or the barrel vault. Both had a long history behind them in the mud-brick architecture of the ancient East, to which they were constructionally well suited and in which they had already achieved monumental expression in the palace facades and city gates of Assyria and Babylonia. Whether or not counterparts of such buildings were to be seen in the western provinces of the Persian Empire, it was unquestionably from deliberate choice, not ignorance, that the architects of classical Greece clung doggedly to their own rigorously rectilinear tradition, whose whole visual impact was dependent on the contraposition of vertical and horizontal members.

Even so, from the fourth century onward we begin to find the arch and the barrel vault steadily infiltrating the repertory of Greek builders—at first mainly in contexts where they posed no visual problems, as in the substructures of the theater at Alinda, in Caria, or in the staircases of the *gymnasium* at Pergamon, but before long in monumental architecture as well. It is no accident that in the latter category the city gate seems to have led the way. Here strong practical considerations favored possible Oriental influences. A gate needed above all to be strong, and a large stone arch is by its very nature more robust than an opening of the same size with a horizontal lintel. By the fourth century arched gateways were well established both in metropolitan Greece and in South Italy: at Oiniadai in Acarnania, for example, where the fine polygonal walls may be as early as the fifth century, or the recently excavated Porta Rosa at Elia (Velia) in Lucania *(Plate 28)*. In Central Italy such gateways were certainly common by the third century: at Cosa already in 273 B.C.; at Falerii Novi soon after 241 *(Plate 25)*; and still later the two magnificent gateways at Perugia *(Plates 26, 27)*.

The precise path by which the idea of the monumental arched gateway reached Central Italy may be disputed. Yet what is certain is that, once established, it took vigorous root. Gateways similar to those of Perugia were the models for the gateways of the colonies and municipalities of Republican North Italy and, through them, of countless later city gates both in Italy and in the provinces. The

balustraded gallery portrayed above the arch of the Porta Marzia and the heads in the spandrels are features that look forward to the first Porta dei Leoni at Verona *(Plate 29)* and to the Arch of Augustus (27 B.C.) at Rimini *(Plates 242, 243)*. The heads on or above the keystone here and at Volterra and Falerii Novi are another feature with close early Imperial counterparts, at Verona (the theater) and at Nîmes, in Provence (the Porte d'Auguste, 16 B.C., *Plate 235*).

Along with the emergence of the monumental arch as an architectural form in its own right we begin to meet another usage which, though less dramatic, was even more far-reaching in its implications— the substitution of an arch for the rectangular opening of a conventional Greek order. To us today the rhythmic deployment of a series of arches or arched openings is an architectural device so familiar that it is hard to appreciate how strange it must have seemed to eyes that were attuned only to the contrasted verticals and horizontals of Greek practice. Once again, however, we must beware of attributing revolutionary visions of the future to builders whose concern was not with innovation as such, but simply with the more practical and economical use of materials at hand.

Increasing familiarity with the curvilinear forms of concrete vaulting must in itself have been a factor in dispelling the prejudice for Greek solutions; and when timber ceased to be an acceptable material for the outer walls of newly commissioned public buildings, the arch offered a simple answer to one of the resulting constructional problems. A horizontal architrave is only feasible where there are supplies of a stone strong enough to carry the intercolumnar load: in most parts of Greece marble, or stone of an equivalent quality, was readily available, but in many parts of the Hellenistic world it was not. One solution to the problem was to use a timber architrave disguised beneath a facing of stucco. Another, used widely in Roman times, was the redistribution of the load by some form of flat-arch construction, as for example that used in the porticoes of the forum at Pompeii *(Plates 19–21)*. A third solution, widely favored by Hellenistic architects in such contexts as the stage buildings of theaters (Priene) and architectural tomb facades (Alexandria, Cyrene), was to narrow the span by widening the vertical member. The column became a rectangular pier with an engaged half-column and the intercolumniation became a large rectangular opening in what was in effect a discontinuous screen wall.

From this third solution it was only a short step to replacing the rectangular opening by an arch. With the hindsight of history one is tempted to stress the element in this that was new; and the explicit acceptance of the arch as a component of the architect's visual vocabulary was indeed full of significance for the future. At the time, however, it must have been seen rather as a manifestation—a bit daring but constructionally quite logical—of a trend long apparent in Hellenistic architecture whereby the Greek orders were losing their exclusively structural role in favor of a variety of wholly or partially decorative usages *(Plates 30, 31)*.

The first steps in this direction had already been taken in the fifth century B.C. in the discreet privacy of the interiors of the temples of Bassae and Tegea; and from the fourth century onward one encounters a steadily growing readiness to use engaged semi-columnar orders as a frankly decorative device, imitating the external forms of real architecture but not its substance. The half-columns that carry the columnar motif of the porch down the flanks of the Rectangular Temple in the Forum Boarium *(Plate 60)* have their exact counterparts in the outer facades of the Bouleuterion at Miletus. Here Roman Republican architecture was merely adopting what was already a commonplace of progressive Hellenistic architecture.

Rome's unique contribution was to combine this superficial, purely decorative use of the Greek orders with the arch; and because it was the arch, not the order, that imposed the structural logic of the underlying building, it was only a matter of time before the order was dropped altogether. The remarkable thing is that for a couple of centuries to come the authority of tradition was still strong enough to ensure its retention in public buildings such as the Tabularium *(Plate 58)*, the Basilica Julia, the Theater of Marcellus, and the Colosseum, where it remained one of the standard formulas of Roman monumental architecture.

What are the principal surviving monuments of this last phase of Republican Roman architecture? Pride of place must go to the three great sanctuaries of Latium: that of Fortuna Primigenia at Praeneste (modern Palestrina), which is variously ascribed to the second half of the second century B.C. and to the early years of the first; that of Jupiter Anxur at Tarracina (Terracina), probably rebuilt soon after 80 B.C.; and that of Hercules Victor at Tibur (Tivoli), which was still being built about the middle of the century. Each in its own way was a remarkable structure, and together they convey, as does no other surviving group of buildings, an impression of the tremendous architectural potential which the political events of the third and second centuries B.C. had awakened in Central Italy.

The Temple of Jupiter Anxur *(Plates 32–35)* owes a great deal to its magnificent situation on a rocky headland that dominates the coast for miles around, and its architect had the good sense to exploit this natural advantage by adhering to an economy of detail that matches the simple grandeur of the basic conception. The eccentricity of the temple with respect to its precinct (an unusual feature in Roman

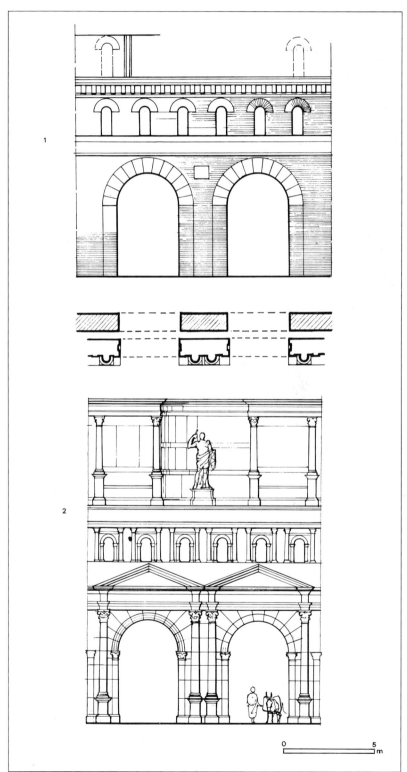

28. *Elia (Velia), Porta Rosa*
29. *Verona, elevations and plan of the Porta dei Leoni. 1) original gateway, mid-first century* B.C.; *2) reconstructed gateway, second half of the first century* A.D.

0   5
m

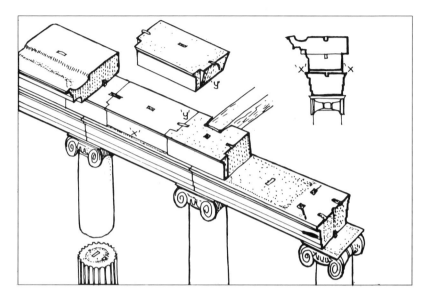

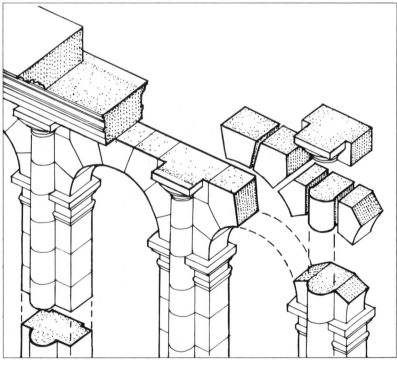

30. *Miletus, diagram of the Ionic portico, a traditional Greek order of the Roman period (first century A.D.)*

31. *Rome, diagram of the portico in the Forum Holitorium, a late Republican arched facade with a purely decorative, applied order*

architecture of any period) was no doubt dictated by the disposition of the earlier Latin shrine which it replaced, although the architect cannot have been unaware that in adopting it he was also enhancing the view of the temple from the town itself and from the Via Appia, the road that brought the traveler in from Rome. His main contribution, however, was the huge terraced platform which carried the precinct out on to the brow of the headland. This was entirely constructed of *opus incertum*—mortared rubble faced with an irregular mosaic of small limestone fragments and contained at the angles by small dressed blocks of the same material. To support this terrace, and at the same time to give it scale and emphasis, the architect faced it with a buttressing arcade of twelve large, severely simple barrel-vaulted recesses, which open at right angles off an inner barrel-vaulted corridor, and which themselves intercommunicate through smaller arched openings. The only ornamental feature was a molding at the spring of each of the arches of the facade.

Although the inner corridor would have been convenient for the storage of temple equipment, the main purpose of these substructures was unquestionably that of supporting the terrace above. In earlier Republican architecture this would have been done by means of a massive, inert, earth-filled platform, as at Alatri or in the Capitolium at Segni. A first step forward was to incorporate vaulted substructures within the platform without substantially modifying its external appearance, as was done in the bastion-like projection from the acropolis at Ferentinum *(Plates 39, 40)*. Now, thanks to an ever-increasing virtuosity in the handling of the new concrete medium, this innovation could be pushed to its logical conclusion, resulting in an exterior architecture which was a direct expression of the structural forms inherent in the medium itself. One is thus witnessing the emergence of a new, functional aesthetic. Although this was not the first time that a plain arcaded facade had been so used—at Tarracina itself the so-called Small Temple must be somewhat earlier, and Roman bridge-builders were already at work on such multiple-arched bridges as the Ponte di Nona on the Via Praenestina *(Plates 41, 42)*—nevertheless, in a context of monumental religious architecture the architects of Rome itself might well have felt constrained to apply a discreet top-dressing of traditional classicism. So bold an application of the new principles shows how far and how fast some of their colleagues were already traveling.

The Temple of Hercules Victor at Tibur *(Plate 36)*, though slightly later in date and far more ambitious in scale, was in many respects a more conservative building. There are, as one would expect, many signs of the influence of its great neighbor at Praeneste, among them the building techniques, the elaborately articulated systems of

32. *Tarracina (Terracina), Temple of Jupiter Anxur, axonometric reconstruction of the temple, portico, and platform*

33. *Tarracina (Terracina), Temple of Jupiter Anxur, detail of substructures of the platform, showing* opus incertum *limestone masonry*

vaulted substructures, and the frontal ramps. But if one makes allowances for the differences in scale, site, and proportions, the elements of the plan—the axial, forward-looking temple, the porticoes that frame it on three sides, the theater-like stepped hemicycle in front of it— these are derived almost directly from an older Latin tradition, of which the sanctuary at Gabii is the outstanding surviving example *(Plate 45)*. In contemporary terms, Piranesi's view of the north flank of the terrace *(Plate 44)* affords a striking and instructive contrast to the monumental simplicity of the platform of the Tarracina temple: a row of great stone buttresses, very much in the manner of those supporting the theater-terrace of Hellenistic Pergamon, and above them an arcade, decorously framed between the half-columns and projecting entablature of an engaged order. This was, one sees, a developing tradition within which architects had a wide range of individual choice.

Both in scale and in conception the great Sanctuary of Fortuna Primigenia at Praeneste is one of the most impressive monuments of classical antiquity. Terraced sharply down the steep hillside *(Plate 46)*, it comprises two main groups of buildings: at the foot of the hill the so-called *area sacra*, and above it the vast terraced complex crowned by the hemicycle of the Palazzo Barberini *(Plates 47, 48)*. The central feature of the lower group was what appears to have been a large transverse columnar hall with a facade of two superimposed porticoes, Corinthian over Doric, and on the other side, set out from the vertical rock face, a curious inward-facing screen wall, with tall, narrow windows and molded labels between the semi-columns of a decorative order; above the latter ran a low arcade. At one end of this central feature lay the oracular cave which had been the nucleus of the old Latin sanctuary, and at the other end, facing outward, a smaller but very richly decorated apsed hall, paved with a magnificent Nilotic mosaic and flanked internally by a pair of molded plinths, each of which carried an engaged, semi-columnar Ionic order and, recessed into the walls, niches for statuary (one of the relatively rare examples in three-dimensional architecture of the illusionistic architectural schemes of the so-called Second Style of contemporary wall painting). With so much that calls for comment, we must be content to emphasize the baroque quality of so much of this detail, inside and out: "baroque" in the sense that the familiar classical elements are taken apart and recomposed in a manner which often bears remarkably little relation either to the proprieties of traditional classicism or to the realities of the underlying structure.

The upper part of the sanctuary at Praeneste, where the architect had a freer hand to develop the sweep of his fancy *(Plate 48)*, defies brief verbal analysis. Here we are confronted by a bewildering com-

34. *Tarracina (Terracina), Temple of Jupiter Anxur, arcaded facade of the platform.*

35. *Tarracina (Terracina), view of the Temple of Jupiter Anxur, showing the corridor which connects the arches of the platform facade*

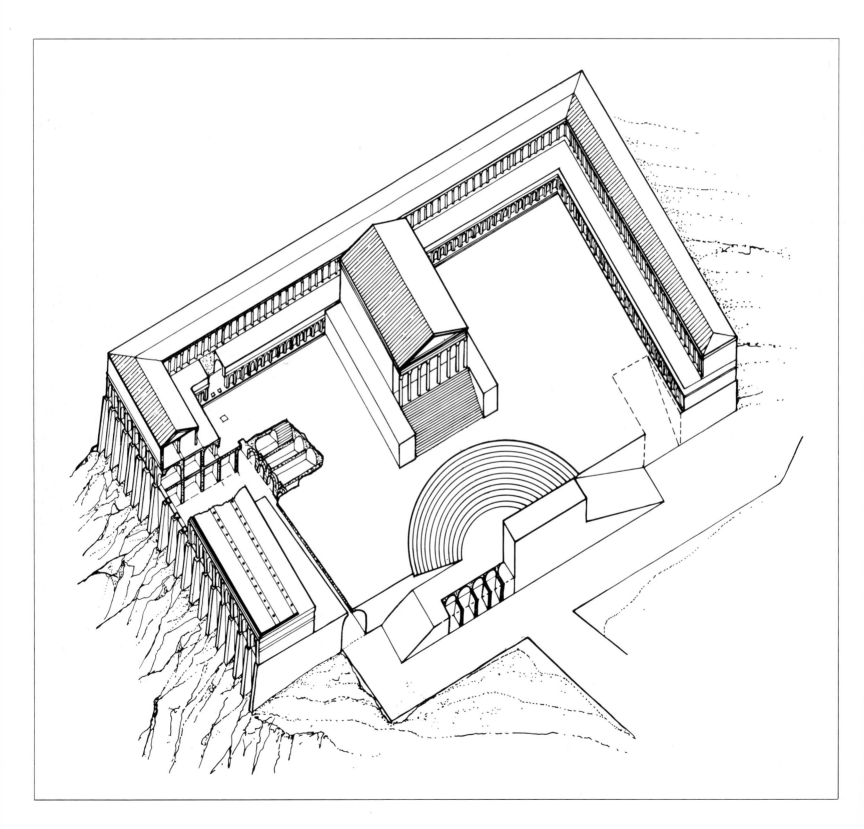

plex of terraces and porticoes, ramps and stairs, gabled columnar façades, screen walls with engaged orders, circular pavilions and hemicyclical reentrants, a sparing but emphatic use of arches to emphasize key elements of the design—all disposed symmetrically about a central axis, but in such a way that the visitor, though never allowed to forget the symmetry, could only experience the totality of it in orderly succession, terrace by terrace and group by group, as he progressed upward. In this respect it affords a remarkable anticipation of later Roman planning. Without this element of an orderly, progressive revelation, poised precariously between calculated anticipation and visual surprise, many later monuments—in Rome itself, the great Imperial bath buildings or the Forum of Trajan, or in the provinces complexes such as the great Sanctuary of Jupiter Heliopolitanus at Baalbek or that of Artemis at Gerasa—would lose much of their meaning. This concept was so utterly alien to Greek ideas of planning, and so far in advance of the simple axial symmetry of earlier Italic practice, that it is startling indeed to find it deployed in so elaborately sophisticated a manner in Hellenistic Latium. One is tempted to see in it a reflection of the influence of Ptolemaic Egypt, a country which had a time-honored tradition of axial progression. But with the buildings of Hellenistic Alexandria irretrievably lost, this can be no more than an educated guess.

The buildings at Praeneste have been variously dated between the mid-second century B.C. and the period immediately after the destruction of the town in 80 B.C. Despite much learned argument, however, we still lack evidence for a firm chronology. Yet what is beyond dispute is that, even if the later date were correct, the buildings would still be remarkably advanced for their age—advanced alike in the principles of their composition, in the virtuosity of their constructional techniques, and in the quality of their detail. Although it is true that the Sanctuary of Aesculapius on Kos and the Acropolis and Temple of Athena at Lindos on Rhodes offer valid Hellenistic precedents for ascending terraced plans of this sort, neither can compare with Praeneste in scale and sheer complexity. We shall be returning to the building techniques in a later chapter. As for details, we must here be content to refer to the coffered vaulting of the hemicycles *(Plate 50)*, the first recorded instance of such work in the new concrete medium; to the sparing but emphatic use of arches *(Plate 49)*; and to the numerous "baroque" elements mentioned above. In much of this too the architect was breaking fresh ground.

The surviving Republican monuments of Rome itself are by comparison far less adventurous. It is true that we lack the fantasy architecture of the temporary theaters, which has left its mark only in the literature and in the architectural schemes of the so-called Third

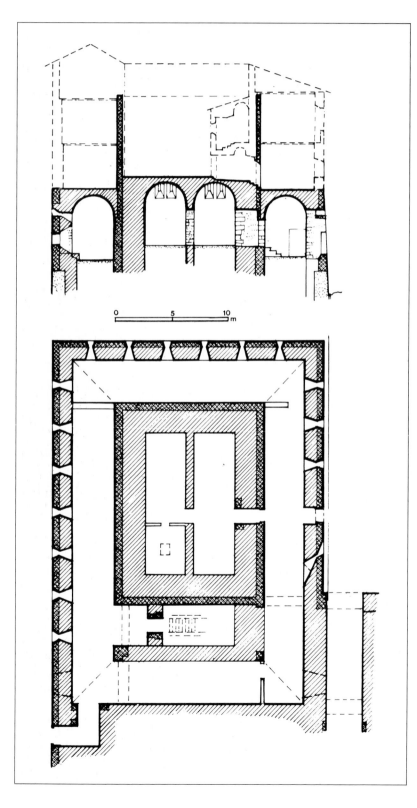

39. *Ferentinum (Ferentino), acropolis. Section and plan of the vaulted substructures of the great bastion*

Style of wall painting *(Plates 52, 53)*. This genre came directly from the courts of the Hellenistic monarchs, from the sort of dream world of which the state barge of Ptolemy IV (221–205 B.C.) was a tangible expression. The impact of such work was sufficient to provoke the disapproval of the conservative-minded Vitruvius, but we are left wondering how far the Theater of Pompey *(Plate 54)*, built in 55 B.C. —the first permanent theater building in Rome—was successful in capturing anything of its spirit. Among the surviving monuments of Republican Rome one looks in vain for the sense of creative adventure of which the sanctuaries of Latium are so striking an embodiment.

One obvious reason for this conservative attitude is that physical conditions within the city were not suitable for this sort of dramatic, scenographic architecture. Another possible reason is the influence of the same "old Roman" minority which had so long been successful in keeping at bay such socially dangerous innovations as permanent buildings for public entertainment. Architects must have found their attitudes very inhibiting. Yet another reason was that the established local materials for monumental architecture—dressed tufa and more recently travertine—simply did not lend themselves to the elaborate flights of constructional fancy for which the limestone concrete of Praeneste and Tibur proved so adaptable and stimulating a medium. The same innovative currents were at work in Rome, but the advance was altogether more cautious.

Almost all of the secular public buildings of Republican Rome were swept away and replaced by Augustus and his successors. We know them today principally from the literature and from occasional glimpses on the coinage: the Senate, or Curia Julia, for example, as rebuilt by Caesar followed the traditional lines prescribed by Vitruvius *(Plate 56)*. The Basilica Aemilia too, after its restoration in 80–78 B.C., was a traditional columnar building with galleries around the central hall *(Plate 57* shows the interior; the circular objects are bronze shields). The only major public monument of the period to have come down to us is the Tabularium *(Plates 58, 59)*, the public record office, which was built *ex novo* in 78 B.C. Here for once there was some scope for landscaping, for converting the rocky slopes of the Capitoline into an architectural backdrop for the untidy complex of ancient and modern buildings which had grown up around the west end of the forum *(Plate 24)*. The solution adopted was simple but impressive: a massive, tufa-faced concrete substructure, incorporating a longitudinal vaulted corridor lit by simple rectangular openings and, resting on this platform, the two stories of a galleried stone facade. The upper story has gone, but the facade and gallery of the lower story are still standing, built of dressed tufa with concrete pavilion vaults and with three of the arches of the facade still facing out over the forum. As at

41, 42. *Ponte di Nona, a Republican bridge on the Via Praenestina*
43. *Rome, Pons Aelius and Hadrian's Mausoleum(Castel Sant' Angelo)*▷

44. *Tibur (Tivoli), Temple of Hercules Victor, showing the northwest facade of the temple platform. Engraving by Piranesi*

45. *Gabii, plan of the sanctuary*

46. *Praeneste (Palestrina), Sanctuary of Fortuna Primigenia, restored axonometric view*

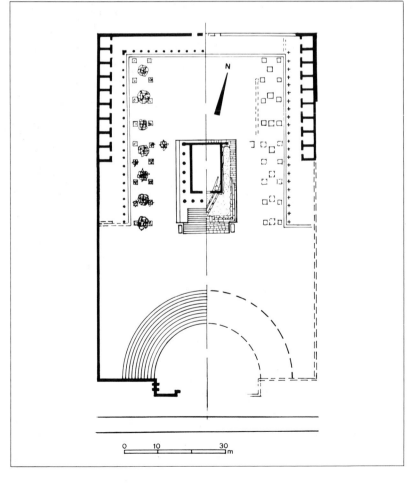

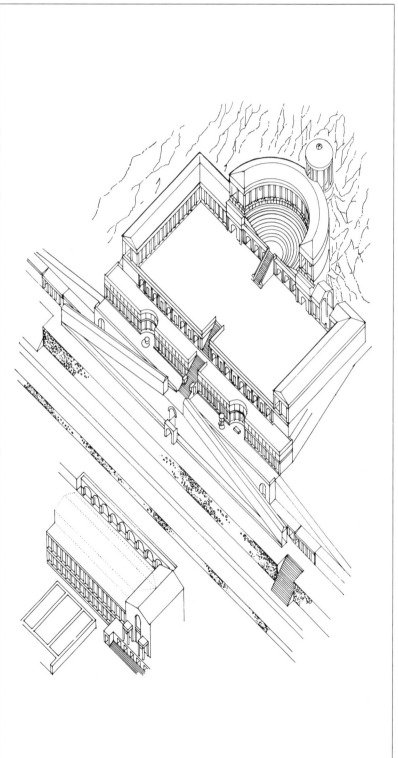

47. *Praeneste (Palestrina), upper part of the Sanctuary of Fortuna Primigenia, seen from the campanile of the cathedral*

48. *Praeneste (Palestrina), model of the upper part of the Sanctuary of Fortuna Primigenia*

49. *Praeneste (Palestrina), terrace and detail of one of the colonnaded hemicycles*

50. *Praeneste (Palestrina), vaulted hemicycle, detail*

51. *Praeneste (Palestrina), ramp (in antiquity there was a portico, facing inward, on the outer side)* ▷

Praeneste and Tibur, the arches (and doubtless also those of the lost upper story) were decorously framed between the half-columns and the entablature of an applied decorative order: here in the heart of Rome it was essential to observe the traditional proprieties. But, for all the sobriety of its design, this was a building in exactly the same tradition as the great sanctuaries of Latium.

Religious architecture is a notoriously conservative field in most societies, and except for the sanctuaries described above Republican and early Imperial Rome produced largely conservative buildings. It took the advent of the Mystery religions of the East to introduce forms that were basically new, and even then change came slowly and reluctantly to Rome. The Underground Basilica just outside the Porta Maggiore *(Plate 55)* is an early and short-lived example of innovative trends, built in the mid-first century A.D. and destroyed very soon afterward. By and large Rome was content to follow traditional lines, the only concessions to the times being the adoption of contemporary materials and the adjustment of the proportions and of the superficial detail to suit contemporary Italo-Hellenistic taste. We have already observed this in what was, in its day, one of the lesser temples of late Republican Rome, the Rectangular Temple in the Forum Boarium *(Plate 60)*, but much the same could have been said of the great state temple of Jupiter Optimus Maximus on the Capitoline. This was burned down in 83 B.C. and was rebuilt and rededicated in 69 B.C. by the same Q. Lutatius Catulus who ten years earlier had built the Tabularium. The plan remained that of its venerable predecessor, but the proportions, though still not as lofty as its builders would have liked, were quite new; so was the classical detail, including the marble columns brought by Sulla from the unfinished Temple of Zeus Olympios in Athens.

There were also, of course, a few real innovations. One such was the introduction of circular peripteral temples modeled more or less directly on those of Greece. The one in the Forum Boarium *(Plates 13, 14)* is still an almost purely Greek building, built in the first half of the first century B.C. by Greek workmen working in Greek materials. The so-called Temple of Vesta at Tibur (Tivoli), a nearly-contemporaneous building, followed similar models but adapted them to suit the local materials and the locally accepted version of the Hellenistic Corinthian order *(Plates 61–63)*. The most notable innovations were the concrete walls of the cella *(Plate 61)* and the substitution of a low, molded podium for the stepped surround of conventional Greek practice. Temple B in the Largo Argentina *(Plate 64)*, though slightly earlier, represents a further concession to Italic tradition by the introduction of a forward-facing, pedimental porch—an architectural solecism by Greek standards, but almost a necessary one in the con-

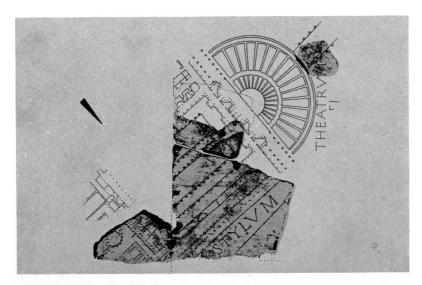

text of a row of small temples of traditionally Italic plan and one with far-reaching implications for the future. Innovations there were, but broadly speaking this was an architecture of gradual adaptation and cautious advance.

The domestic architecture of the last centuries of the Republic presents an altogether livelier picture. The censorious might voice their disapproval of the outpouring of wealth on private luxury, as happened around 100 B.C. when Lucius Crassus, the orator, used six columns of imported Hymettan marble for the atrium of his house on the Palatine. But the existence of that wealth could not be disputed, and despite many pious protestations of admiration for the old-fashioned virtues of hard work and frugal living, most of the newly moneyed classes were eager to spend it. One result was an orgy of private building. Again Rome was not, architecturally speaking, a front runner. The wealthy families maintained their town residences as a convenience, enriching them with every available luxury. But the new Italo-Hellenistic architecture called for space, and that was a commodity in short supply in Rome itself. It was in their country houses, in their suburban villas, and, in the last century of the Republic, along the coasts of Latium and Campania that the rich could indulge their fancy to the full *(Plate 53).*

This fact needs to be borne very clearly in mind in any discussion of the domestic architecture of the later Republic. Although this architecture has been the subject of much debate in the past (much of it highly speculative), interest in it has almost all focused on one particular type, the atrium house. This was the standard type of town house of the well-to-do citizens of Pompeii and Herculaneum; and since in this respect they were echoing Roman urban practice, it was an important component of the domestic architecture of its time. But one must remember that it was only one aspect of the larger picture.

For example, by Augustan times the atrium house had at least three centuries of continuous use behind it, and it was reasonable enough for contemporary scholars to regard it as in some sense ancestrally Italic—very possibly Etruscan *(Tuscanicum),* as both Varro and Vitruvius believed. So far as the atrium itself is concerned, they may well have been right. A rectangular, timber-roofed hall, symmetrical along its longer axis and lit and ventilated through an opening in the center of the roof *(Plates 65, 66):* this is a fairly basic type of dwelling, and with a little ingenuity plausible analogies can be found for it in the rock-cut tombs and terracotta models of classical Etruria. But houses of this sort are as yet notably absent from Rosellae, from Acqua Rossa (the sixth-century Etruscan predecessor of Roman Ferentinum, near Viterbo), and from the city blocks of fifth-century

Marzabotto. Until excavation can give us a more comprehensive vision of Etruscan and early Italic cities, the protohistory of the atrium is probably best left to the archaeologist. The architectural historian must rest content with the unquestionable fact that by the turn of the fourth and third centuries a type of house centered on the atrium had taken shape and was already in use in the country towns of Samnite Campania.

Pompeii and Herculaneum can only give us a partial view of the picture. We can see, for example, that even in the towns of Campania there were already population pressures and that land values were rising quickly; the town houses became more compact, often with an upper story around the atrium and with galleries facing onto the street. Valuable street frontages were converted into shops *(Plate 67)*, and many of the wealthiest families moved out of town altogether. What these towns cannot show us is the result of similar population pressures in Rome itself, where the multi-storied, timber-framed tenement houses of the popular quarters were already a by-word for poor living conditions. But they are vividly described in the contemporary literature, and under the Early Empire we have the apartment houses at Ostia, which were in many respects their successors.

Another notable gap in our knowledge of Roman domestic architecture arises from the fact that not one of the large Republican country or suburban residences has been the subject of serious excavation. We know a great deal about them and about their artistic contents from contemporary writers, but the architecture of the buildings themselves has been sadly neglected. Many stood on terraced platforms which incorporated galleries and other substructures: the northwest facade of the Villa of the Mysteries at Pompeii *(Plate 73)* is arcaded in the manner of the Temple of Jupiter Anxur at Tarracina. We know that they borrowed freely from contemporary urban practice, and we may confidently assume that because many of the living rooms were designed to look outward onto the surrounding landscape, not inward upon their own courtyards and gardens, they in turn inspired what is one of the most distinctive trends in the last phase of the architecture of Pompeii and Herculaneum. But we must admit that, with such rare exceptions as the Villa of Pompey at Albano *(Plate 72)*, we know little about what seems to have been one of the most exciting, forward-looking trends in late Republican architecture.

It is, therefore, only about the town house that we can speak in any detail. Here at any rate, in a building such as the House of the Surgeon at Pompeii *(Plate 68)*, we are on firm ground in stating that by about 300 B.C. all the elements of the typical atrium house had already taken shape: a small axial entrance hall *(vestibulum)* flanked by

58. *Rome, Tabularium, facade overlooking the Forum. The three arches were originally part of a continuous arcade*

59. *Rome, Tabularium, interior staircase*

53

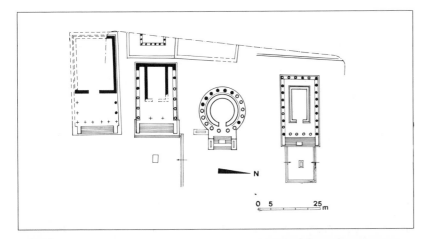

a pair of service rooms; a much larger central hall *(atrium)* with bed chambers down either long side (the central basin, or *impluvium,* is in this case a later addition); at the far end of the atrium a vestigial transverse corridor *(alae);* and beyond it the main living rooms, of which the central one (the *tablinum*), originally the family archive and perhaps also the master bedroom, came in time to be the principal reception room, closed off from the atrium by wooden screens or curtains and looking out through windows onto the garden beyond. Another early (third century B.C.) Pompeian residence is the House of Sallust *(Plate 70),* occupying an irregular city block, some of whose frontages were from the outset rented out as shops.

The subsequent development of the town house followed a predictable course. Apart from the results of the social pressures referred to above and from a steady improvement in building materials and techniques, the main formative influences came unquestionably from the Greek world: at first, as the detail of the architectural ornament shows, directly from that part of it for which Tarentum was at the time the most influential center, and then more generally from the Hellenistic world at large. One far-reaching innovation was the replacement of the old walled garden by the peristyle, an elegant porticoed quadrangle containing a formal garden, fountains, and statuary, toward which in the course of time many of the living rooms of the house inevitably gravitated *(Plate 74).* Another was the Hellenization of the atrium by the introduction of supporting columns, four at first, at the angles of the central fountain basin (the so-called tetrastyle atrium of Vitruvius), and then six or more (the "Corinthian" atrium), turning it in effect into a miniature peristyle. The luxurious second-century B.C. House of the Faun at Pompeii illustrates both of these trends *(Plate 69).* As the architecturally more versatile peristyle took over, so inevitably the importance of the old Italic nucleus dwindled. In a building such as the House of the Stags at Herculaneum *(Plate 75),* built not long before A.D. 79, the atrium has become little more than a vestibule, with the living rooms disposed symmetrically around the central courtyard and around the terrace beyond it, looking out over the Bay of Naples. Here and there atrium houses of the old type lingered on—three are still shown in one of the fragments of the Severan marble plan of Rome, dating from soon after A.D. 200—but the essential steps in the transformation of the old Italic house to the forms current under the early Empire had already taken place in the second and first centuries B.C.

To the sanctuaries, the public buildings, and the private houses of Republican Central Italy we must add one final category—that of harborworks, granaries, and warehouses, of which more and more were needed as Rome became the commercial and political center of

66. *Pompeii, House of the Menander, atrium*
67. *Pompeii, shops with residential upper stories overlooking the Via dell'Abbondanza*
68. *Pompeii, House of the Surgeon, plan of the earliest structures (third century B.C.)*

69. *Pompeii, plan of the House of the Faun, a large house of the second century B.C., with two atria and two peristyles*

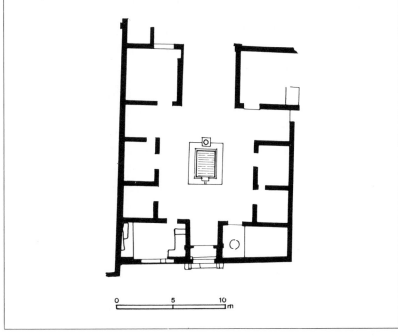

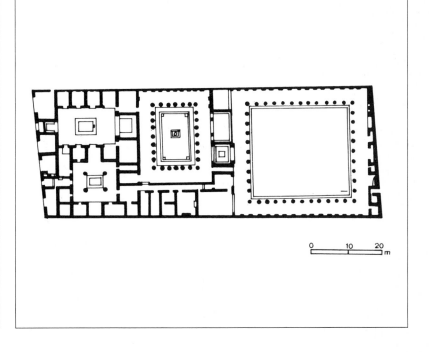

70. *Pompeii, House of Sallust, second century* B.C.: *The street facade was occupied in the latest period by shops, a bar, and a bakery*

71. *Pompeii, Villa of the Mysteries, plan showing the complex at the moment of its maximum prosperity, before the earthquake of* A.D. *62*

the Mediterranean world. By a happy accident one of these warehouses, the Porticus Aemilia, built in 193 B.C. and restored in 174 B.C., is still partially standing *(Plate 77)*. Although it is the earliest concrete-vaulted building preserved in Rome, its preservation is not perhaps quite so fortuitous as it might seem, for it was precisely in utilitarian buildings such as this that architects were most free to develop the functional, durable forms for which the new material was suited, without any prior conceptions of what was architecturally fitting. This is a subject to which we shall be returning in a later chapter; it is sufficient here to note that once again it was in the last two centuries of the Republic that the foundations of subsequent Roman architectural achievement were well and truly laid.

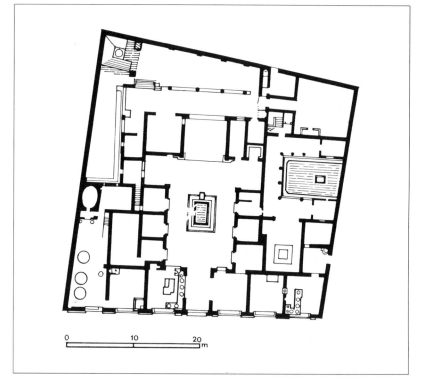

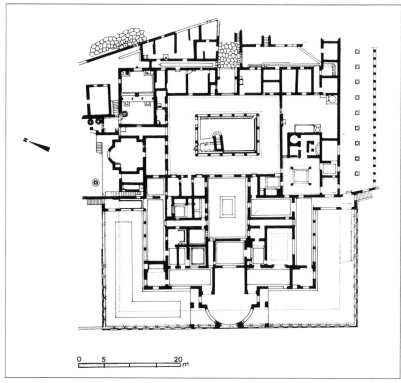

72. *Albanum (Albano), Villa of Pompey. The platform is that of the original building; the angled rooms belong to a reconstruction of the first century* A.D.

73. *Pompeii, Villa of the Mysteries, northwest facade*
74. *Pompeii, House of the Vettii, peristyle*

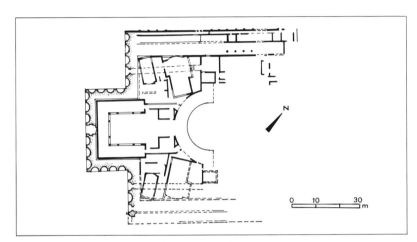

75, 76. *Herculaneum, House of the Stags and House of the Mosaic Atrium, plan and restored view of the south facade, built over the old walls*

77. *Rome, Porticus Aemilia, warehouse adjoining the Tiber River. Second-century* B.C. *construction*

78. *Rome, underground sanctuary of Mithras, beneath the church of San Clemente*

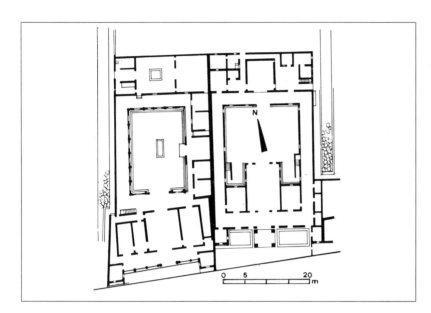

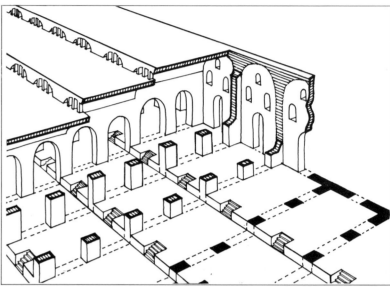

Chapter Two   AUGUSTAN AND EARLY IMPERIAL
ROME: THE CONSERVATIVE TRADITION

The victory of Caesar's nephew and heir, Octavianus, over Marcus Antonius and Cleopatra at Actium in 31 B.C. was one of the decisive events of history. It put an end to the bitter struggle for power which for half a century had periodically divided the Roman Republic into two warring camps. For the next half-century until his death in A.D. 14 Octavianus, better known as Augustus (the title which was conferred on him four years later by a grateful senate), was undisputed master of the Mediterranean world. He left to his adopted heir, Tiberius, and to the latter's successors the framework of a system of authoritarian rule which, though power was to change hands violently many times within it, was in itself never again seriously challenged from within. This was the system we refer to as the Roman Empire.

The term, like many other universally accepted terms, is equivocal, applicable alike to the political unit which was the result of the establishment of Roman rule over a large part of the civilized world and to the system of government whereby Rome exercised that rule through the authority of an emperor who was an absolute monarch in all but name. The Roman architecture of our era was a product of the Empire in both senses of that term, and we do well at this point to discuss briefly a few of those aspects which most directly concern the study of the architecture of the period.

In the first place it should be emphasized that as a physical entity the Roman Empire had largely already come into being during the last two centuries of the Republic. Another hundred and fifty years were to pass before the tide of Roman expansion reached its peak, under Trajan, and almost everywhere there existed the huge task of consolidation and organization. But with the annexation of Egypt Augustus was able to complete the effective reunion of the Hellenistic world. In the preceding chapter we discussed the impact of Hellenistic civilization on Central Italy, which had hitherto lain outside the main cultural stream. In the eastern Mediterranean, on the other hand, despite the political divisions of the Hellenistic age, there was already a secure common basis of Greek language, Greek thought, and—in a variety of lively local forms—Greek material culture. Augustus's achievement was to bring about the peace and prosperity resulting from a common political framework, thus enabling the old Hellenized civilizations of Greece and Asia Minor, Syria, and Egypt to meet and mingle in a renewed ferment of creative activity.

In the West matters were different. Here, outside the Mediterranean coastlands where Greek and Roman settlement had established a narrow fringe of Hellenized urban life, there were vast areas which in this respect were almost virgin territory. Some of these, such as Gaul, had recently been conquered; others, such as the Alpine valleys and Dalmatia and the lands along the Danube, had still to be brought under control. In both it was initially Rome—the Hellenized Rome of the late Republic and the newly established Imperial Rome, capital of the civilized world—which was called on to supply the models.

Underlying the newly found political unity of the Roman world there was therefore a profound difference between the Greek-speaking East and the Latin-speaking West, between those areas where Rome was heir by adoption to an older civilization and those where she was herself the principal source of such civilization. Between the two there were of course innumerable points of contact, points of mutual interaction and assimilation, and as the Pax Romana took root and flourished, these contacts grew stronger daily. But at every turn one is made aware also of the differences in historical background and tradition, which were at once a source of weakness and of strength, and which left their mark on almost every aspect of daily life.

Another fact of empire, namely the concentration of power into the hands of a single man, the emperor, was more varied in its impact. Monarchs are almost by definition builders, either from personal taste or because they are the ultimate source of public patronage; and since Rome was both the seat and the symbol of authority the personality of the reigning emperor was almost bound to be a major factor in shaping public taste. Outside Rome too the authority of a strong central government had a powerful unifying effect, which was greatly accelerated as increasing numbers of citizens from the provinces came to hold high imperial office and in due course the imperial throne itself: Trajan (A.D. 98–117), from Italica in Spain, was the first non-Italian emperor, Septimius Severus (A.D. 193–211) the first non-European. With the consolidation of the monarchy and the steady growth of the ceremonials of an imperial court there was also a call for new types of building. Where Augustus had been content—ostentatiously so—with the house of a well-to-do private citizen, barely a century later Domitian (A.D. 81–96) had built the great imperial residence on the Palatine, the architectural prototype of a long series of imperial and vice-regal residences throughout the Empire and the building from which all subsequent "palaces" derive their name. This was all familiar ground: the Hellenistic monarchs had indulged in their own forms of architectural pomp, and many of the victorious generals of the Republic had chosen to spend part of their booty on lavish public building. Mausolus of Halicarnassus, Eumenes of Pergamon, Sulla, and Pompey had all left the mark of their personal taste on the architecture of their day. What was new was that all of this was now concentrated in the hands of a single man, the emperor, and for a time at any rate within a single city, Rome. With the accession of Augustus we turn a page in the history of classical architecture.

For one who was served by the greatest writers, architects, and artists of his day and on whom the spotlight of history shone so fiercely for more than half a century, Augustus's personal taste in the arts remains tantalizingly elusive. Augustus the man was too successfully buried beneath the sedulously fostered image of Augustus, Pater Patriae, the father of his country. It is a reasonable guess that his patronage of the arts was less the result of any deep personal artistic conviction than a conventional response to a familiar situation. Artistic patronage was not only one of the accepted duties of a public figure: as Sulla, Pompey, Caesar, and others before him had realized, it could also be a powerful political weapon. A building such as the Temple of Divus Julius, his adopted father, or that of Mars Ultor ("Mars the Avenger") was as loaded with political meaning as Vergil's *Aeneid* or the reliefs on the Ara Pacis. That the markedly conservative flavor of most of the artistic output of Augustus's reign was in tune with his personal taste is another reasonable guess, although even here we must reckon with the fact that such attitudes were also good politics. As a professed upholder of the traditional Roman virtues, he stood to gain nothing by offending the sort of die-hard conservative sentiment which Pompey and Caesar had disregarded to their cost. With the Theater of Pompey an accomplished fact, the addition of two others, that of Lucius Cornelius Balbus (13 B.C.) and that built by Augustus himself in memory of his nephew, Marcellus *(Plate 79),* was evidently felt to be acceptable; but it can hardly be an accident that the amphitheater built in the Campus Martius by Statilius Taurus in 30 B.C. and destroyed by the fire of A.D. 64 was still a semipermanent building, with a superstructure of timber on stone foundations. In Campania, a modest country town such as Pompeii might already boast a permanent stone-built amphitheater, but in Rome it still paid to tread cautiously.

It is by his works that Augustus the builder must be judged, and this assuredly is how he would have wished it. A large section of his official testament, the *Res Gestae Divi Augusti*, is devoted to the list of monuments built or restored during his long reign, and Suetonius records his boast that "he found Rome a city of brick and left it a city of marble." Much of the earlier part of his vast building program was shaped by the legacy of ideas and uncompleted projects inherited from Julius Caesar, but it was the hand of Augustus that guided them to completion. Later emperors might add, restore, and otherwise embellish, but they did so within a framework whose broad outlines had been firmly established by Augustus.

Was there a single "Augustan" style of architecture? Many architectural historians have felt that such a unified building program should generate a recognizable style and, failing to find it, they have picked on this or that particular monument as typical, banishing from

the corpus of known Augustan monuments any buildings that do not happen to conform to that model. Such tidy-minded attitudes disregard both the historical and the archaeological facts: for one thing it must be remembered that Augustus's reign was a long one, and much can happen in half a century; for another, with so many buildings going up at one time every conceivable workshop must have been pressed into service. Augustus himself, as Caesar's executor and heir, was already actively at work very soon after the latter's murder in 44 B.C., and there were many others no less active. Over the next twenty or thirty years a great deal of building in Rome was in fact still being promoted and financed, just as it had been under the Republic, by public-spirited or politically ambitious individuals. Most of these buildings are lost, but enough remains of some of them to show that they do indeed represent a wide variety of workshops and styles: the Regia, for example, restored in 36 B.C. by Cnaeus Domitius Calvinus and the first building in Rome known to have used marble from the newly opened quarries at Carrara; the Temple of Divus Julius, built by Augustus himself and dedicated in 29 B.C.; the Temple of Saturn, rebuilt by C. Munatius Plancus (the founder of Lyon) probably soon after 30 B.C.; and the Temple of Apollo in Circo, built by C. Sosianus around 20 B.C. At this time at any rate there was not one prevailing style but many.

Later, as what had initially been a temporary political settlement hardened gradually into an established system, more and more of the real patronage fell into the hands of Augustus himself, to be exercised through men of his own choice. If there is any single building that deserves to be singled out as representative of the Augustan age, it is unquestionably the great state monument of this later period, the Forum Augustum, together with the Temple of Mars Ultor. Even so, the major temples of the later part of his reign, those of Castor and Pollux *(Plates 80, 81)* and of Concord, both built by his stepson Tiberius and dedicated respectively in A.D. 6 and A.D. 10, still display so marked an individuality that several eminent scholars have felt it necessary to postulate an otherwise unrecorded rebuilding of the former later in the first century A.D. They are certainly mistaken: the building as it stands is undoubtedly the work of Tiberius. But the dilemma will serve to emphasize that even at this late date there was still no single, all-embracing Augustan style. As we shall see, a pattern was emerging, and the story of monumental building in Rome during the rest of the first century A.D. does indeed follow a broadly uniform stream of development. But it was still a stream of many currents.

What were the essential constituents of the architecture of the Augustan age? One was clearly the mixture of native Italic and imported Hellenistic ideas, materials, and practices which constituted the architecture of the last two centuries of the Republic. A second was the legacy of ideas and of uncompleted buildings which Augustus inherited from his adopted father, Julius Caesar, a legacy which absorbed a very large part of his own building activity during the thirty years following Caesar's death. A third strand in the fabric was the triumphant affirmation of marble as an essential part of the monumental builder's repertory; and a fourth, intimately connected with the introduction of marble, was the emergence of the sort of classicizing taste of which the Forum Augustum is the outstanding representative. A fifth and very important element was the steady development of Roman concrete as an all-purpose building material; but since this was an aspect of the Republican heritage to the formal development of which the architects of the Augustan age seem to have given very little explicit thought (although they were always glad to use it wherever conventionally appropriate), it will be discussed in the next chapter, which deals specifically with Roman concrete construction.

As we have seen, the Hellenized Italic architecture of late Republican Rome was a rather sober plant, its full potentialities exploited only outside the capital, in some of the outlying sanctuaries of Latium, and very possibly also in the domestic architecture of the wealthy villas. But its roots ran deep. Along with such elements of the older Italic tradition as the monumental use of dressed stone and the frontally disposed Italic temple, Roman architectural thinking had accepted and absorbed more recent innovations such as concrete vaulting; a general abandonment of the forms and proportions of the older Italic stone and timber architecture in favor of the traditional Greek orders; the arch, with or without (but in urban monumental architecture still usually with) a veneer of decorative classicism; and a number of relatively recent hybrid creations, such as the basilica and the Roman theater. There were still a few venerable buildings remaining from earlier times, but by the middle of the first century B.C. these had long acquired the status of historical monuments. Contemporary architectural taste had successfully come to terms with the results of belonging to the larger Hellenistic world.

This established late Republican tradition was the inevitable point of departure for the architects of the Augustan age. At the level of building materials and practices it could hardly be otherwise. These were the materials that local contractors had at hand and this was how they were accustomed to using them. In matters of design too and, for a time, of architectural ornament there was a marked strain of cautiously experimental conservatism. Although the permanent theater was a relative newcomer to the capital, the arcaded outer facade of the Theater of Marcellus (which in this

80. *Rome, Temple of Castor and Pollux, as rebuilt in* A.D. *6*

81. *Rome, Temple of Castor and Pollux, detail of an Augustan capital*

respect may well have been following a precedent established by the Theater of Pompey) could be treated in precisely the same way as the Republican Tabularium *(Plate 24)*. Structural arcades framed within the compartments of a decorative order were ideally suited to the needs of an architecture in which the element of sheer size posed ever-increasing problems for a more conventional use of the classical orders. They could be applied with equal success to the basilicas of the Forum Romanum, to porticoes, to commemorative arches, to family mausoleums—in any context in fact where the newly evolving architecture called for a decorous top-dressing of traditionally acceptable classicism. Nearly a century later the outer facade of the Colosseum was still following faithfully a tradition established in Republican Rome.

Another, but more recent and potentially more adventurous, legacy from the past was that of the buildings begun or projected by Julius Caesar. Here we may usefully distinguish between two groups: those buildings that were started and brought to varying stages of completion during his lifetime, many of them planned as early as 54 B.C. on the proceeds of his conquest of Gaul; and those which still lay partially or wholly in the future at the time of his death in 44 B.C.

Of the earlier group, the most substantial enterprise was nothing less than an attempt to bring order to the west end of the Forum Romanum, a work which Sulla may be said to have begun twenty-five years earlier by commissioning the building of the Tabularium. Caesar's project involved the complete rebuilding of one of the old Republican basilicas, the Basilica Sempronia (henceforth to be known as the Basilica Julia), and the restoration of another, the Basilica Aemilia; the moving of the Rostra (the orators' platform) and of the Curia (the Senate), the former to an axial position in the middle of the west end of the Forum and the latter to a new site with a frontage related to that of the Basilica Aemilia; and behind the Curia, and carefully aligned with it, the construction of a whole new forum of his own (the Forum Julium)—a long, narrow, rectangular enclosure flanked by porticoes, at the end of which was incorporated, after his victory over Pompey at Pharsalus in 48 B.C., a temple in honor of the divine ancestress of the Julian family, Venus Genetrix *(Plate 82)*. Though still incomplete, some of these buildings were sufficiently advanced to be dedicated in 46 B.C., while others can barely have been started in the year 44. But the main lines of the scheme were established before Caesar's death, and in this case it only remained for Augustus to finish what had been begun by siting the new Temple of Divus Julius at the east end of the Forum, facing down the axis toward the new Rostra *(Plate 83)*. Given the number of venerable monuments that had to be respected, the result was a commendable attempt to invest the heart of the capital with an order and a dignity appropriate to its new status.

One other of Caesar's earlier projects calls for brief mention—Rome's first public library. A librarian had been appointed (Marcus Terentius Varro, the historian and philologist), and a start made on the collection of books, but whether a building to house them had been begun before Caesar's death we cannot say for certain. It was completed by Asinius Pollio in 39 B.C.

In all of this Augustus and (in the earlier years) his contemporaries were following lines already broadly established, so that wherever we find a departure from traditional architectural practice there is a reason for it. The surviving remains of the Basilica Julia, for example, are not those of Caesar's building, which was burned down, probably about 12 B.C., but those of its later Augustan replacement, dedicated in A.D. 12. The plan and the exterior followed conventional lines, but the internal ambulatory galleries, instead of being carried on columns and being timber-roofed, as were those of the Basilica Aemilia or, a century later, those of the Basilica Ulpia, consisted simply of a treble ring of cruciform piers, externally of marble and internally of travertine, which carried concrete vaults, leaving only the central hall to be roofed in the traditional manner. The intention was presumably to reduce the risk of fire. In such a place and context this must all have seemed startlingly modern, though the modernity was carefully tempered to public taste behind a conventional facade—an art at which the Romans were adept in every walk of life, none more so than Augustus himself.

Of Caesar's grandiose ideas for the formal enlargement of Rome by building out into the Campus Martius (which was itself to be enlarged by diverting the course of the Tiber between the Pons Mulvius and the Vatican) we know little more than the barest outlines, as recorded in one of Cicero's letters. A planning expert was, it seems, brought in from Athens, and the formulation of the project had reached the point where detailed provisions for it could be incorporated into the Town Planning Act of 45 B.C. (the *Lex de Urbe Augenda*); but little if any action can have been taken before Caesar's death.

It was left to Augustus to convert the vision into reality. He set about the task with an eye for the long-term requirements of the project, which is all the more remarkable in that work was started in 33 B.C., two years before the battle of Actium. He delegated the work to his faithful friend and colleague Marcus Vipsanius Agrippa, who more than any other single man may be held to have shaped the course of contemporary architecture at this critical moment of its development. It was Agrippa who in the year 33 restored Rome's

82. *Rome, the Imperial Forums. 1) Forum Julium and Temple of Venus Genetrix; 2) Forum Augustum and Temple of Mars Ultor; 3) Northwest end of the Templum Pacis; 4) Forum Transitorium and Temple of Minerva; 5) Forum of Trajan: a. monumental entrance; b. equestrian statue of Trajan; c. Basilica Ulpia; d. Column of Trajan; e. libraries; f. Temple of Divus Traianus; g. Markets of Trajan*

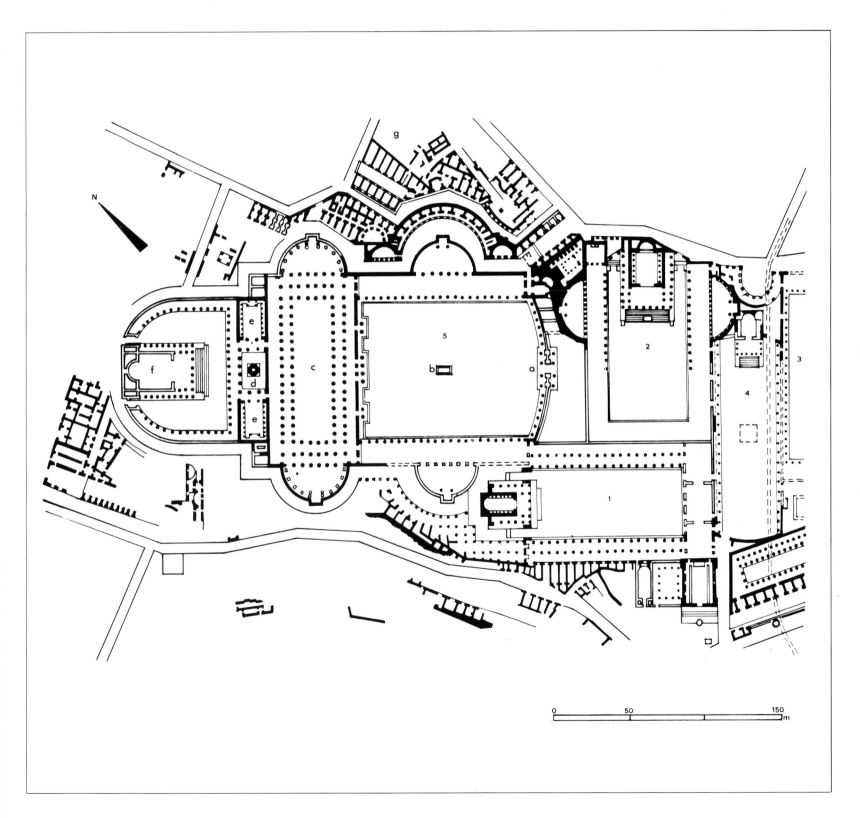

four existing aqueducts and added a fifth, the Aqua Julia—was this too one of Caesar's projects?—while also starting the colossal task of modernizing the city's drainage system. The scheme to divert the Tiber was dropped, but the embankments were repaired and modernized and the low-lying ground alongside the river raised. At the same time work was begun on the addition of a whole new monumental complex in the Campus Martius, beyond the Circus Flaminius and the Theater of Pompey. This included the Saepta (projected by Caesar himself in 54 B.C., but only finally completed in 26 B.C.), the Pantheon, the Basilica of Neptune, and—the most startling and appreciated innovation—Rome's first public bath building, the Baths of Agrippa. All of this was laid out in a landscaped setting which included porticoes, gardens, a canal, and an artificial lake, and which in time came to incorporate many other monuments, including the Mausoleum of Augustus and the Ara Pacis. Agrippa's work was all swept away in the fire of A.D. 80, and the Pantheon, although it still bears his name *(Plate 153),* is in fact the work of Hadrian. But we do know two things about its predecessor, which was finished in 25 B.C. One is that its plan was unusual, seemingly a cella wider than it was deep, with a narrower porch in the middle of one long side. The other is that it incorporated marble caryatids carved by an Athenian sculptor, Diogenes. It is tempting to believe—though this can only be a guess—that it was deliberately planned as a free adaptation of the Erechtheum in Athens.

It is very likely that the marble quarries of Carrara (ancient Luni) were yet another legacy from Caesar. A new quarry takes years to become operative, and marble from Carrara was already reaching Rome in time to be used in the rebuilding of the Regia in 36 B.C. Both white and colored marbles had been imported in increasing quantities during the last century of the Republic, the former from Attica, the latter from Numidia and from several quarries in the Aegean; but it was the opening up of the Carrara quarries which in a few decades transformed what had been an exotic luxury into a standard building material for certain types of monumental architecture. Marble was still expensive, and except for columns, capitals, entablatures, and pavements it was normally used only as a veneer for other, cheaper materials. A building such as Augustus's own Temple of Apollo on the Palatine, the walls of which were of solid marble, remained the exception rather than the rule. But the wholesale adoption of marble in Rome by Augustus—and his claim to have left it a city of marble was no idle boast—was an important event. It established new standards of opulence for the capital and inevitably affected taste throughout those parts of the Empire which did not have an established marble architecture of their own. Within a

generation the results were making themselves felt in buildings such as the now-lost Temple of Rome and Augustus at Narbonne and the Maison Carrée at Nîmes *(Plate 219).*

The culmination of the Augustan building program was the Forum Augustum. The Temple of Mars Ultor ("Mars the Avenger"), which stood in the same relation to the Forum Augustum as the Temple of Venus Genetrix did to the Forum Julium, had been projected as long ago as the battle of Philippi in 42 B.C.; but it was still incomplete when the Forum Augustum itself was inaugurated exactly forty years later, and much of the work of both temple and forum undoubtedly belongs to the last decade of the first century B.C. Here, if anywhere, we are confronted by the architecture of the Augustan age at the moment of its full maturity *(Plates 85, 86).*

The plan was essentially that of its predecessor, the Forum Julium (which Augustus himself had completed), enriched by the addition of a pair of semicircular courtyards opening outward off the flanking porticoes. This refinement may well have been suggested to the architect in the first place by the shape of the ground available —Suetonius tells us that Augustus was unable to purchase as much land as he wished—but in any event it allowed for the introduction of a lively and characteristically suggestive cross-axis on a line coinciding with that of the facade of the temple. A century later Apollodorus of Damascus was to use the same motif with great effect in the Forum of Trajan. Today, with the porticoes leveled, it is the flanking courtyards and the great enclosing wall of the Forum Augustum that dominate one's vision, giving a false impression of spaciousness *(Plate 85).* In antiquity, with the porticoes marching up either side of the paved open space and tightly framing the temple, which stood at one end on its lofty podium, dominating the whole, the feeling must rather have been one of enclosure *(Plate 87),* relieved only by a cross-axis which was all the more effective for being suggested rather than baldly stated.

All of this was still very much in the old Italic tradition, more tightly knit, more self-consciously monumental, but still calling to mind a complex such as the remodeled forum at Pompeii *(Plate 19).* What was new here was in the first place the scale and wealth of the materials: gleaming white marble for the temple and other architectural details, set off by the colored marbles of the columns of the porticoes, the pavements, and the facing of the inner walls; and secondly the detail of the craftsmanship, which reveals unmistakably the hand of workmen brought from Athens for the purpose. This appears most conspicuously in the caryatids from the attic stories of the porticoes, where they alternated with huge *clipei,* carved medallions with a central human head; or again in the graceful Pegasus

83. *Rome, Forum Romanum. 1) Curia (Senate); 2) Basilica Aemilia;*
3) Temple of Antoninus and Faustina; 4) Temple of Divus Julius;
5) Regia; 6) Arch of Augustus; 7) so-called Temple of Vesta; 8)
House of the Vestal Virgins; 9) Temple of Castor and Pollux; 10)
Vestibule to the Domus Augustana; 11) Basilica Julia; 12) Temple of
Saturn; 13) Temple of Divus Vespasianus; 14) Temple of Concord;
15) Arch of Septimius Severus; 16) Rostra

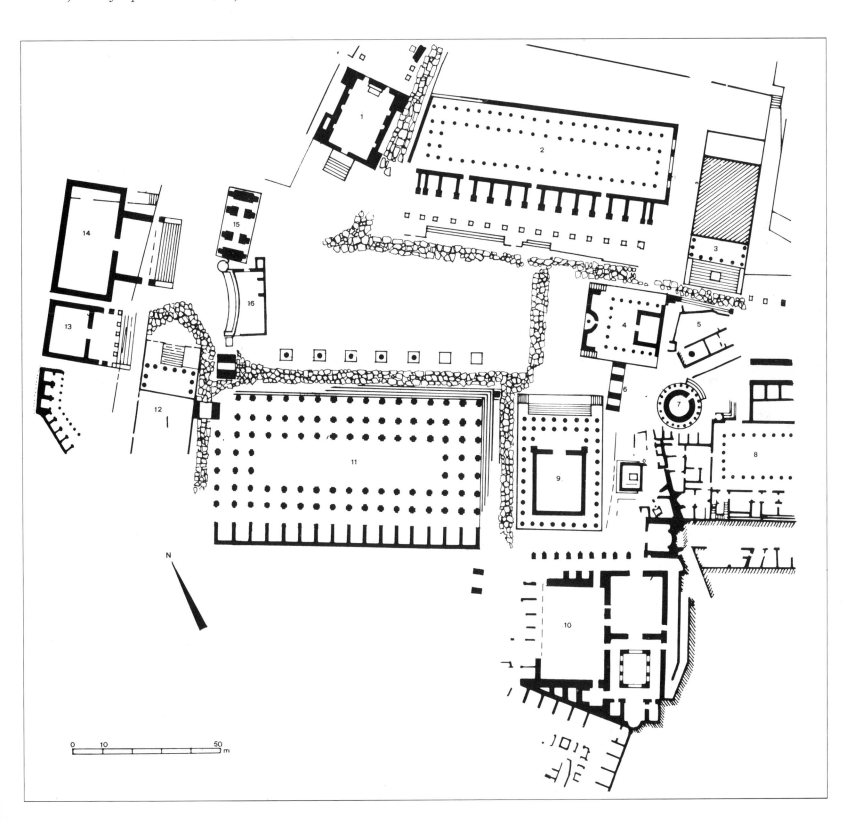

pilaster capitals from the interior of the temple, the models for which can be seen at Eleusis in Attica. But Attic influence is in fact implicit in almost every detail of the marble carving *(Plate 84)*.

This Attic influence was nothing new; and although under the Republic it meant some buildings that were Greek in both materials and workmanship and the presence in Rome of Greek architects such as Hermodorus of Salamis in the later second century B.C. (almost certainly selected as a specialist in marble work) or the town planner brought in by Caesar to advise on the extension of the city, the influence was at any rate partly reciprocal. The summoning of Marcus Cossutius to Athens by Antiochus IV of Syria (175–164 B.C.) to undertake the rebuilding of the Temple of Zeus Olympios is an unusually clear and early indication of the reputation abroad of Roman architects; this was reinforced by the veteran settlements at Corinth in 44 B.C. and, after the Civil Wars, at Philippi and Nicopolis near Actium, where there are clear traces of the influence of contemporary Italian architecture, particularly that of Campania. Agrippa himself, in building the Odeion in the Agora of Athens, was undoubtedly drawing on this source.

There was, then, already a healthy element of give and take between Greece and Rome. But if we are right in regarding the Forum Augustum and the Ara Pacis as the state monuments *par excellence* of the mature years of Augustus's reign, there can be no doubt that here in the capital the scales were weighted heavily in favor of what Greek skills and Greek craftsmanship had to offer Rome.

In terms of techniques and quality of workmanship this was a natural, almost inevitable, product of the shift from local materials to marble. Whatever one's opinion of the quality of contemporary Greek art (and more particularly of contemporary Attic art, since it was predominantly Athens which supplied the master craftsmen for these aspects of the Augustan program) there can be no doubt about the Attic artists' consummate technical skill and versatility. The severest critic of Augustan art will not deny its professionalism and its manifest mastery of the media employed.

It is only when one pauses to reflect on the products of these technical skills that doubts arise. State art is rarely disinterested. Even the Parthenon was created to be the visible symbol of a particular political situation. If it is also an outstanding work of art, this is due to the happy accident that permitted its creators to draw upon the resources of a great artistic tradition at the moment of its full maturity. Augustan Rome had few such resources of its own and (as we shall see) those which it had it was reluctant or unable to recognize as adequate for the task. Consequently it was very largely dependent on the skills of others, and except for certain of the minor arts—

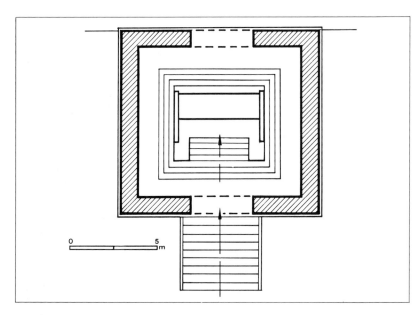

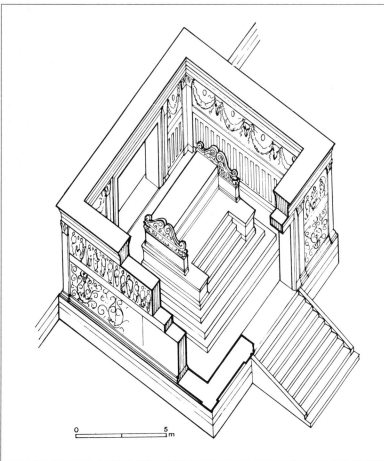

decorative stuccowork, for example *(Plate 88)*—the principal source upon which it chose to draw was Athens; and Athens was itself by this time creatively bankrupt.

The results are plain to see on the Ara Pacis (Altar of Peace), which stood at the northern end of the Campus Martius, alongside the Via Flaminia. Decreed by the Senate in 13 B.C. and dedicated four years later, its object was to embody in visible form the gift of peace which Augustus had bestowed upon a war-weary world. Whatever the tribesmen of the Alps or of the mountains of northwestern Spain may have felt about the Pax Romana, there is no doubt that to the ordinary citizen of the Roman world, worn out by the uncertainties of a century of civil war, this unaccustomed feeling of stability and security was what Augustus stood for.

The form chosen to symbolize this gift, an altar tightly enclosed within a rectangular precinct *(Plates 89, 90),* seems to have been a free adaptation of the Altar of Pity in the Agora at Athens, and it was carried out in Italian marble under the direction of Attic sculptors. The inner face of the precinct perpetuated in monumental form the pavilion-like wooden enclosure, hung with sacrificial garlands, within which we may imagine the initial consecration ceremony to have taken place. The outer face was divided by a strip of *maeander* ornament into two horizontal zones *(Plate 91)*. All around the lower part ran a continuous dado of stylized acanthus foliage *(Plate 92),* of a type which stems ultimately from Hellenistic Pergamon but which by this date was preserved only in the archaizing repertory of the Attic workshops. The upper part displayed on the two short ends figured panels symbolic of the historic destiny of Rome, and on the two longer sides a frieze with a lifelike representation of the solemn procession of priests, state officials, and members of the imperial family who on July 9th of the year 13 B.C. had consecrated the site.

The first—and most obvious—thing to be said about the Ara Pacis is that it was essentially a monument with a message. Opinions may vary as to its architectural qualities, but to its creators this aspect would have seemed largely irrelevant. They were concerned not with the production of a work of art as such, but with projecting an image. The public they were addressing was not the sophisticated citizenry of Periclean Athens; it was one to whom the opulence and virtuosity of the carving would have been far more eloquent than any aesthetic nuances of design.

Art in the service of a political ideal: countless examples from our own time show the depths of tastelessness to which such an attitude can lead. The Romans were fortunate (or unfortunate, depending upon one's point of view) in that their preferred models

were Greek. Bianchi Bandinelli has argued, on the whole most persuasively, that in the field of sculpture the result of this preference was to set the creative genius of Italy back by a couple of centuries or more; it was not simply that the models chosen were Greek, but that they were indiscriminately Greek, of all styles and periods, chosen for the authority conferred on them by their country of origin rather than for any real sympathy with the style or the taste which they represented.

So far as pure sculpture is concerned Bianchi Bandinelli may well be right. But in those cases where sculpture impinges on architecture (as in classical architecture it did at every turn) one finds it less easy to condemn out of hand the success story which the Augustan monuments represent. Even if the acanthus ornament of the Ara Pacis can be shown to be a synthetic re-creation of models which had gone out of fashion in Pergamon a century before, it clearly struck an authentic note in contemporary decorative taste. Within Augustus's own lifetime the acanthus scroll had become part of the standard repertory of architectural ornament in Italy and the western provinces. As for the figured frieze, it too was an instant success. Aesthetically speaking, both the overall design of the altar and the rather banal academicism of the frieze are open to criticism. But as a clear visual projection of a vital contemporary issue, pitched at just the right emotional level and placed in such a way that all could see and study it in its every detail, it would be hard to beat.

It is instructive to compare the placing of the Ara Pacis frieze with that of the great frieze on the Parthenon, which depicts the Panathenaic procession. This too was in its own very different way a lively statement of a contemporary theme; and yet, though a work of far greater intrinsic merit, positioned with all the feeling for architectural niceties which is so characteristically Greek, it was so placed that even with the aid of color its message must always have had to be sensed rather than "read." One can only suppose that to a contemporary Athenian, living in an age which suffered few doubts about its own intellectual and aesthetic values, this did not really matter; the message was already an integral part of himself. In much the same way a medieval sculptor, living in an age with few religious doubts, could afford to carve his masterpieces to the greater glory of God, often with very little regard for the convenience of the human observer. To Augustus and his contemporaries, the heirs to a century of travail and uncertainty, such an attitude would have been incomprehensible. The frieze of the Ara Pacis was artistically meaningful precisely to the extent that it could be easily seen and understood. The measure of its success is the long line of state reliefs on monumental arches and other public monuments of which over the next two hundred years it was the lineal ancestor.

It is the architectural historian's duty to record and to interpret facts, not to praise or condemn. If we have lingered over the Forum Augustum and the Ara Pacis as the two surviving state monuments which between them represent the official Augustan attitudes to the problems of architecture and architectural sculpture, it is not because of their intrinsic aesthetic merits, but because by any reckoning they constitute a milestone in the history of Roman architecture. For historical reasons it could hardly have been otherwise, and before we end our discussion of the Rome of Augustus we shall do well therefore to attempt a brief assessment of the place his great building program has within the larger framework of Roman architectural history.

In one respect it undoubtedly represents a step backward, a closing of doors. Just as during the last century and a half of the Republic the prestige of Greek sculptural art had effectively stifled native Italian taste, so now one promising current within the mainstream of native architectural inspiration, faced by the challenge of the grandiose Neo-classicism of Augustan court taste, was forced into other channels. The great Sanctuary of Fortuna Primigenia at Praeneste had no direct successors: the sort of artistic sensibility which it represented found a partial outlet in the landscaped villas of the wealthy, but monumentally it remains one of the tantalizing "might-have-beens" of architectural history.

Fortunately, as we have already observed during the late Republic, architecture is less vulnerable than sculpture or painting to arbitrary shifts in taste: it touches on matters of everyday habit and social convenience at too many points to be lightly swayed. Over most of the range of contemporary building, including many branches of public architecture, the impact of the renewed Augustan classicism was in fact largely superficial. Theaters, amphitheaters, basilicas, and buildings dedicated to utilitarian and commercial uses continued to follow very much the same lines as before, differing from their predecessors only in the wider variety of building materials employed and, if decorated, in the character and opulence of such decoration. We shall be looking at some of these buildings in the concluding sections of this chapter.

On the level of design the Augustan building program may have closed off several existing lines of development, but on the level of decorative detail it opened up many others. Marble, for example, both white and colored, had come to stay, bringing with it many fresh opportunities as well as problems. It was the opening of the quarries at Carrara which had made this aspect of Augustus's program possible. Now, under Augustus himself and his immediate successors, existing sources for marble were developed *(Plates 93, 94)* and new sources were explored (notably the granites and porphyries

of Egypt); and the entire system of production and distribution was overhauled and rationalized under state control so as to ensure an abundant and varied supply. Marble, which almost within living memory had been a rare luxury material, within a few decades had become a commonplace of public building. In the form of paving tiles and wall veneer it soon spread also into domestic use, and appreciable quantities were reaching even a small country town such as Pompeii before its destruction in A.D. 79. The full implications of the new material, both structural and decorative, were still to make themselves felt, but in this field, as in so many others, it was the Augustan period which set the stage for future development.

One aspect of the increased use of marble which did make itself felt immediately was, as we have seen, that many foreign craftsmen came to Rome to work it, mostly from Attica; and the prestige of buildings such as the Forum Augustum was such that within a generation the motifs and the mannerisms which these craftsmen introduced were accepted in Rome as the basis of the standard repertory of carved architectural ornament. As one might expect, the latter rapidly developed iconographic and stylistic characteristics of its own. Julio-Claudian and Flavian architectural ornament were as Roman as their antecedents had been Greek. Yet the accepted point of departure (to which Trajan's architects were to return a century later) remained the classicizing ornament of Augustan Rome. What had been lost was the corresponding Republican tradition, which was itself based on classical models, but whose development had been shaped by the use of tufa or travertine, normally faced with stucco. In the capital this Republican decorative tradition went out of use almost overnight, never to return. Only in provincial Italy can one find any substantial survivals of it into the Imperial age.

What first strikes the eye about the Augustan buildings of Rome is their lavish top-dressing of *nouveau riche* opulence, coupled with strong overtones of Attic Neo-classicism. This was indeed an important element in the Augustan program: although it may not be to everybody's taste today, it did unquestionably suit the mood of the times, expressing precisely the note of prosperous stability which the Augustan regime wished to convey. But while it is the great state monuments which catch the eye, it must be remembered how much of Augustus's building activity lay in such prosaic but necessary fields as roads and bridges, water supply and drainage, and other practical aspects of urban development. Side by side with the Attic sculptors and the marble workers were innumerable firms of builders, great and small, all working in (and slowly perfecting) the traditional materials which they had inherited from their fathers. Theirs was the "grass-roots" architecture of the day and, as we shall see in the next chapter, they were busy preparing the ground for one of the most spectacular advances in the history of architecture. Seen in this perspective, Augustan Rome is important not so much because of what it actually was as because it set the stage for what was shortly to come.

Whatever the future might hold, however, the immediate effect of the Augustan building program was to accentuate the attitude that for certain categories of public monument the only acceptable style was one which observed the superficial proprieties of the classical Greek orders. This attitude was inevitably strengthened by the deliberately classicizing trend of so much of Augustus's own work. It was only at the other end of the scale—in the sort of commercial and utilitarian constructions where no such prejudices existed—that the native Roman school, working in concrete, was genuinely free to develop along its own lines. There was of course much common ground, and by the middle of the first century A.D. there can have been few buildings which were not drawing to some extent upon both traditions. Nevertheless, in terms of the accepted norms of contemporary architectural thought the distinction is a valid one, determining the face which a particular monument was likely to present to the world; and of the many possible ways of classifying Roman building it is probably the one which at this period is most meaningful in terms of later Roman architectural history. Not until the Renaissance did the older Greek-inspired tradition come fully back into its own, crystallizing for posterity a vision of "Roman" architecture which in reality does scant justice to those aspects of it which were most genuinely and characteristically Roman.

The rest of this chapter will, accordingly, pass in brief review some of the principal monuments of the last phase of the conservative, classicizing, Italo-Hellenistic tradition. In the chapter that follows we shall examine the other face of the coin, tracing the processes which led to the general acceptance of the new architecture which was to be Rome's great original contribution to the sum of European architectural experience.

In many societies the most conservative of all conservative elements is that of established religion. Rome was no exception. Its official temples were all decorously classical buildings, occasionally circular, but far more commonly rectangular, with gabled columnar facades. A few, such as Hadrian's Temple of Venus and Rome, a deliberately archaizing building, were still free-standing in the old Greek manner and colonnaded on all four sides; but the great majority, both in Rome and increasingly in the provinces, followed the Italic model, which stood on a podium and was accessible only from the front, up a flight of steps and through a gabled porch. This was the type which we have already encountered in the Imperial Forums,

95. *Rome, Forum Romanum. Left, Arch of Septimius Severus, Curia, and Temple of Castor and Pollux. Right, Temple of Antoninus and Faustina*

96. *Rome, Temple of Antoninus and Faustina and, built into it, church of San Lorenzo in Miranda (nineteenth-century print)*

a familiar later example being the Temple of Antoninus and Faustina *(Plates 95, 96)*, begun in A.D. 141, which survived until modern times as the church of San Lorenzo in Miranda. Even so revolutionary a building as Hadrian's Pantheon felt it necessary to follow convention in presenting to the outer world a decorously gabled facade.

The fact that the creative future lay with an entirely different type of building does not mean that these temples were not architecturally important in their day. It is true that in the capital their importance was already dwindling: the religious aspirations of the age were increasingly turning to the Oriental Mystery religions, whose more intimate rituals called for an altogether different architectural expression; in this respect the meeting places of the followers of Mithras are typical. The three great state temples of the third century A.D. were anachronisms, grandiose buildings of conventional classical type dedicated to newcomers from the East: Caracalla's gigantic Temple of Serapis on the Quirinal (211–217), the Temple of Sol Invictus Elagabalus *(Plate 97)* on the Palatine (218–222), and Aurelian's Temple of the Sun in the Campus Martius (273–275). It was left to Constantine to make the final break with tradition, when he chose a secular type, the basilica, as the standard place of worship for official Christianity.

However, it is outside of Rome, and particularly in the western provinces, that the type of temple characteristic of Augustan Rome achieved its full architectural significance. Here, in the provinces, a Temple of Rome and Augustus or a Capitolium was often the ultimate symbol of Roman authority, and as such they played an important part in disseminating the outward forms of a traditional classicism. Such buildings include the Maison Carrée at Nîmes *(Plate 219;* dedicated in the names of Gaius and Lucius Caesar, who were at the time Augustus's destined heirs) and the *capitolia* of Sbeitla *(Plate 233)*, Thuburbo Maius *(Plate 274)*, and Dougga *(Plate 275)*, all in North Africa. The forms vary in detail. At Sbeitla, for example, each of the divinities of the Capitoline triad had a separate shrine. But the basic type is clearly derived from the Italic temple of late Republican and early Imperial Italy.

We must remember also that the fusion of the Greek and Italic types of temple could not be without effect on the norms of even conventional architectural taste. Specifically one can trace a steady shift in the acceptable proportions of the Greek orders, involving an ever-increasing emphasis on the component of height. The preference of the Hellenistic age for the slender elegance of the Ionic order was given fresh impetus by the introduction of the podium. A building such as the Temple of Castor and Pollux or that of Mars Ultor was meant to dominate the space in front of it by its height; and from

97. *Rome, coin from the time of Severus Alexander showing the Temple of Sol Invictus Elagabalus, rededicated to Jupiter Ultor*

98. *Rome, Forum Transitorium, facade of the Templum Pacis* ▷

temple architecture the podium passed easily to use in other types of buildings, notably in the form of the plinth which now regularly supported the applied decorative orders of both domestic and monumental usage. Starting as shallow, half-columnar imitations of actual three-dimensional orders, these soon developed characteristics of their own. One such is illustrated by the flanking orders of the Forum Transitorium, completed by Nerva in A.D. 96–97. The columns are free-standing and only bracketed into the wall at entablature level; in this particular instance *(Plate 98)* there is no plinth, but there is an attic to give added height and, incidentally, to emphasize the horizontal rhythm of the projecting features. Another version of the same theme can be seen in the facade of Hadrian's Library at Athens, where there is no attic but the columns are upraised on free-standing molded plinths *(Plate 370);* and yet another in the outer facade of the amphitheater at Nîmes (second half of the first century A.D.), where the actual projection is small but runs right up through all the elements of both orders *(Plate 229).*

Many of the same trends can be observed in the development of that characteristically Roman institution, the commemorative arch. In simple form both plinth and attic were already part of the scheme of the Arch of Augustus at Susa *(Plate 100),* in Piedmont (9–8 B.C.); and very little if at all later, at Pola in Istria and at Glanum in Provence we find plinths, entablatures, and attics being broken out in conformity with the patterns established by the angle-columns or paired columns of the framing order. The subsequent development of the type is largely one of the elaboration and refinement of this horizontal articulation, almost always in conjunction with a strong emphasis on height, further accentuated in antiquity by the groups of statuary for which these arches constituted the monumental base. The scheme was capable of considerable baroque elaboration, as in the two closely related Flavian gateways of Verona, the Porta dei Borsari *(Plate 99)* and the reconstructed Porta dei Leoni. The more strictly classicizing development is exemplified by three well-known Italian monuments: the Arch of Trajan at Benevento (A.D. 114; *Plate 101*), the late first-century Arch of Titus in the Forum Romanum, and the Arch of Trajan at Ancona (A.D. 115; *Plate 102*).

To complete this account of the final stages of the conservative classicizing tradition we must be content to glance briefly at four representative Roman monuments: the Porta Maggiore, Vespasian's Templum Pacis, the Colosseum, and Trajan's Basilica Ulpia.

The Porta Maggiore *(Plates 103, 104)* is the monumental double arch built by Claudius to carry his two new aqueducts, the Aqua Claudia and the Aqua Anio Novus, over the Via Praenestina and the Via Labicana just before these two roads converge at the entrance to

Rome. The aqueducts themselves were of contemporary brick-faced concrete, but the arches were built throughout in the old-fashioned manner of dressed travertine, the lower part of which is heavily rusticated. Unlike the superficially similar masonry of the Porta Nigra at Trier, which is simply work that was never finished, the rustication here is a deliberate mannerism found only on a small group of mid-first century monuments, among them the terminal arch of the Aqua Virgo (another Claudian monument) and the terraced substructures

of the Claudianum, or Temple of Claudius *(Plate 105),* which was completed by Vespasian. As a feature of contemporary Roman architecture it is a curiosity of rather marginal importance. Its significance lay in the future, since it was undoubtedly from Roman work of this sort that Michelozzo and Bernini drew the inspiration for their own use of rustication.

Vespasian's Templum Pacis *(Plate 106)* was in fact if not in name an addition to the complex of Imperial Forums, and like Augustus's Ara Pacis it was designed to identify the new dynasty with the blessings of peace after a period of civil war. It was a large, nearly square enclosure, laid out as a garden and framed on three sides by porticoes. The actual temple was a modest building. It had no podium, and it was placed in such a way that the gabled facade occupied the middle of the southwest portico, with the cella projecting beyond it. To right and left were a library and galleries, in which were displayed the trophies from Jerusalem and, later, the Severan marble map of Rome.

The formal precedents for the Templum Pacis are to be found not in Rome, but in Campania, where colonnaded enclosures with a gabled porch in the middle of one side are a common feature of both public and private architecture. Half a century later, for example, the plan of the market building at Puteoli (modern Pozzuoli) offers a close parallel to that of the Templum Pacis. Even closer, and very possibly a deliberate adaptation of it, is that of Hadrian's Library at Athens. To Pliny the Elder, the Templum Pacis was one of the three most beautiful buildings in the Rome of his day (the others being the Forum Augustum and the Basilica Aemilia). Allowing for Pliny's decidedly conservative taste, which was no doubt influenced by the sheer wealth of the fittings and statuary, this was probably a fair comment on what was in fact one of the last great buildings in the old Italo-Hellenistic tradition.

Much the same could be said of the Colosseum *(Plates 107–109),* except that, unlike the Templum Pacis, it belongs to a formal tradition which had long been established in the capital. Built by Vespasian on the site of the artificial lake around which Nero had grouped the buildings of his Domus Aurea, its outer travertine facade is in a direct line of succession from the Tabularium, the Basilica Julia, and the Theater of Marcellus. The interior, with its lavish use of stone and rather limited use of concrete, was hardly less conservative. Although to Renaissance architects the Colosseum was to become the epitome of Roman architectural achievement and a living textbook of the classical order, it in fact represents a tradition which in Rome was nearing the end of the road. The city's last public monument comparable to it in style and materials was to be the Stadium of Domitian, today the Piazza Navona.

106. *Rome, Templum Pacis (Forum of Vespasian), reconstruction*
107. *Rome, Colosseum, exterior* ▷

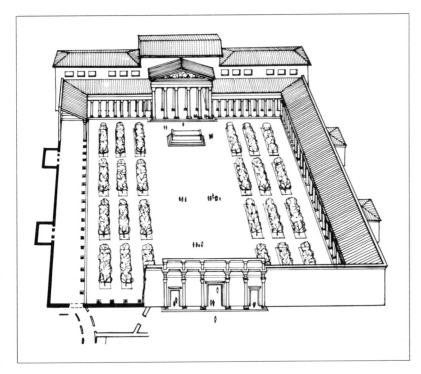

108. *Rome, Colosseum, exterior*
109. *Rome, Colosseum, interior, view of the substructures of the seating area and the service galleries beneath the pavement of the arena* ▷

Apart from its breathtaking size, the main interest of the Colosseum to the historian of Roman architecture lies in the evidence it affords of Roman working methods. Structurally the success of the enterprise lay in the superb quality of the foundations (there is hardly a trace of settlement) and in the carefully selective use of proven materials. The main load-bearing skeleton was of dressed stone masonry throughout, travertine externally and tufa internally; concrete was limited to the vaults and upper internal walls and, to minimize the thrust of the uppermost tier of seating against the unsupported outer wall of the attic, the seating was of timber. All of this was old-fashioned but predictably effective, and the fact that the building could be inaugurated (admittedly with the upper story still incomplete) barely ten years after its inception shows that the architect knew how to deploy effectively and economically what must have been a huge labor force. To speed construction the work was broken down into four quadrants, each further subdivided by materials into what must have been a very carefully scheduled working program. And though the materials and style may have been traditional, the organizational skills were timeless, resulting in a formidable achievement. It is a great pity that so little remains of the Baths of Titus, built just across the street for the inauguration ceremonies of the Colosseum. Presumably the Baths were strictly contemporary buildings of brick-faced concrete, and they would have afforded an interesting confrontation of styles and methods.

The Forum of Trajan, dedicated in A.D. 113, the last and greatest of the Imperial Forums, was yet another monument built to convey a message, this time that of the Pax Romana imposed upon Rome's enemies by the victories of her great soldier-emperor. To make way for it the slopes of the Quirinal hill were cut back and the spur linking it with the Capitoline was leveled. A grandiose entrance led into a large open square flanked by porticoes, the central feature of which was a gilded bronze equestrian statue of Trajan; at the far end of the square, instead of the usual axial temple, there rose the transverse bulk of the Basilica Ulpia; and beyond this again, in the center of a smaller galleried courtyard flanked by a pair of libraries, stood the Column of Trajan, carved with an ascending spiral of reliefs depicting his Dacian victories *(Plate 110)*. The whole complex was lavishly adorned with polychrome statuary symbolic of the emperor's triumphs *(Plates 111, 112)*. After Trajan's death the scheme was completed by the building of a huge temple at the far end, facing the Column and the Basilica.

The work of Apollodorus of Damascus, the Forum of Trajan was a singular monument, a calculated evocation of an architectural tradition that was passing, but couched in terms of such magnificence

111. *Rome, coin showing part of the facade of the Basilica Ulpia, with elaborate statuary*

112. *Rome, coin showing part of the facade of the Forum of Trajan. The statuary includes a chariot drawn by six horses and trophies of war*

that for centuries to come it was to be the visible symbol of Rome's greatness. Apollodorus, it will be remembered, was also the builder of the Baths of Trajan and thus a master of the contemporary manner. His work was not blindly derivative: the Column of Trajan, for example, was a unique creation whose sculptures mark the first real break with the classicizing tradition of state reliefs, establishing in its place an alternative tradition which exercised a profound influence upon the sculpture of later antiquity. The architectural detail, on the other hand, while breaking decisively with the florid fashions of Flavian workshops, marks a deliberate return to the classicizing motifs and styles established in the Forum Augustum—a building which obviously also inspired the flanking porticoes and exedras of the Forum of Trajan. Yet the combination of basilica and forum as it is used in the latter was a newcomer to the capital, imported from the northern provinces where (as we shall see in a later chapter) such basilica-forum complexes had long been one of the standard formulas of Roman town planning.

Except for the apses at either end of the main hall (for which too there were probably provincial precedents, and which in any case neatly balanced the exedras of the forum), the Basilica Ulpia was, both in its design and its materials, a distinctly conservative building—all the more so for the starkly contemporary character of the adjoining market buildings. With its ambulatory colonnades, its galleries, and its coffered wooden ceilings, it was a building which Pliny would unhesitatingly have added to his list of the most beautiful monuments in Rome. Indeed, although it was the last building of its sort to be built in Rome, it was greatly admired and widely imitated in the provinces (the Severan Basilica at Leptis Magna is an outstanding example) and with the passage of time its prestige steadily grew. Among other buildings, Constantine must assuredly have had the Basilica Ulpia in mind when he selected the timber-roofed, clerestory-lit basilica to be the standard type of building for the practice of the rituals of the newly enfranchised Christian religion. It is recorded that when the emperor of the East, Constantius II, visited Rome in A.D. 356, this was the monument that excited his admiration above all others, and that he expressed the wish to copy the equestrian statue in the center of the forum; to which one of his entourage replied, "First, sire, command a like stable to be built, if you can." Such was the judgment of antiquity, and it affords a fitting note on which to close this account of the heroic age of early Imperial architecture.

Chapter Three   ROME: THE NEW CONCRETE ARCHITECTURE

In the preceding chapters we have followed the course of Roman architecture from its first modest beginnings in Central Italy and through the processes of absorption, adaptation, and transmutation of Greek ideas whereby this native tradition gradually emerged as a lively Central Italian member of the larger family of regional Hellenistic architectures; and we have witnessed the final affirmation of this vigorous hybrid as the essential basis of the great Augustan building program in the Roman capital. As we shall see in a later chapter, it lay at the root also of a great deal of the early Imperial architecture of the western provinces. In tracing this history we have deliberately refrained from making more than passing reference to the development of Roman concrete, an aspect of Republican Roman architecture which in fact constitutes a consistent counter-motif to the main theme, slowly but steadily building up until in the first century A.D. it finally breaks through to become itself the dominant theme of later Imperial architecture. Since the realization and exploitation of the inherent possibilities of this new material are generally held to be Rome's greatest single contribution to the history of European architecture, it is now time to retrace our steps and to say something of its genesis and early development.

First a word of definition. Roman concrete (*opus caementicium*) was neither a cement nor a concrete in the modern sense of these terms. It was a material composed of lumps of aggregate (*caementa*) laid in mortar of a quality such that it could be used not only as an inert fill but also as a building material in its own right. Walls were commonly, though by no means invariably, faced with courses or panels of some other material, either stone or brick, or some combination of both, and it is usual to classify the masonry in terms of this facing, which is the visible and most distinctive feature of the finished product. We shall have to say something about these facings at a later point in this chapter, not only because of the conspicuous position which they occupy in any view of a Roman concrete structure, but also because they played an important, albeit secondary, part in the processes of construction. Nevertheless, the essence of the structure was the core behind the facing. Here the *caementa* might consist of lumps of whatever material happened to be available, or they might be specially selected for their purpose. Heavy, compact stones were preferred for foundations, light stones for vaulting. An extreme case of such selection is the Pantheon, where there is a careful gradation of the *caementa,* from the volcanic basalt of the footings to the pumice of the crown of the dome.

Although in antiquity the term *opus caementicium* would almost certainly have been applicable to any form of mortared rubblework, in modern usage it is convenient to term "Roman concrete" only those forms of it in which the mortar was strong enough to constitute a vaulting material in its own right. The distinction between such work and the superficially similar work in which the mortar could be used as little more than a medium for binding the bricks or stones of a conventional vault was, as we shall see, based on factors of which the Romans had no theoretical knowledge. They simply knew from experience that the materials available in some localities would produce a mortar of unprecedented strength and that in others it would not. Distinctions based on the rule-of-thumb wisdom of generations of builders are bound to be imprecise, and there are also bound to be borderline cases that are hard to classify. Nevertheless, in terms of the sort of building that could be undertaken with it, it is unquestionably useful to distinguish the "Roman concrete" of Rome itself and of Central Italy from the superficially similar mortared rubblework which one finds in large parts of western Asia Minor, for example.

The earliest uses of mortar in Central Italy need no long discussion. The employment of mud or clay to fill the interstices between lumps of stone—although in certain specialized forms it survived into historic times—belongs properly to the prehistory of formal architecture. The first significant step forward was the realization that the same function could be achieved better by using a mixture of lime and sand. It is indicative of the Romans' empirical approach to building that the resulting mixture, which we call mortar, has no direct equivalent in the Latin language. Our word, "mortar," is derived from *mortarium,* the receptacle in which the lime and sand were mixed, and even so specialized a writer as Vitruvius is content to use the generic word *materia* in many passages, a word quite as indefinite as its modern linguistic derivatives. Where greater precision was needed, as for example in the well-known building contract of 106 B.C. recorded in an inscription from Puteoli, it was necessary to specify the mixture's ingredients, *calx* (lime) and *arena* or *harena* (sand).

The lack of a clear, precise terminology for the mortar mixture is a logical expression of the piecemeal, empirical processes whereby the Romans came to a working knowledge of this all-important building material. Like so much else, the first knowledge of lime mortar almost certainly reached Rome from Greek South Italy and, although many details still elude us, it was certainly in established Roman use by the first half of the third century B.C. The town walls of Cosa, built in 273 B.C., are an important archaeological landmark in this respect. The lower parts were built in the massive polygonal masonry traditionally appropriate to this limestone region, but the upper parts were something quite new, a rubblework of small irregular limestone nodules laid in a generous mixture of lime mortar.

As early as 273 this was evidently recognized as a medium strong enough for such superstructures and at the same time far more flexible than any traditional material of equal strength.

The subsequent development of this commonplace building material into "Roman concrete" was a direct consequence of the fact that large areas of western Italy, from Lake Bolsena southward, are superficially of very recent volcanic origin. Ordinary lime mortar depends for its strength on the chemical processes induced by successively dehydrating limestone through burning, by mixing the quicklime with sand, and then by rehydrating the mixture of quicklime and sand so as to create what is in effect an artificial limestone. What the builders of Republican Latium and Campania discovered, by accident in the first place and subsequently by cautious experiment, was that certain types of local "sand," known today as *pozzolana,* were capable of producing a mortar far stronger than that produced by other ordinary sands.

To Vitruvius, who in such matters faithfully reflects the accumulated empirical experience of generations of working builders, this *pozzolana* was just another type of sand, known professionally as *harena fossica* ("quarry sand") to distinguish it from the sea and river sands that were already in common use. What Vitruvius and his contemporaries did not and could not know was that it was not really a sand at all. Sand consists essentially of particles of rock, minutely abraded by natural processes of weathering, whereas *pozzolana,* for all its gritty, sandlike appearance, is a volcanic deposit. Its chemical composition, and in particular its high silica content, gives it a number of properties valuable to the builder. For one thing, a mortar mixed with *pozzolana* instead of with river or sea sand will set under water, making it an unrivaled medium for embankments, bridges, and harborworks. For another, it requires proportionately less lime than do ordinary sands, and the resulting chemical fusion is more complete. In experienced hands it can be used to create a compact substance which is not only capable of bearing great weight, but which also possesses a surprisingly high degree of tensile strength. No precise figures seem to exist for comparing this latter property with that of the fine building stones used in antiquity. For large unsupported horizontal members it was clearly no substitute for traditional materials, but for curvilinear vaulting it was not only far stronger in proportion to its weight, but also incomparably cheaper. The largest monolithic roof surviving from antiquity is the shallow dome over the Mausoleum of Theodoric at Ravenna (d. A.D. 526; *Plate 114*). This is carved out of a single block of Istrian limestone and has an unsupported internal diameter of $29\frac{1}{2}$ ft., or 9 m. (the corresponding figure for the dome of the Pantheon is 142 ft., or 43.20 m.).

In the absence of any true theoretical knowledge of the principles involved, progress in working with mortar was inevitably a matter of trial and error, with a liberal admixture of luck. The Porticus Aemilia *(Plates 77, 115)* shows considerable mastery of the medium of which the builders of the capital, using the local "quarry sand," were already capable in 174 B.C. The Sanctuary of Fortuna Primigenia at Praeneste is another outstanding example. But there were still many practical difficulties to be overcome, one of the most serious being that the deposits available in the subsoil of Rome itself and of the Roman Campagna are extremely variable in quality, some being so contaminated with ash and other impurities as to be virtually useless for building purposes. Lacking any valid theoretical criterion for making a choice, the only way Roman builders could find out which were suitable and which were not was by experiment; and while such practical experience may be an excellent teacher, it can also be a slow one. To judge from the poor, friable quality of much of the mortar used in and around Rome during the late Republic, for a long time many contractors preferred to continue using whatever supplies were available locally, regardless of quality.

One of the reasons for this continued use of inferior materials was undoubtedly a matter of organization and of cost. Even when it had been learned which deposits were suitable for the production of a superior mortar, it was still cheaper and easier to use local supplies. It took the sort of organization which came with the centralization of authority under the emperor to make the better qualities widely available at a reasonable price. The name *pozzolana* itself is significant. It is a corruption of the Latin name *pulvis puteolanus* ("Puteoli powder"), which was given to superficially different but chemically similar volcanic deposits quarried around Puteoli (modern Pozzuoli). It was evidently in this area that the hydraulic properties of *pozzolana* were first discovered, possibly in the second century B.C., and its reputation was such that at least as late as the reign of Claudius (A.D. 41–54) shiploads of it were still being imported for the great harborworks at Ostia. This information, which we owe to Pliny, offers a vivid glimpse of the mentality that lay behind much early Roman building: a mentality which was founded on a slow, rather cautious accumulation of empirical know-how, and which, though not closed to worthwhile new ideas, lacked the theoretical knowledge that might have made for more rapid progress, preferring on the whole to solve familiar problems by familiar methods. At the same time it illustrates the readiness to organize the supply of valuable building materials which was to remain one of the great strengths of Roman building practice.

In one respect, then, the early history of Roman concrete is one

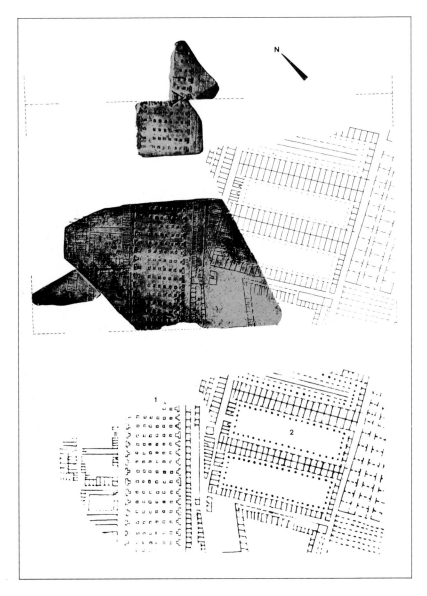

115. *Rome, the Porticus Aemilia (1) and the Horrea Galbana (2), as portrayed on the Severan marble plan of the city. The parts now missing were seen and drawn in the Renaissance*

of the accidental discovery and slow, empirical exploration of the properties of *pozzolana* as an ingredient of a lime mortar far stronger than any previously known. By the end of the Republic there was an explicit awareness of the hydraulic properties of *pulvis puteolanus*, and a growing realization that the better qualities of Roman "quarry sand" shared these properties. Vitruvius may have been old-fashioned in many of his architectural ideas, but in matters of materials and techniques he does give a very fair idea of the resources available to the Roman builder in the third quarter of the first century B.C.

What was the impact of the new material upon the architecture of the late Republic? The first and most obvious result was its steady infiltration into the building trade as a cheap and often more efficient substitute for traditional materials. The use of concrete vaulting would not have made the rapid progress it did had it not proved its value in both respects. It was particularly well adapted to the sort of cellular structure which, as we have seen, played so large a part in the planning of the sanctuaries of Latium, of the villa platforms of the wealthy, and of such new types of building as the amphitheater and the Roman theater; this fact must in turn have been a stimulus to the development of newer and more flexible methods of vaulting. The earlier concrete vaults had been built up around an inner facing of elongated, radially laid *caementa* which served, or were believed to serve, much as the bricks or voussoirs of a conventional barrel vault *(Plate 141)*. The mature Roman vault was laid in exactly the same horizontal coursing as the walls from which it sprang *(Plate 184)*. It stood, not because of any dynamic interrelation of the individual *caementa*, but by virtue of the tensile strength of the mortar in which the latter were incorporated. The older forms inevitably lingered on for a time, side by side with the new; but by and large one may say that the builders of the Augustan age were already fully masters of the new material.

Alongside this increasing mastery of the medium we can also detect a cautious advance toward new constructional forms. As yet these forms were not chosen for their own sake: concrete was still the agent, not the inspiring force. It remains nevertheless a significant fact that among the new types of building for which concrete was admirably suited there were at least two, the amphitheater and the free-standing Roman version of the Greek theater, which were both vaulted and markedly curvilinear. It was perfectly possible to construct the wedge-shaped substructures of such a building in dressed stone—witness, for example, the stadium at Perge in Pamphylia *(Plate 116)*—but it must always have been a laborious and therefore costly procedure. With experienced planning and the services of a skilled carpenter a wedge-shaped chamber could be vaulted in concrete at only marginally greater cost than a rectangular chamber of the same size. The lesson must have been observed; it only remained now to exploit it.

Yet another aspect of this formative stage of the use of Roman concrete was the selectivity of its application. As we have already had occasion to remark, the replacement of traditional materials was socially more acceptable in some branches of architecture than in others. This is a very familiar phenomenon. The emergence of cast iron as a building material in England at the time of the Industrial Revolution took place within a remarkably restricted range of buildings, predominantly utilitarian in character and mostly associated with industry, commerce, and transportation. In just the same way temples in classical Rome were among the very last buildings to be vaulted, while many branches of civic architecture were only marginally less inhibited by the inherited proprieties of their own past. If vaulting was to be introduced into the construction of the new Basilica Julia, it was something to be done discreetly behind a facade of conventional materials: Rome had to wait another three hundred years for a basilica that was openly and unashamedly vaulted. Meanwhile, it was in commercial buildings such as the Porticus Aemilia *(Plates 77, 115)*, in aqueducts *(Plate 117)* and (rather cautiously) in bridges, and in such relative newcomers to the architectural scene as bath buildings, theaters, and amphitheaters that the new material first came into its own.

By the time of Augustus Roman concrete had long established itself as a cheap, strong substitute for stone and timber in an ever-widening range of contexts; and there must have been a growing awareness among the more adventurous of its users that in some of those contexts at any rate there were exciting new possibilities in architectural design. One is left wondering just what remarkable innovations the Augustan rebuilding of Rome might have embodied, had it taken place under different political circumstances. As it was, the accent of Augustan officialdom was on the re-establishment of the traditional Roman values, which in terms of architecture meant the showier externals of a traditional classicism, with a top-dressing of Neo-Attic craftsmanship that had nothing whatever to do with the latent possibilities of Roman concrete. As far as the latter was concerned, the only serious innovation of the Augustan period was the rapid spread of brick as a facing material. It was already sufficiently established in Rome to be used prominently by Tiberius in the outer walls of the Castra Praetoria, or camp of the Praetorian Guards (A.D. 21–23; *Plate 118*), and it was to remain thereafter the preferred constructional facing material right down to late antiquity.

It is difficult for us today to realize quite how new the new concrete architecture was when it did finally break through. The notion

of the manipulation of interior space as one of the fundamental concepts of architecture is so deeply ingrained that it calls for a conscious intellectual effort on our part to accept that it was once a startling innovation. The architecture of Greece, and of the ancient East before it, had been based almost exclusively on the rival concept of architecture as structure: a building was conceived in terms of the sum of its masonry masses. An envelope, it is true, is bound to enclose space, just as four walls and a roof enclose a room. But it was essentially upon the rational, harmonious organization of the envelope and its appropriate disposition within the surrounding space that Greek architects had lavished their formidable talents.

How fundamental this concept was to Greek architectural thinking can be seen on the relatively rare occasions when the Greeks or their predecessors had to face up to the problem of constructing a hall capable of housing large numbers of people. The Persian audience hall or throne room was simply a large square hall with a flat ceiling supported by a regularly disposed forest of columns. Mesopotamia and Egypt must always have relied to some extent on imported timber. From their own resources they were limited absolutely to the space that could be spanned by a mud brick vault and a stone slab, respectively. The proportion of solids to voids in the great hypostyle halls of the Egyptian temples is tolerable only as a self-conscious statement of the majesty of matter.

As for Greece, nothing has come down to us of the Odeion of Pericles, which was in its day notorious for the bad visibility occasioned by its numerous supporting columns. But we can reconstruct the successive phases of the great assembly hall, the Telesterion, at Eleusis, and these show that even in the hands of Ictinus, the outstanding architect of his day, this was at best an uneasy compromise between the physical requirements of the situation and an aesthetic tradition to which such problems were essentially alien. Even in the second-century B.C. Bouleuterion (the meeting place of the City Council) at Miletus, one of the most successful of such large covered buildings, the result was only achieved by stretching to their limits the available constructional resources. There is no hint of any radically fresh architectural thinking. Lacking the technical resources which might have stimulated the creation of an authentic architecture of interior space, the Greeks were content to refine upon what they already had; and they were at their best precisely where, as in the great Hellenistic stoas, they frankly accepted the limitations of their own time-honored tradition.

It was only on Italian soil that the Greeks and the Romans between them (the precise division of responsibility is, as we have seen, uncertain) succeeded in producing a building type which, though conceived within the framework of the traditional orders and of traditional materials, managed to look inward as well as outward. This was the basilica *(Plate 412)*. The architectural vocabulary was unchanged, but the syntax was new. Not only was the sense of enclosure of the central nave notably diminished by framing it within a colonnaded ambulatory (which for many purposes could be treated, visually as well as functionally, as an extension of the nave itself), but the clerestory lighting also introduced a strong centralizing accent—an accent, moreover, that was conceived in terms of illumination rather than of structure. To a lesser degree something of the same result was achieved in a building such as the Covered Theater at Pompeii. These were "compromise" buildings, but they were successful compromises, the basilica in particular. Despite the totally different medium of expression, by the very fact of contriving to enclose a large volume of space that was both uncluttered by supports and centrally lit, the basilica must be seen as a significant step toward the achievement of the new concrete-vaulted architecture.

It is against this background of converging, though as yet only partially acknowledged, architectural practices and ideas that we must view the explosive emergence of a new architectural vision. Suddenly, it seems, architects became aware that interior space might be something more than the void defined by four walls and a roof, and that it could itself be treated as the *raison d'être* for the envelope which enclosed it. For such a concept concrete vaulting, thanks to its strength and flexibility of form, was to prove an almost ideal medium. In place of a tradition which went out of its way to stress the elementary facts of construction—a tradition in which the horizontals of ceilings and architraves were clearly displayed as resting upon the verticals of walls and columns—Roman architects found themselves confronted by the almost totally unexplored possibilities of an architecture in which the traditional structural verities yielded pride of place to purely visual, and often deliberately elusive, effects of space, light, and color. To any architect endowed with creative imagination, this was an intoxicating situation. To understand what the Roman Architectural Revolution was about one has only to contrast the concept of architectural perfection embodied in the Parthenon or the temples of Paestum with that embodied in the interior of the Pantheon, of Hagia Sophia, or of one of the great Gothic cathedrals. This was indeed one of the turning points in architectural history.

The first major monument in which we can see clear traces of an awareness of these revolutionary new possibilities is the Domus Aurea, or Golden House *(Plates 119–123)*. This was the sumptuous villa which Nero built in the heart of Rome after the great fire of A.D. 64, expropriating some 300 to 350 acres in the middle of what had been the old town in order to create an elaborate residential park, which was to combine the formal rusticity of the great suburban villas of the capital and the more relaxed architectural landscaping of the wealthy coastal villas of Latium and Campania.

With one notable exception, the novelty of the Domus Aurea lay less in its architecture than in its setting (in the crowded heart of Rome) and in the ingenuity and extravagance of its fittings. The residence, terraced into the slopes of the Esquiline and overlooking an artificial lake on the site of the later Colosseum, was built in the contemporary manner: vaulted concrete faced with a wealth of marbles, stuccoes, gilding, and mosaics. The plan was conventional enough, being in essence that of a contemporary seaside villa whose porticoed facade fronted onto a terrace; many examples of just this sort of building are portrayed in the wall paintings at Pompeii and Stabiae *(Plate 53)*. The only major planning innovation was the room which occupied the middle of the east wing. This was in the shape of an octagon, with secondary chambers radiating from five sides, while the remaining three sides opened directly or indirectly off the frontal portico. The whole complex was vaulted, the central chamber with an octagonal vault which merged imperceptibly into a dome with a circular oculus, and the radiating chambers with barrel vaults and cross vaults. The latter were further enlivened by a number of decorative recesses and, on the main axis, by a cascade, and they were lit by an ingenious system of downward plunging windows opening onto a shallow light well between the extrados of the central dome and the vertical upward extension of the piers of the inner octagon. The plan is not without its awkward features: for example, the clumsy roofing of the triangular, corridor-like spaces between the radiating chambers, or again the crude way in which the oblique members of the octagon were fitted into the otherwise rectangular scheme of the wing as a whole. Today, stripped of its marbles, mosaics, and statuary and devoid of light and color, it is a sorry shadow of its former self; but to eyes accustomed to the simple, four-square conventions of most contemporary planning it must in its day have seemed a very startling break with tradition.

That so daringly original a design was realized for the first time in the Domus Aurea seems unlikely. It may well have been the first time that a plan of this sort had been incorporated into the framework of an otherwise conventionally rectangular structure; and this in turn would doubtless have suggested a number of refinements of detail. But both the plan of the octagon complex and the rather clumsy manner of its incorporation into the east wing suggest that the prototype was conceived originally as an independent unit and was only subsequently adapted to its new role. The milieu to which one

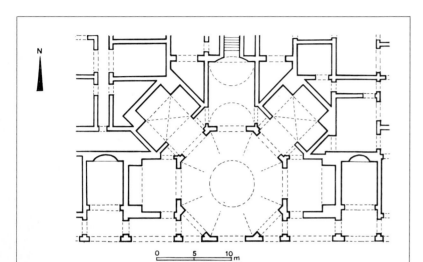

the ground for the sober good sense of the new, planned Rome of which Ostia is today the tangible memorial. We shall return to Ostia later in this chapter; at this point let us restrict ourselves to the more heady vision implicit in the octagon of the Domus Aurea and follow the architects of the next two generations briefly on their epoch-making voyage of architectural discovery.

If it is natural that the first exploratory steps should probably have taken place under private patronage and should first have found official expression in a highly experimental private residence of the emperor, it is no less natural that, once embodied in a building as notorious as the Domus Aurea, much of the subsequent development should have taken place in the public domain. It was largely in the official monuments of the capital that the ideas implicit in the new vaulted architecture were carried through to their logical conclusion, and we are fortunate in possessing substantial remains of most of those monuments which marked the stages of that development—Domitian's state residence on the Palatine, the Domus Augustana; the Baths of Trajan and the market buildings adjoining his Forum; and Hadrian's Pantheon and his magnificent private villa near Tivoli. All of these monuments, it will be noted, belong in varying degrees to the categories of building for which concrete had long been an accepted medium. Side by side with them the same emperors continued to erect buildings in the conservative manner still considered appropriate to many forms of public architecture, buildings such as the Colosseum, Vespasian's Templum Pacis, the Stadium of Domitian, and the Forum of Trajan. Official religious architecture was even more doggedly conservative: even the builder of the Pantheon felt it necessary to preface the rotunda with a gabled porch, and for the next hundred years the state temples of Rome continued to be gabled columnar buildings of the familiar type. The first major state temple to have broken with tradition in this respect was Aurelian's Temple of the Sun.

Domitian's great residence *(Plates 124–132),* known officially as the Domus Augustana and in popular usage as the Palatium, is one of the relatively few great Roman buildings of which we know the architect's name—Rabirius. Inaugurated in A.D. 92, it was situated on the irregular saddle between the two spurs of the Palatine hill, a site which posed a number of planning problems. To the west and south-west it was restricted by existing monuments and, in addition to the differences of level dictated by the terrain, it called for two asymmetrically opposed facades, one facing northward toward the Forum valley and the other southward toward the Circus Maximus. The solution adopted by Rabirius was to group the state apartments together on a partly artificial platform so as to form a virtually in-

naturally turns for such a prototype is that from which the Domus Aurea itself was derived. The landscaped villas of the wealthy would have been the natural breeding ground for such frankly avant-garde architectural experimentation; and it is by no means impossible that the immediate model was some artificial grotto or fountain building in one of Nero's own previous residences—at Anzio, Subiaco, or in Rome itself before the fire, in the Domus Transitoria. We may never know for certain, but we can be reasonably sure that this was the sort of setting in which architects first became consciously aware of the revolutionary possibilities inherent in the use of Roman concrete.

The fire of A.D. 64, at the same time as it made way for the megalomaniac fantasies of Nero's private residence, was also clearing

dependent west wing, dominating the approach from the forum, while the private residence occupied the Circus Maximus frontage, at a lower level. The two blocks were formally linked by a pair of large peristyle courts, which together constituted a single cross-axis. To the east, balancing the state apartments in plan but not in visual bulk, lay an elongated sunken garden (the "Stadium"), beyond which were later added a number of supplementary structures, including a bath building. The entire complex was served by a branch of the aqueduct built by Nero to supply the Domus Aurea.

The official wing of the palace comprised three elements: the state apartments proper, terraced out above the head of the valley that leads up from the Arch of Titus; beyond them a large peristyle courtyard containing a formal garden, flanked by two ranges of smaller rooms (the precise function of which we can only guess at); and, opening off the far end of the peristyle, the massive bulk of the great banqueting hall.

The state apartments formed a virtually independent rectangular block which stretched right across the north frontage, facing outward and communicating with the peristyle only through secondary doorways. At the west end was the Basilica, where the emperor sat in judgment. In the center lay a huge audience hall, conventionally known as the Aula Regia, which must have been used for such state occasions as formal appearances of the emperor or the reception of foreign embassies. At the east end was a smaller hall, which is sometimes identified as the Lararium, or palace chapel, but which is perhaps better regarded as an antechamber and guardroom, serving the main hall. Behind it lay a service room giving access to the only staircase of which there is any trace in this part of the palace. Around the north and west sides of the block ran an outer portico with projecting balconies opposite the entrances to the three main halls.

The constructional medium throughout the Domus Augustana was a fine brick-faced concrete, built up on massive foundations and liberally laced with horizontal leveling courses of tile. Virtually nothing of what one sees today was visible in antiquity: the walls throughout were faced with other materials—marble veneer and decorative marble orders in the main rooms, plaster in the service rooms. The vaults were almost certainly stuccoed, probably gilded in places and perhaps already alternating with some use of mosaic (in the semidomes of the apses, for example). One of the great difficulties in studying the more monumental aspects of this Roman concrete architecture is that what confronts us today is only one stage nearer to the finished building than the reinforced concrete skeleton of a modern apartment block. We may deduce something of the finished appearance, but we cannot truly experience it.

124. *Rome, plan of the Domus Augustana (Palace of Domitian). 1) basilica; 2) Aula Regia; 3) so-called lararium (vestibule?); 4) peristyle courtyards; 5) triclinium (state baqueting hall); 6) domestic wing; 7) stadium (sunken garden); 8) libraries; 9) facade overlooking the Circus Maximus*

125. *Rome, Domus Augustana, restored axonometric view* ▷

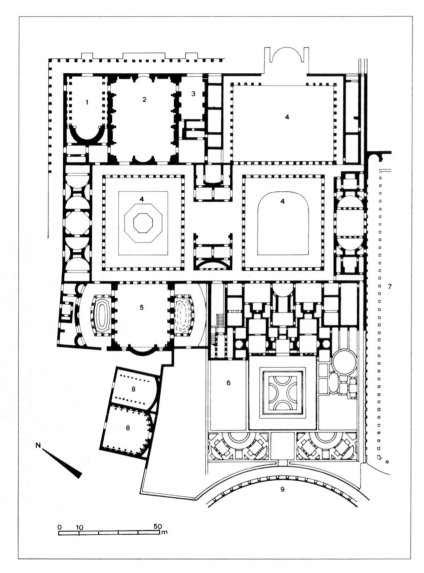

N

0   10   50
                 m

The planning of the two main halls has one feature in common, namely the apse or apsidal recess in the middle of the south wall—a feature which here makes its first formal appearance in Roman architecture as the setting for the semi-divine majesty of the emperor. In other respects, despite the common constructional medium, the Basilica and the Aula Regia embody two very different architectural traditions. That of the Basilica is one which in a variety of related forms goes right back to late Republican and Augustan times. The essential elements of this tradition were the apse and the rows of columns set out from the two side walls, leading the eye from the entrance to the focal point of the composition within the apse. In one branch of this tradition, taken up for example in the temples of Venus Genetrix and of Mars Ultor, the apse housed the cult statue of the divinity; and since at this stage the roofs of temples were still regularly of timber, the flanking colonnades (which in Greek temple architecture, before the development of the roof truss, had served the practical purpose of helping to support the roof) were normally relegated to a purely decorative role, resting on a continuous plinth. Another related branch, we may suspect, was that of the audience halls *(basilicae)* in the villas of wealthy private citizens. Yet another branch is that embodied in the late Republican Nymphaeum of the so-called Villa of Cicero at Formiae *(Plate 133)*, in which the flanking colonnades resume their structural function of reducing the span of the coffered concrete vault.

Domitian's Basilica unites all these traditions, placing them in the service of an autocracy which was with every passing day taking on more of the external forms of a cult of the living emperor. Although the roof is not preserved, there seems no reason whatever to question the generally accepted belief that it took the form of a concrete barrel vault. The span ($47\frac{1}{2}$ ft., or 14.5 m.) is perfectly credible, and the fact that this corner of the building had to undergo heavy buttressing within a generation of its construction strongly supports such a hypothesis.

The Aula Regia was a far more self-consciously contemporary building. The markedly static, centralizing proportions (about 7:8) were deliberately emphasized by treating all four walls alike. A discreet note of axiality was introduced by the shallow apse in the middle of the south wall, a requirement of court ceremonial; but even this was reduced to a minimum by setting it within one of the series of near-uniform bays into which the entire circuit of the lower walls was subdivided. These bays, alternately curved and rectangular, were framed by projecting piers, against which stood the fluted marble columns of a continuous semiengaged order—very much in the manner of the almost exactly contemporary Forum Transitorium,

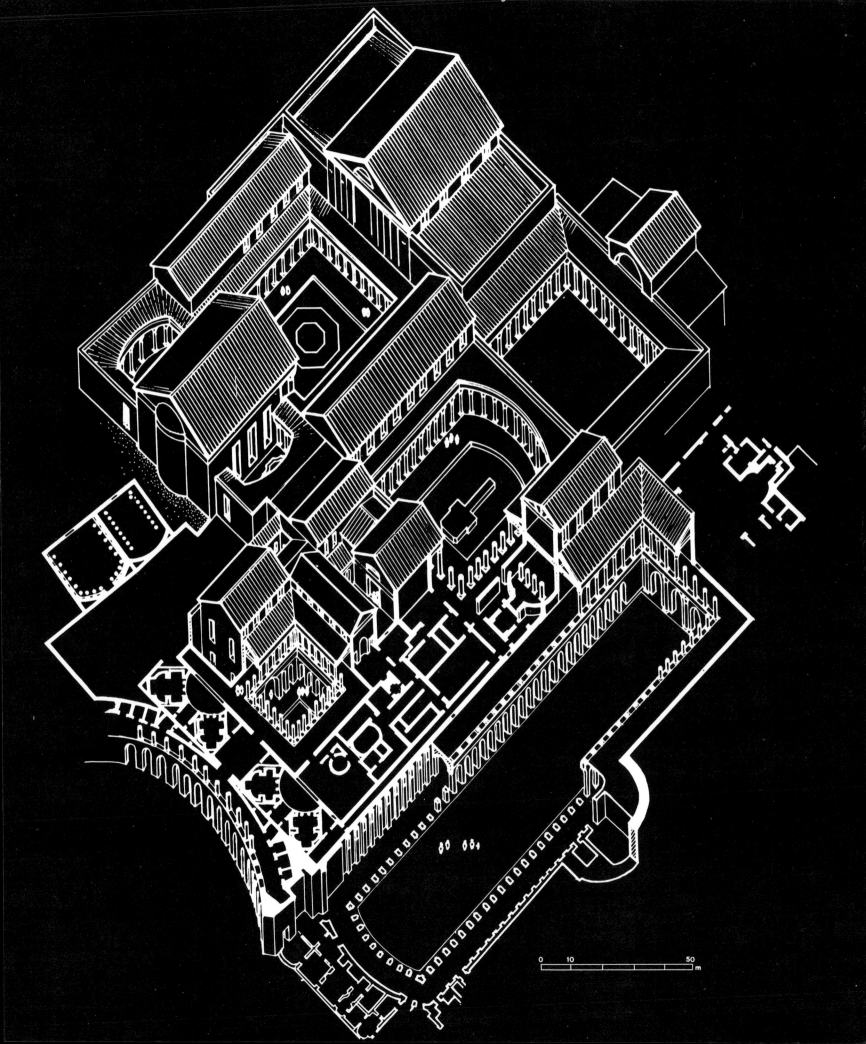

126. *Rome, Domus Augustana, staircase in the domestic wing*
127. *Rome, Domus Augustana, courtyard of the domestic wing with central fountain* ▷

except that in this case there may well have been an upper order of comparable dimensions. Seven of the bays contained doorways, and one the apse; the remaining eight held projecting columnar (and presumably pedimental) aediculae adorned with statuary. The lower walls were thus articulated into a complex series of projecting and reentrant features in what was clearly a deliberate attempt to play down the massive, load-bearing qualities of the walls themselves. Taken separately, there was nothing new in the use of engaged orders, of alternately curvilinear and rectilinear features, or of decorative aediculae to give life and movement to the wall surfaces of such monumental architecture. But used together, as they are here, to break up the tangible properties of the walls and to create a studied sense of spatial ambivalence, they constitute a decisive step in the direction of the sort of "dematerialization" of which later Roman architects were to make such effective use.

The upper walls of the Aula Regia are nowhere preserved and speculation about the form of the roof is at best a matter of informed guesswork. The span was a very large one (at least $93\frac{1}{2}$ ft., or 28.5 m.), and it has even been suggested that this must have been an open courtyard. But the span of the banqueting hall is only one meter less, and in this case we can be quite sure not only that there was a roof but also that it was of timber: the unbuttressed flanking walls and columns could never have supported the weight and thrust of a vault. The walls of the Aula Regia are more substantial, and they were firmly buttressed by the adjoining halls. Even so, it may be doubted whether they could have supported the load of the concrete barrel vault which many scholars believe them to have carried; nor indeed would such a vault have been appropriate over a nearly square room. It seems far more likely that here too the roof was of timber and that the reason the walls were stouter was that they had to rise clear of the roofs of the adjoining buildings in order to light the central hall.

In these great state rooms we see Domitian's architect, Rabirius, pressing the new concrete medium to its limits (and in one case, the Basilica, even beyond the limits of safety) in the search for grandiose effects of enclosed space. Formally the Basilica was based on familiar precedents, but the Aula Regia was a boldly innovating conception. The banqueting hall was more conventional: in this case the almost square plan was traditional, and there are precedents in the private houses of Pompeii and Herculaneum for the gabled facade which marked the passage from the peristyle to the hall itself. But once again the scale was unprecedented, and the opening of the side walls onto a pair of symmetrically placed courtyards with fountains was a startling translation into real, three-dimensional architecture of the illusionistic vistas of architectural landscapes and gardens which had figured so largely in the paintings of the Augustan age.

129. *Rome, Domus Augustana, detail of masonry showing cracks due to settling of the foundations*

130. *Rome, Domus Augustana, view of the stadium (right rear, the domestic wing)*

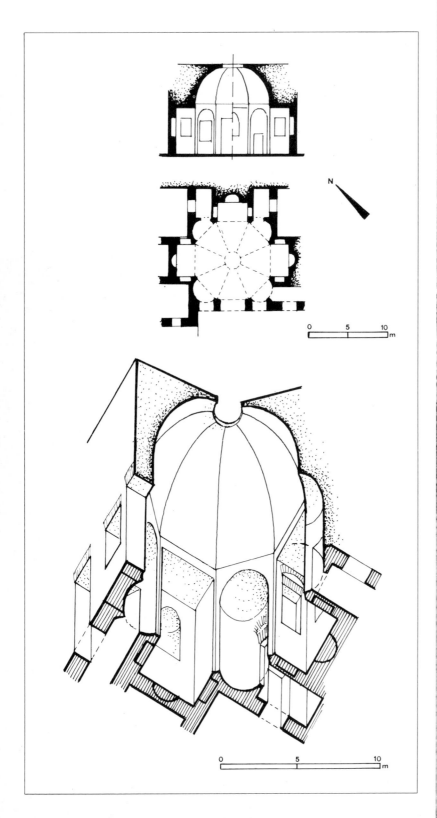

131. *Rome, Domus Augustana, section, plan, and axonometric view of the domed octagonal room in the lower story of the domestic wing*

132. *Rome, Domus Augustana, facade overlooking the Circus Maximus* ▷

With the fountain courtyards we find ourselves confronted by yet another innovating trend, namely the exploration of curvilinear form for its own sake. Both the fountains themselves, with their oval shapes and intricately scalloped profiles, and the courtyards might well be the work of some seventeenth-century architect. We find the same frankly experimental attitude expressed very clearly in the west wing of the peristyle, where Rabirius was able to indulge his fancy, uninhibited by any practical or ceremonial considerations. Even a generation earlier the uncompromisingly antifunctional shapes of some of these rooms would have been quite unthinkable. These were rooms to be admired rather than lived in. Convention evidently still demanded a traditionally rectilinear exterior; but within this framework the elaborate interplay of barrel vaults, domes, and semidomes implicit in the plan could only have sprung from a quite explicit recognition of the fact that with concrete vaulting the only formal limitations lay in the strength of the concrete itself. The shapes chosen were no longer an expression of the structural logic of the materials but of the architect's whim.

The domestic wing was partly terraced out from, and partly dug into, the steep upper slopes of the hill overlooking the Circus Maximus at a point where there was already a natural reentrant. It was no doubt this characteristic of the terrain which suggested the creation of a residence on two levels, around a square garden courtyard. Today this courtyard has been stripped of all detail except for the core of the central fountain, but it seems certain that it was surrounded at both levels by porticoes and that those of the lower story at any rate were vaulted, with arcades resting on piers of brick-faced concrete. The rooms of the lower story were lit from the courtyard or from a series of rectangular, shaftlike light wells. At the upper level, on either side of the entrance from the peristyle court, there was a series of four or more halls facing northward, which may have been of a semipublic character, since they had only very limited direct communication with the more intimate domestic quarters around the courtyard. The north wing is the only part of which there are substantial upstanding remains, but the plan must have conformed fairly closely to that of the lower story. The materials and building techniques throughout are identical with those used in the state apartments.

There is so much that is novel about this remarkable building that we can only select here a few of the more significant features. The very fact of being planned at two levels of equal importance was itself a novelty: there was to be no *piano nobile* resting on substructures, but (or so it seems) two equal levels designed for use on different occasions and at different seasons. This fact is closely related to the wholehearted acceptance of the formal logic of the new concrete medium, which favored development in elevation. For a century past the domestic architecture of the capital had been moving in this direction in its widespread adoption of the barrel vault in place of the traditional wooden ceiling. The Casa dei Grifi, preserved through the lucky accident of its incorporation within the terraced footings of the palace Lararium, shows how far this tendency had already progressed by the end of the Republic. From the scanty remains of the subsequent domestic architecture of the city center we can only guess at the extent to which in the intervening period urban pressures had provoked the formulation of new, more strictly contemporary forms. It seems very likely that the decisive step was taken in the town houses of the new Rome which emerged from the ashes of the fire of A.D. 64 (as we shall see later in this chapter). But nothing of this phase has survived. It is in the Domus Augustana that we can first document the transformation of the relaxed, predominantly single-storied planning of the old atrium-peristyle house into the more compact, multi-storied forms to which the brick-faced concrete medium lent itself so admirably.

Here, in the domestic wing, there was no call for the prodigies of soaring space characteristic of the state apartments. Instead we are faced by the expression of two complementary and contrasting trends. One of these, which we have already met in the western section of the peristyle of the official wing, is admirably exemplified in the series of rooms opening off the north side of the garden courtyard at the lower level. Two of these rooms are domed octagons whose sides are articulated into alternately curved and rectangular recesses, of which the latter are in turn broken out into similarly alternating secondary niches (Plate 131). Here we are faced, although in another form, with the same systematic exploration of the geometric properties of enclosed space, all the more impressive in this case for the ingenuity with which the constituent parts interlock to form a coherent unity capable of supporting the related (but in detail different) plan of the upper story. The fountains of the courtyard and of the light wells are another expression of delight in the intricacies of geometric form. At the other extreme we have the austere, functional simplicity of the staircases and the light wells themselves, and the lost arcading of the central courtyard. Pitched on a correspondingly sober note, but contrasting impressively with the strict rectilinearity of the rest of the outer perimeter, is the shallow reentrant curve of the facade toward the Circus Maximus (Plate 132).

Domitian's other surviving buildings in Rome belong, as we saw in the last chapter, to an earlier, more conservative tradition. The Domus Augustana and, to judge from the ill-studied remains, his villa near Albano were the only monuments in which he and Rabirius felt free to develop the possibilities of the new concrete architecture

unhindered by the restraints of customary taste. The same duality of architectural sensibility continued to prevail under Trajan, another great builder, who succeeded in A.D. 98. There were still many categories of public building for which only one of the two available styles of monumental architecture—the traditional and the contemporary—was deemed appropriate.

The Forum and Basilica of Trajan were in many respects ultraconservative, even deliberately archaizing. The scale was new, and there were certain innovations of detail, such as the famous Column on which was carved the story of Trajan's Dacian victories (Plates 134, 135); but even this, for all its formal novelty, was conceived in the spirit of the Ara Pacis. Both the planning and the constructional practice were based on the models established a century earlier in the Forum Augustum. Such evocations of the founder of the principate, the historic source of imperial authority, were quite deliberate, and they show how strong was the feeling for the meaning of certain forms of public architecture, and how explicit were the political overtones. Just as in the time of Augustus and of the more far-sighted of his successors, this was still architecture with a message.

This was one side of the coin. But side by side with the conservative, classicizing pomp of this sort of official public architecture we find Trajan and his architect, Apollodorus of Damascus, indulging no less freely in the contemporary concrete idiom wherever this was appropriate. Apollodorus was by training an engineer as well as architect—if indeed such a distinction would have been meaningful in classical Rome. His recorded works comprised a bridge over the Danube near the Iron Gate; an otherwise unknown Odeion, or concert hall; a great public bath building, the Baths of Trajan, on the site of the Domus Aurea; and what was referred to by Dio as the "Agora." It has sometimes been maintained that Dio used this term to distinguish the Forum of Trajan (and by implication the Basilica Ulpia) from the adjoining market buildings, and that the markedly conservative style of the former reflects Apollodorus's Syrian upbringing. Such a view is untenable. Not only is it evident that all these buildings were part of a single, organically conceived project but, as the builder of the Baths of Trajan, Apollodorus was by definition a master of the contemporary concrete medium. Whatever his wider tastes and abilities, in this aspect of his work he was a product of the same metropolitan Roman tradition as his immediate predecessor, Rabirius.

With the Baths of Trajan the type of bath building which is conveniently referred to as "imperial" came to full maturity (Plate 139). Roman bath buildings had, it seems, first taken shape in the second century B.C. in Campania. Initially they may have been served

by hot springs, but this very soon developed into an artificial, wood-fired heating system whereby the hot air circulated beneath concrete floors that were raised on brick *suspensurae* and, with increasing sophistication, passed upward through hollow jacketing in the walls, to be discharged through vents in the roof. The system was in essence that of a Turkish bath. Rooms of graduated heat were supplied with plunge baths of correspondingly hot or cold water; dressing rooms, a lavatory, and some form of exercise yard *(palaestra)* completed the essential equipment of what, in an infinite variety of layouts of every degree of complexity, by early Imperial times had already become one of the hallmarks of Roman culture, both in Italy and the provinces, and at every social level.

From the very outset such bath buildings were quick to adopt the use of concrete vaulting. For one thing, the material was extremely practical for the purpose and, for another, a building with no social precedents was free from the restraints of conservative sentiment which limited experiment in other, longer established types. In the Stabian Baths *(Plates 136, 138)* and the Forum Baths *(Plate 137)* at Pompeii one can see the considerable progress already made in the first century B.C., while the so-called Temple of Mercury at Baiae *(Plate 140)*—a thermal rotunda $71\frac{1}{2}$ ft., or 21.5 m., in diameter—with a dome lit by a central oculus, illustrates the very considerable technical skills achieved by the Campanian architects as early as the Augustan period.

Rome itself was a relative latecomer to the field. The first public baths established in the capital were those built by Agrippa in the Campus Martius, near the Pantheon. Though part of a larger complex which included gardens and porticoes, all that we know of the actual bath buildings indicates that they were of the Pompeian type, comprising a rather informal agglomeration of functionally vaulted structures. For half a century they were the only public baths in Rome. Then Nero built new *thermae* and a *gymnasium*, which were much admired. "What worse than Nero, what better than Nero's baths?" was Martial's comment. Unfortunately for our knowledge of Nero's work, they were rebuilt between A.D. 222 and 227 by Severus Alexander; and although the remains were recorded by Palladio and Antonio da Sangallo, it is now impossible to determine how much of Nero's plan Severus incorporated. It is a reasonable guess—but little more—that Nero's bath building was a monumentally planned symmetrical structure, and that it was located beside, if not actually integrated structurally with, the *gymnasium*. If that is so, once again Nero's was the decisive contribution to the creation of one of the most characteristic and impressive of all Roman building types, that of the great "imperial" *thermae*.

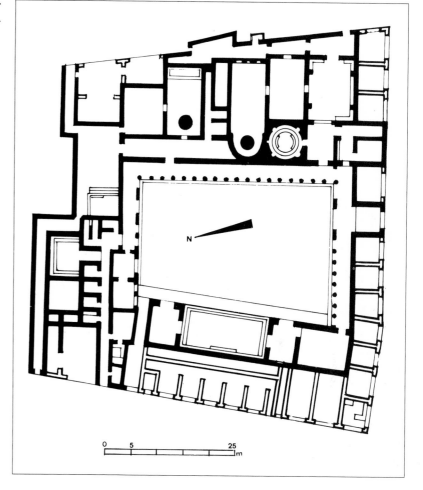

In the absence of unequivocal documentation for the form of Nero's building, the first known example of this type is the Baths of Titus, begun by Vespasian on the lower slopes of the Esquiline beside the Domus Aurea and completed by Titus in time for the inauguration of the nearby Colosseum in A.D. 80. They too are known only from a measured sketch by Palladio, but in this case there is no doubt about the main lines of the plan: a symmetrical, near-rectangular, terraced enclosure of which the northern half was occupied by a bath building which was itself symmetrical along its shorter, north-south axis. At the north end of this axis lay the main cold room *(frigidarium)*, a large vaulted hall of three bays; at the south end, projecting into the open courtyard, was the main hot room *(caldarium)*, which in this case was a pair of rooms; the rest of the south facade was occupied by the secondary hot rooms, and behind these lay a pair of porticoed courtyards for exercise *(palaestrae)* and other service rooms. Both the scale (the whole enclosure measured barely 4 acres) and the development of the vaulted halls was modest by comparison with the giants that were to follow; but in essence this was the "imperial" plan.

The Baths of Trajan, built between A.D. 104 and 109 on the site of the residential wing of the Domus Aurea (which thus disappeared from sight barely forty years after its construction), were a far more ambitious affair, occupying a total area of nearly 23 acres. The entire layout was again symmetrical along the north-south axis, but in this case the bathing block, which itself occupied nearly 10 acres, took up only a part of the north side of the enclosure, from which it projected inward. An important addition to the scheme of the Baths of Titus was the incorporation of a large swimming pool *(natatio)* to the north of the *frigidarium*, which was moved to a central position at the intersection of the two principal axes. Architecturally as well as functionally the *frigidarium* now became the focal point of the whole complex. Other important innovations were the bold use of rows of windows along the south facade, a development made possible by the steadily increasing use of window glass, and the incorporation into the outer perimeter of a number of lecture halls, with fountain-buildings, sculpture galleries, libraries, and shops. What had been two distinct buildings, the bath building and the *gymnasium* (in the Greek sense of the latter word, as a center for educational and cultural as well as athletic activities), now became one. Henceforth these huge complexes were to take their place as the great popular centers of social life, both in Rome itself and in the provinces.

Although the Baths of Trajan made considerably more use of curvilinear shapes than those of Titus, the functional requirements of the main building dictated a certain restraint in this respect. There

139. *Rome, plan of the Baths of Trajan. 1)* natatio *(swimming pool);* *2)* frigidarium *(cold room); 3)* caldarium *(hot room); 4)* palaestrae *(exercise yards)*

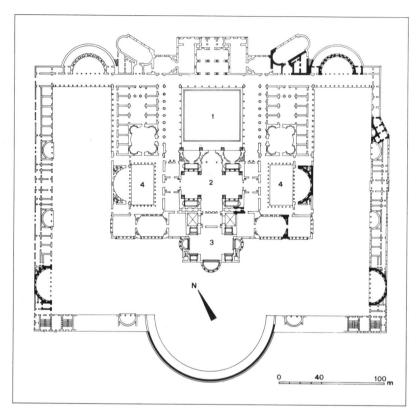

was even less room for pure fantasy in Apollodorus's other master-piece in the contemporary manner, the Markets of Trajan *(Plates 142–149)*. These were a new commercial quarter, terraced at a bewildering variety of levels into the steep slopes which had been created by cutting back the saddle that linked the Esquiline and Capitoline hills in order to create a level space for the forum-basilica complex. The plan is one that should be studied by anyone who believes that Roman architects were blind slaves to the dictates of formal symmetry. It is true that there were certain categories of monumental public architecture for which axial symmetry was one of the established conventions to which an architect was expected to conform. It is also true that, all else being equal, both by training and by temperament a metropolitan Roman architect was more likely to adopt a tidy, axially symmetrical solution than one of his Greek colleagues. But where there were no restraints imposed by convention, or where the nature of the site called for a more relaxed, informal treatment, his skills were readily adaptable, and vaulted concrete was an ideal medium for such situations.

The site chosen for the Markets was emphatically one that called for lively, imaginative planning. The scheme adopted envisaged access from three horizontal or gently sloping streets, which followed the contours of the hillside and were linked by stairways. One of these streets, at the foot of the slopes, clung to the outer perimeter of the forum and basilica, with a reentrant, hemicyclical facade matching the projecting curve of the forum exedra. This facade was two stories high and the related buildings backed onto a second street, which followed a gently rising contour at a higher level and which survived into modern times as the Via Biberatica. Rising three stories above the north end of this second street was the west facade of the market hall, while variously grouped along the rest of it, at more than one level, were rows of shops, some of them facing outward onto intermediate terraces. Towering above the south end of the street were the three-story west facades of several distinct blocks of mixed shops and apartments, of which the east frontage opened off a third street which followed the slopes at a yet higher level.

Within this vast complex we must be content to single out two units. One is the block which lay between the Via Biberatica and the northeast corner of the forum, a difficult site in the shape of an irregular polygon, with street frontages on four or more distinct alignments and at two sharply contrasted levels. Here, and here alone, in order to give an element of formal unity to a very awkward site, Apollodorus allowed himself the luxury of some fanciful planning, placing a large semicircular, semidomed hall across the frontage between the two projecting curves of the basilica and the forum, and

140. *Baiae (Baia), dome of the so-called Temple of Mercury*

141. *Baiae (Baia), detail of late Republican or Augustan vaulted masonry. The tufa, which is softer than the mortar, is laid radially around the arches and horizontally between them*

then picking up the curve of this hall as a reentrant feature in the middle of the facades of each of the two terraces which carried the complex upward and backward toward the Via Biberatica.

The site chosen for the market hall itself presented fewer problems. A line of six shops facing onto the Via Biberatica supported the west frontage of what was a near-rectangular platform terraced sharply into the hillside. On this terrace, parallel with the Via Biberatica, was set the main building, whose central hall, instead of the customary barrel vault, was roofed with six equal cross vaults corbeled out on travertine brackets. This arrangement made possible the incorporation of two tiers of barrel-vaulted shops, six pairs at each level, of which the lower ones opened directly off the hall, the upper ones off a gallery-like corridor, which served also to light the interior by means of skylights from the terrace roof above. Flights of steps connected the three levels, continuing up to what appears to have been a fourth tier of shops over the eastern wing. The whole complex displays the deceptive simplicity of design that springs from skillful planning—a far cry from the stolid bulk of the old Republican market halls at Tivoli and Ferentinum *(Plate 150)*, of which it is the direct descendant.

From the point of view of construction, the Markets of Trajan were as strictly contemporary as the Baths or as Domitian's palace. Nevertheless, as one steps into them, one is at once conscious of having moved into a quite different level within the hierarchy of Roman architectural sensibility. For all the breadth and sweep of the planning, there are none of the studied effects of soaring interior space which we have encountered in the state apartments on the Palatine and again in the Baths. The market hall is a relatively modest building; what impresses is not its scale but the logic of its planning. Nor again is there any suggestion of the exploitation of geometric shapes for their own sake. The form of the hemicycle was imposed by that of the adjoining forum, while the interlocking curves of the block that lies between the Via Biberatica and the northeast corner are a direct response to the problem of giving some measure of unity to the frontage of a difficult site.

As was appropriate to an essentially utilitarian complex, the Markets' simplicity of design was matched by an extremely sparing use of architectural ornament. Outside the central hemicycle, it was left almost exclusively to the patterns of doors, windows, and balconies to enliven the wall surfaces, patterns rendered more emphatic by the tendency of the windows themselves to grow in size and number (a fact we noticed also in the south facade of the Baths). The eight large windows of the semicircular room opposite the northeast corner of the forum occupy fully two-thirds of the upper wall sur-

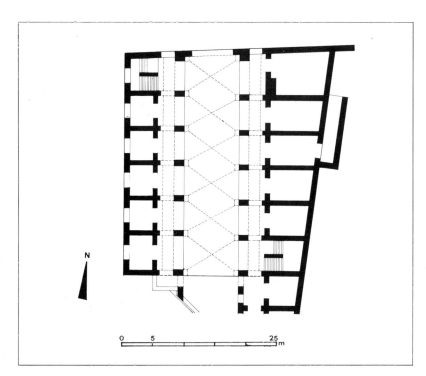

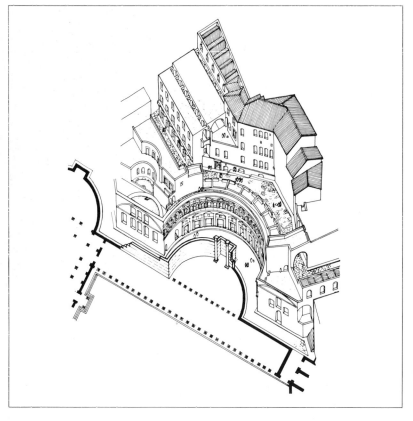

145. *Rome, Markets of Trajan, the former Via Biberatica. On the left, the west facade of the market hall*

146. *Rome, Markets of Trajan, the central market hall*

147. *Rome, Markets of Trajan, facade of semicircular hall with semidome
and eight large windows*

face of the interior, reducing the actual wall to little more than the framework necessary to support the vault *(Plates 147, 148)*. From the exterior the facade of this room was a very prominent feature of the design, and yet the only conventional ornament was a tiny molding framing the three upper windows, little more than a stringcourse in the shape of a segmentally arched tympanum. It was the windows themselves which were made to tell the architectural story.

Not only was the ornament far more sparingly used, but such of it as there was was also very different in character. As a concession to the pomp of the adjoining forum the windows of the upper story of the hemicycle were framed with a delicate decorative order, which bears (and was no doubt meant to bear) a superficial resemblance to the framing orders so common in late Republican and early Imperial monumental architecture. But the resemblance is only skin-deep. Although the orders of the outer facades of the Theater of Marcellus or the Colosseum were already purely decorative, they were still formally true to their actual structural origins, as befitted the offspring of a marriage between the classical order and the arch. The decoration of the hemicycle is something quite different: though loosely linked into the semblance of a classical order by continuous moldings, the elements of the design are in fact a series of independent aediculae, every fourth one of which had a triangular pediment and alternated with groups of three in which a low, segmentally curved pediment was framed by two half-pediments. The elaborate counterpoint of this design was never meant to be viewed frontally and fully displayed—as one cannot help viewing it today—but obliquely and partially, disappearing suggestively around the curve of the street. Nor did it have any antecedents in actual architecture. It sprang from the world of decorative pseudo-architecture that we see, for example, portrayed in the later wall paintings at Pompeii. Reinterpreted in actual brick construction, such fantasy architecture inevitably took on a certain substance and structural logic; and in this new guise it came to enjoy a certain popularity in the domestic and funerary architecture of second-century Rome and Ostia *(Plate 151)*. But its shallow, delicate relief and rather intimate proportions caused it to remain closely linked to the brick medium of which it was a manifestation. Whether in any particular instance the brick surfaces were left exposed or were faced with stucco, such ornament was always used to enhance the underlying structure, never to conceal it.

It was doubtless this last quality which made the decoration of the hemicycle acceptable in the otherwise remarkably austere setting of the Markets of Trajan. The free articulation of the constituent masonry masses, the bold, rhythmical patterns of doors and windows, the sweeping horizontals of cornices and balconies—these were the

qualities which Apollodorus was out to exploit, and they were all qualities inherent in the brick-faced concrete medium. After centuries of deference to the superficial proprieties of the Greek architectural tradition, Rome had at last acquired an architectural language of her own—and was beginning to have the courage to use it.

It was in the commercial and domestic architecture of first-century Rome and Ostia that this new, functional, concrete-vaulted architecture had taken shape. We shall be returning to this later in the chapter. Here we must be content to take note of it as only one of several components of an architecture which, at the turn of the first and second centuries A.D., was rapidly moving toward a new synthesis.

On the one hand there was the conservative, classicizing tradition of monumental public architecture, still powerful enough to dictate the concept of the Forum of Trajan and the Basilica Ulpia. There was still life in this tradition insofar as religious buildings were concerned, but in secular architecture Trajan's Forum was to be its last great monumental expression in the capital. At the other extreme there was the rapidly developing tradition of the contemporary brick-faced concrete medium, a tradition within which we may distinguish several convergent but still distinct currents. There was the frankly innovating, exploratory quest for novel spatial effects represented in the octagonal hall of the Domus Aurea and in many parts of the Domus Augustana. There was the dramatic exploitation of this new awareness of the architectural properties of interior space in order to create ever grander versions of familiar themes, as in the state rooms of the Domus Augustana. Allied to both these trends, but conditioned by the specialization of its functions, there was the architecture of the great bath buildings. And last, but far from least, there was the utilitarian, secular architecture, which by its sheer quantity and by the directness of its impact on the man in the street must have provided much of the momentum which carried the Roman Architectural Revolution from its tentative beginnings in Julio-Claudian times to its triumphant conclusion barely a century later.

The monument which beyond all others can be seen to have assimilated all these diverse trends into a single coherent entity is Hadrian's Pantheon *(Plates 152–156)*. Rebuilt from its foundations between A.D. 118 and 128, it is by a happy accident one of the rare Roman buildings to have come down to us in a form which allows us not merely to reconstruct the architect's original intentions but also to experience them directly.

Where there has been most change is where it matters least, namely in the exterior. Today, standing in the street, one is almost equally conscious of the great columnar porch and of the huge ma-

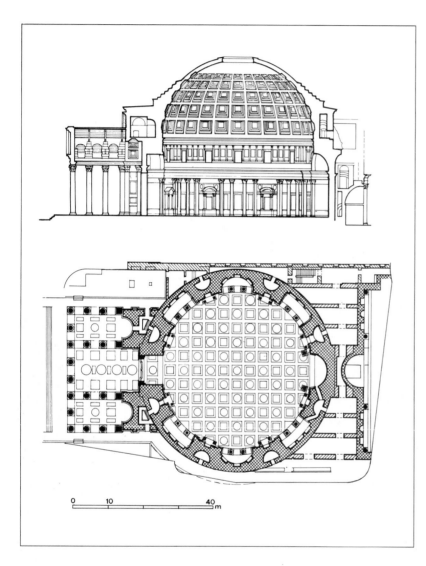

sonry mass of the rotunda from which it projects, but in antiquity the latter was almost entirely masked from sight by other buildings, now demolished. From the front one would have been aware, and indeed one was meant to be aware, of little more than the familiar spectacle of the gabled facade, on its eight 40-ft. (12.2 m.) high columns of Egyptian granite, rising majestically at the far end of a long, rather narrow, porticoed forecourt, very much in the manner of the Temple of Mars Ultor at the far end of the Forum Augustum. A gabled porch was still a necessary concession to the conventional proprieties. The rotunda could not be completely masked from sight, but it was very effectively pushed into the background.

All of this changed dramatically as one stepped across the threshold into the rotunda itself. The very conception of the sanctuary of a temple as something more than a rigidly enclosed rectangular, or occasionally cylindrical, box was in itself a revolutionary innovation; and the first impact of the rotunda, with its soaring coffered vault and the light streaming in through the central oculus, must always have been one of the great architectural experiences. There had been precedents, in the centrally lit, domed rotundas of Baiae *(Plate 140)* and, quite recently in Rome itself, in the Baths of Trajan; but nothing on this overwhelming scale, nothing of the same breathtaking simplicity and dignity of conception.

The formal scheme of the Pantheon's interior is extremely simple —a cylindrical drum (142 ft., or 43.20 m., in diameter), surmounted by a hemispherical dome, of which the crown was exactly the same height above the pavement as the internal diameter of the building. Cornices divide the walls internally into two zones and externally into three, of which the uppermost external zone corresponds to the lower part of the dome as seen from within. This difference between interior and exterior was dictated by structural necessity, since the equilibrium of the dome demanded a heavy load on the shoulders, and it explains the rather squat, saucer-like outer profile of the dome, which is patently a by-product of the vaulted space within. Inevitably there were concessions to the outward appearance of a building which, as today, would have been a conspicuous landmark from the surrounding hills —the cornices themselves and perhaps also the gilt-bronze tiles with which the outer face of the dome is said to have been covered until they were removed by the Byzantine emperor Constans II in A.D. 663. Or were these last perhaps only on the porch? On the dome thin bronze sheeting (as still survives around the oculus) would seem a more logical answer. Be that as it may, our main concern is with the interior of the rotunda. This unquestionably is the feature around which the thinking of Hadrian and his architect took formal shape.

The construction of a dome fractionally larger than that of St.

Peter's would at any time have been a formidable engineering enterprise, and the undertaking of such a project demonstrates the overwhelming confidence which its builders felt in their materials and in their own ability to handle them. Out of the many factors which contributed to the success of the project we may select four for special mention.

One that by this date could be taken for granted was the sheer strength of the mortar mix. Auguste Choisy's description of the dome as an "artificial monolith" captures the essence of such architecture. The architect of the Pantheon was prepared to push this element to its known limits, and beyond. And time has proved him right.

A second factor was the strength of the foundations. The need for such had been learned the hard way: some of Rabirius's work on the Palatine was already showing signs of dangerous settling *(Plate 129)* and had to be heavily buttressed during Hadrian's reign. The architect of the Pantheon was determined to make no such mistake. The rotunda rests on a solid ring of concrete, about 24 ft., or 7.30 m., wide at the base and 15 ft., or 4.50 m., deep, and this was strengthened during construction by the addition of a concentric, benchlike outer ring of footings.

A third factor was a selective grading of the *caementa* of the aggregate in terms of weight and compressive strength—travertine in the foundations, alternate layers of travertine and tufa in the lower drum, tufa alone in the upper drum and the two lower rings of coffering of the dome, a band of tile and tufa corresponding to the third ring of coffering, and above this line nothing but light yellow tufa and pumice. At the crown of the vault the estimated weight per unit of volume is barely two-thirds of that in the footings. By this means and by diminishing the thickness of the envelope from 20 ft., nearly 6 m., at the shoulder to 59 in., barely 150 cm., at the crown, it is estimated that the moment of flection was kept very nearly uniform throughout the envelope—a crucial factor in ensuring the stability of the finished structure.

Fourth and last were the numerous cavities carefully disposed within the body of the drum. Besides facilitating the drying out of the vast mass of the concrete core, these cavities served to lighten the sheer dead weight of masonry and in particular, during construction, to relieve the load over the entrance and the seven radiating chambers which constitute the principal decorative articulation of the interior. In this they were helped by the great relieving arches which are such a conspicuous feature of the brickwork of the exterior of the drum and by the liberal use of leveling courses of tile.

Two other aspects of the Pantheon call for brief discussion—the proportions and symbolism of its design and the interior decoration.

From the literary sources and from the monuments themselves alike it is evident that both proportion and symbolism regularly played a substantial part in determining the design of classical architecture, the latter particularly in buildings that were directly or indirectly religious in character. We have already observed the apse and semi-dome taking their place in Domitian's palace as part of the religious-inspired ceremonials of the imperial court. In the case of the Pantheon we can hardly question the cosmic symbolism of the basic design or of the seven recesses which, together with the door, divided the interior into eight equal segments. Beyond this point one almost inevitably begins to stray into the realms of guesswork, and there is much to be said for the belief that, once the basic form was established, its detailed development was primarily determined by more strictly architectural and constructional considerations (which might well in their turn have been given symbolic significance in the final ordering and decoration of the building). The sort of rules concerning proportions given by Vitruvius arise naturally in an architecture which depended heavily for its execution on the use of multiples of some basic unit, or module, or on simple geometrical derivatives thereof. Vitruvius (in quite a different context) describes exactly how the architect of the Pantheon, in laying out the plan, must have begun by subdividing the circumference of the inner circle successively into 4, 8, 16, and 32 symmetrical parts; and (to take a single unusually clear example) it can hardly be an accident that in elevation the distance from the cornice of the lower order to the crown of the dome is the same as the side of the square inscribed within the same circle.

Such relationships between the major dimensions are fully credible. This was how Roman architects were trained to think and, however much improvisation of detail there may have been as the building went up, the principal vertical dimensions must have been established from the outset. Beyond this point anyone with a ruler and compass can find various other numerical coincidences which may or may not be significant—mostly one suspects not, except as an inevitable by-product of modular construction. A feature for which no really satisfactory explanation has ever been offered is the choice of 28 as the number of coffers in each ring. Did the sophistication of the architect extend to using the subtle shift of rhythm from 8 to 7 in order to emphasize the formal break between drum and dome? Intentional or not, this is the result and, together with the central lighting of the dome, it is one of the reasons why the latter seems to float almost weightlessly above the spectator.

To the student of Roman architecture the Pantheon must occupy a central position. Not only is it, by any reckoning, one of the great buildings of antiquity; not only does it mark the coming of age of the concrete-vaulted architecture which was Rome's unique contribution

157. *Praeneste (Palestrina), limestone* opus incertum *masonry*

158. *Ostia, Piazzale of the Corporations, tufa* opus reticulatum *masonry. The mosaic pavement displays the emblem of the merchants' guild whose office this was*

159. *Rome, Mausoleum of Augustus, tufa* opus reticulatum *masonry* ▷

to the history of European architecture; but we can also see it very much as the Romans saw it in their own time. Thanks to its consecration as a church in A.D 608–610 the Pantheon has been in continuous use since antiquity, and because it could not easily be subjected to the sort of modifications which overtook so many more conventional basilican churches it has come down to us in a form very like that which it presented in antiquity. The interior of the cupola has lost its decoration, which probably consisted of metal rosettes within a framework of molded stucco, the whole lavishly gilt; and the marble veneer of the upper order was replaced by Pope Benedict XIV (1740–58), with only a small section of it recently restored to its original form— but in other respects, including the splendid marble floor and the marble columns, aediculae, and veneer of the lower order, it is substantially as it was in antiquity.

To appreciate what this means one has only to contrast the Pantheon with what in their day were comparable buildings: the *caldarium* of the Baths of Caracalla, for example, or Tor Pignattara (the Mausoleum of Helena). These are today mere skeletons, to be viewed —according to one's taste—as romantic ruins, as object lessons in Roman building skills, or as the basis for laborious deductive reconstructions of their original appearance. Here in the Pantheon we can for a moment see with our own eyes what this architecture of light, color, and space was all about.

If we review the development of concrete architecture in Rome during the period from the second century B.C. to the first half of the second century A.D., we may distinguish two broad phases. During the first phase architects were principally concerned with the cheaper, more efficient execution of architectural concepts that were already familiar. Formal innovation was restricted largely to the fields of utilitarian and commercial architecture (harborworks, warehouses, aqueducts) or else—discreetly masked beneath a veneer of orthodox classicism—it was applied to types of public buildings which were relative newcomers to the social scene (amphitheaters, Roman-type theaters, bath buildings). The new technology was already busily at work, but the range of new formal possibilities which it offered had not yet been fully accepted, much less comprehended and exploited.

The second phase, that which we have termed the Roman Architectural Revolution, is distinguished by a growing awareness of these new formal possibilities and by an increasing readiness to use them for the creation of an architecture that was not merely more efficient and cheaper but also profoundly different in character from

anything that had preceded it. In terms of architectural form this difference involved an explicit awareness of space as a medium to be exploited in its own right and a recognition of the fact that concrete could be used as an envelope for the enclosure of that space in a variety of ways for which there was little or no architectural precedent. We shall never know which architect or architects of the Augustan age first consciously recognized these new concepts; but we do possess substantial remains of many of the buildings in Rome in which they first achieved monumental expression. Constructionally as well as aesthetically it was a moment of high architectural adventure. The sixty-odd years that separate Nero's Domus Aurea from Hadrian's Pantheon may fairly be said to have changed the entire face of European architecture.

What had made this architectural revolution possible was a notable advance in building technology. To understand fully the products of the new Roman architecture one has also to understand something of how a Roman builder went about his task, and it is accordingly to his prosaic, everyday practices that we must now briefly turn our attention.

The Romans did not invent lime mortar. Their contribution was to recognize that by substituting for ordinary sand the sandlike *pozzolana* characteristic of the volcanic regions of Latium and Campania they could produce a lime mortar of quite unprecedented strength. The story of the first two hundred years of Roman concrete construction is largely one of the exploitation of the properties of that medium by successive generations of working builders. Lacking as they did any possible understanding of the chemical processes involved, their skill could only be acquired by trial and error, and formal innovation could only come about within the framework of established building practices. Sometimes, as in the Porticus Aemilia or at Praeneste in the Sanctuary of Fortuna Primigenia, progress was remarkably rapid and efficient. At the opposite extreme, whether due to the incompetence or to the deliberate negligence of the contractors, there is the notorious instance of the aqueducts begun by Agrippa in 33 B.C., almost all of which had to be rebuilt within a decade or two of their construction. But such differences are the inevitable result of large numbers of builders working in a material whose properties they still did not fully understand. In competent hands by the second century B.C., Roman concrete—conceived originally as an inert mass to fill the spaces within or behind a framework of traditional masonry —had already achieved independent status as a medium for building walls and simple vaults.

In free-standing walls it was almost always used with some sort of facing, at first almost invariably made of the same material as the

163. *Ostia, wall of* opus testaceum *brickwork, with* opus mixtum *wall visible beyond*

164. *Ostia,* opus testaceum *brickwork with decorative joints*

165. *Ostia, late Roman masonry in alternate courses of tufa and brick, showing scaffolding holes*

147

166. *Rome*, stadium *of the Domus Augustana, entrance doorway with a flat architrave and relieving arch above it, showing the non-structural character of the arch*

aggregate *(caementa)* of the core; and it is with the successive development of these facings that scholars have mainly concerned themselves—naturally enough, since it is often the facing which provides the best guide to the date of the associated structure. From the irregular lumps of stone in the primitive mortared rubblework at Cosa *(Plate 113)* it was a natural step to the interlocking patchwork facing *(opus incertum)* typical of the great Republican sanctuaries of Latium *(Plate 157)*. In Rome, with its softer, more tractable tufas, this in turn was gradually drawn into a pattern, developing imperceptibly into the *opus reticulatum,* literally "network masonry" *(Plates 158, 159),* of which the remains of the Theater of Pompey (55 B.C.) offer the earliest example. This reticulate work could be used in combination with small squared facing blocks of tufa *(tufelli)* or, increasingly, with brick *(opus mixtum; Plates 160, 162)*. Under Augustus and Tiberius brickwork *(opus testaceum; Plates 163, 164)* began to take over as a facing material in its own right, at first reusing broken tile but very soon employing flat bricks that were manufactured specifically for the purpose. The camp of the Praetorian Guards (A.D. 21–23) was a pioneer monument of the new fashion *(Plate 118)*. There were survivals or revivals of earlier styles—for example, the reticulate work of Hadrian's Villa at Tivoli *(Plate 161)*; but apart from a growing tendency in cheaper work to alternate courses of brick with courses of *tufelli,* brickwork remained the preferred facing right down to late antiquity.

These styles of facing (of which there were countless provincial equivalents) were those most widely current in Central Italy. Today, stripped of their former coating of plaster or marble, they are a conspicuous feature of this masonry. In terms of construction, however, it was the development of the quality of the core itself which represented the more significant advance. Here it is very easy to be misled by the analogy with modern concrete. Exceptionally (for example in footings laid under water) the mass of mortar and rubble may have been poured indiscriminately, as modern concrete is poured; but normally the rubble was laid by hand in roughly horizontal courses, with a lavish admixture of mortar, and it was the fusion of the mortar of the successive courses into a single monolithic whole which constituted the strength of the finished product. Here the lapse of time between one stage of the work and the next, while fresh scaffolding and shuttering were being erected, posed a real problem, one with which many late Republican builders were still having trouble. The Palaestra at Pompeii and the Villa of Livia at Prima Porta are only two of the many surviving monuments which illustrate their difficulties. It was not until the general adoption of brick as the standard facing material that the problem was satisfactorily resolved by the insertion of courses of large tiles *(Plate 165)* which served the double

168. *Rome, Severan additions to the Domus Augustana. Barrel vault with constructional ribs of brickwork*

169. *Rome, Tor Pignattara (Mausoleum of Helena). Large earthenware jars (pignatte) were used to lighten the shoulders of the vault* ▷

at the shoulders of a concrete vault—as in Tor Pignattara *(Plate 169)* and the Circus of Maxentius—and the use of a self-supporting inner framework of hollow, interlocking tubes *(Plate 170)*. The latter were developed in North Africa, where timber for shuttering was always scarce, and do not seem to have reached Rome before the fourth century. Another latecomer to Italy was vaulting in brick, which was already being used in Asia Minor as early as the second century.

The discrepancy between the structural realities of this concrete masonry and its superficial appearance can be very misleading. The brick relieving arches which regularly accompany doors, windows, and other openings convey the impression of a "live" architecture in which such devices are used to discharge the load that would otherwise bear directly down upon the voids below. In walls of modest dimensions (not more than two Roman feet in thickness) most such arches are structural in the limited sense that they penetrate the full thickness of the wall. One sees this, for example, in the walls of the Capitolium at Ostia, where the relieving arches of the exterior reflect the pattern of the recesses inside the cella *(Plate 197)*. In larger walls more often than not such features prove to be purely superficial, related to the outer facing but not extending through the core of the masonry. The great relieving arches of the Pantheon are quite exceptional in this respect *(Plate 167)*.

All of this is intelligible only if one recalls that, although in the finished structure it was the core and not the facing that did the work, the latter nevertheless played a very important part during the actual processes of building. It was by using the surfaces of the brick that the builder was able to control accurately the vertical and horizontal alignments of his work and to handle such features as doors and windows. Moreover, by building from the outside toward the center, using the brickwork facing itself as a framework to shape and to contain the core, he was able not only to maintain precision but also at the same time to keep the timber shuttering down to a minimum. During construction the arches were in fact an actively functioning part of the brick framework. It was only after the mortar of the concrete core had finally dried out that they lost their structural meaning —indeed that, in the event of any settlement, the vertical joints of the arches became a positive source of weakness.

The Roman builder was always glad to be able to economize on timber. Major vaults and arches can only have been constructed upon a forest of heavy scaffolding, with the coffering built up over a series of precisely carpentered wooden forms. But lesser arches were regularly constructed upon a much lighter framework of planks, or of tiles resting on planks, which were supported in turn by centering that rested on timbers socketed into the spring of the arch or—in

purpose of capping each successive stage of the work and of giving the builder a good working surface on which to prepare for the next stage and to take his levels.

Arches and vaulting presented comparable problems. Right down to the early Empire many builders preferred to play safe by selecting the innermost courses of *caementa* and laying them radially, like the bricks of a conventional brick arch or vault *(Plate 141)*. It was not really until the first half of the first century A.D. that it became general practice in Central Italy to build arches and vaults in the same horizontal coursing as the walls on which they rested. The finished structure took its shape from the wooden centering on which it was laid and, once set, it stood by virtue of the monolithic qualities of the concrete mass of which it was composed. This might seem to be belied by the not infrequent incorporation of ribs of brickwork *(Plate 168)*, already used tentatively in the Colosseum and more and more commonly in late antiquity. On close examination, however, these can be seen to have had no independent structural function, being built up simultaneously with the rising courses of the concrete envelope. They must have been used to help achieve an accurate curvature, and at the same time to subdivide the fluid mass of concrete into smaller, more manageable compartments.

Other vaulting devices which belong predominantly to late antiquity were the introduction of large hollow jars to lighten the load engineering work such as the Pont du Gard (*Plate 246*)—on bosses or ledges that were left projecting for the purpose. Foundations were often built in timber-shuttered trenches, but the upstanding walls needed only a minimum of light, movable scaffolding to form a platform for the masons. The sockets ("putlog holes") for the small timbers which carried these platforms are one of the common features of Roman masonry of all periods (*Plate 128*).

The builders of these great Roman vaulted monuments did not operate from scale drawings as we understand the term today. They could and did survey accurately, and they did unquestionably use plans that were worked out in considerable detail and marked up in Roman feet or, in the provinces, whatever other unit of measure was appropriate. They also prepared drawings and, on occasion, models to give the client an impression of the finished building. But it is very doubtful indeed whether they prepared elevations drawn to scale, or that the masons would have known how to use them. The principal heights were certainly estimated in advance; the architect must also have known the general relationships of the proposed elevation, including such matters as vaulting, lighting, and the discharge of rainwater; templates were prepared for moldings; and during construction some details were drawn out in full to help the sculptors and stonemasons. An example of such detailing which happens to have come down to us is a full-size drawing of one of the arches of the amphitheater at Capua incised, joints and all, on the slabs of the adjoining pavement. Nevertheless, as in much medieval building, a great deal was left to the skill and experience of the builder. There were certain points where coordination was required—for example, the leveling up of the seatings for the architrave of a colonnade or the springing line of a vault. But it is one of the conspicuous qualities of Roman building that it knew how to achieve such results with a minimum of fuss. In an architecture which depended so largely on light and color, rigorous accuracy was not called for at every stage, and a great deal could be left to the good sense of the specialist in charge of each working group.

There were a great many of these specialists. Not only was it customary to subdivide any large task into smaller units (as was done regularly in military architecture), but—as we saw when discussing the Colosseum—there was a strong tendency to specialization at every level of Roman craftsmanship. A common stonemason would not ordinarily be expected to be able to work in marble, and one of the main tasks of the architect in charge of any large enterprise must have been the organization of his labor force in such a way as to minimize overlapping and time-consuming delays. In addition to the architect himself and his immediate staff of surveyors, operators of

machinery, and general assistants, any large project would have involved stonemasons, bricklayers, carpenters, hauliers, smiths (to maintain tools and to provide the stonemasons with dowels and cramps), plumbers, sculptors and marbleworkers, stuccoists, mosaicists, and a large number of unskilled or semiskilled laborers working under the orders of the individual master-craftsmen. Every now and then we catch a glimpse of this labor force in the literary sources, as in Frontinus's account of the *familia* (the permanent staff of slaves) which maintained the water supply of Rome, for which he had been commissioner under Trajan. From the tombstones of individual craftsmen we learn that these were largely hereditary skills, passed from father to son and from master to slave or freedman. Another valuable source of training and recruitment was the army: as a young man Vitruvius had maintained military engineering equipment under the future emperor Augustus, and it was by bridging the Danube for Trajan's armies that Apollodorus seems first to have made his name. A capacity to organize and to discipline a large and varied work force was a gift without which no architect of any major public project could hope to be successful.

To specialization of craftsmanship and to its rational organization we may add the systematic, orderly supply of materials, many of them in standardized, prefabricated form. There had long been a lively production of roof tiles in the lower Tiber Valley; and with the realization that a narrow, tilelike brick made an admirable facing for concrete construction, it was natural that this industry should also take over the production of such bricks in a series of standard sizes, mostly based on simple multiples or fractions of the Roman foot. Thanks to the habit of stamping many of the larger pieces with the name of the owner and very often with the name of the brickyard and the date, we can follow the history of the industry in considerable detail *(Plate 171)*. We note that, whereas in the first century A.D. it was still largely in private ownership, there was a steady trend away from the small owner producing for a limited market toward larger, industrialized production. The builders of the great imperial monuments and of the domestic and mercantile quarters of post-Neronian Rome and Ostia could order their materials in any quantity and in any of the standard sizes, ready for immediate delivery.

The same held true for marble. The marble that reached Rome during Republican times from Greece and Africa had come in relatively small quantities from sources owned by private individuals or cities. The opening of the Carrara quarries greatly increased the amount of white marble available in Rome; and the annexation (30 B.C.) of Egypt, with its fine supplies of decorative stones and its long tradition of specialized craftsmanship, showed the advantages of state ownership and control. Tiberius took over the principal mines and quarries throughout the Empire, and he and his immediate successors followed this up with a radical reorganization of the whole system of production and supply. Instead of the direct relationship between customer and quarry of classical Greek practice we now begin to encounter a system of production in bulk, and of storage against demand at the quarry depots and at the marble yards of the great ports of the Roman world. The principal marble yards of Rome lay beside the Tiber, below the Aventine, and here in the nineteenth century were found hundreds of blocks of rough marble and columns, many of them bearing the accounting inscriptions which are one of our chief sources of knowledge about this commerce.

The essential features of the Imperial marble trade were the following: production in bulk at a limited number of high-quality sources, chosen wherever possible so as to take full advantage of water transport; standardization of certain dimensions, notably those of monolithic columns; and a substantial measure of actual prefabrication (sarcophagi, columns, and other architectural elements). The columns of the porch of the Pantheon are of two qualities of Egyptian granite prepared to the standard dimension of 40 feet (12.2 meters). A 50-ft. (14.85 m.) column of the same material was used in A.D. 161 for the commemorative monument of Antoninus Pius in the Campus Martius; it had been quarried in the year 106 and had presumably

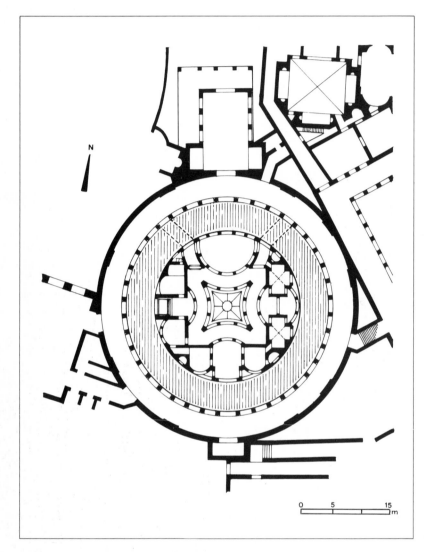

lain in the marble yards ever since. Three more 40-ft. columns were available when it was decided (in 1626 and again in 1666) to replace the missing columns along the east side of the porch, and of these two are known to have come from the ruins of the Baths of Severus Alexander (A.D. 222–227). Even a building of the size of the Pantheon could have been supplied in part from stock.

Mass production, organized marketing, accumulation of stocks, standardization of qualities and dimensions, a substantial measure of prefabrication and corresponding economies in the cost of what must always have been an expensive commodity—this all has a very modern ring, and illustrates one of the cardinal secrets of Roman architectural success. Only on the basis of an orderly production and supply of essential materials would it have been possible to achieve such feats of construction as the building of the Pantheon in not more than ten years (between A.D. 118 and 125–128) or of the Baths of Diocletian in not more than eight (between A.D. 298 and 305–306).

To conclude this account of the emergence of the new Roman architecture, we shall glance briefly at the changes in domestic and utilitarian building which accompanied its more monumental manifestations. For this we may select two groups of buildings which represent the two poles of its development: Hadrian's sumptuous country residence near Tibur (Tivoli), and the early Imperial refashioning of Rome's harbor town, Ostia.

Hadrian's Villa *(Plates 172–196)* is a monument as tantalizing as it is fascinating. As an architectural concept it falls readily enough into place at the end of the long line of luxurious country residences which includes the seaside villas of Cicero's friends and contemporaries, the villas of Augustus and Tiberius on Capri, of Nero at Anzio and Subiaco, and of Domitian at Albano—all elaborately landscaped agglomerations of dwellings, summer houses, bath buildings, libraries and sculpture galleries, small temples, sheltered promenades, pools, formal gardens, and statuary. Both socially and formally the English country house of the eighteenth century—with its lakes, its *tempietti,* its fountains and follies, its alternation of formal gardens and parkland, its elaborately contrived vistas—offers a close parallel.

To a second-century Roman all of this was well-trodden ground. What was new and strictly contemporary, however, was the architecture of most of the individual buildings; and here we are confronted by a situation as paradoxical as it was characteristically Roman. As an institution the Roman villa was itself already something of a paradox. A feeling for landscape was one of the most genuine and endearing qualities of Roman taste, and the villa was a rich man's device for en-

177. *Tibur (Tivoli), Hadrian's Villa, the Teatro Marittimo*

178. *Tibur (Tivoli), Hadrian's Villa, aerial view of the Teatro Marittimo with (left) the residential nucleus and (right) the Sala dei Filosofi and part of the Stoa Poikile (Pecile)*

179, 180. *Tibur (Tivoli), Hadrian's Villa, the Teatro Marittimo*

181. *Tibur (Tivoli), Hadrian's Villa, plan of the pavilion of the Piazza d'Oro*
182. *Tibur (Tivoli), Hadrian's Villa, plan of the Nymphaeum near the Stoa Poikile (Pecile)*
183. *Tibur (Tivoli), Hadrian's Villa, vestibule of the Piazza d'Oro* ▷

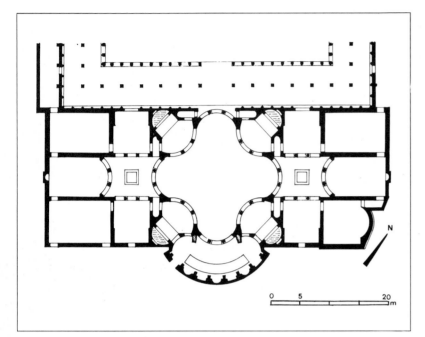

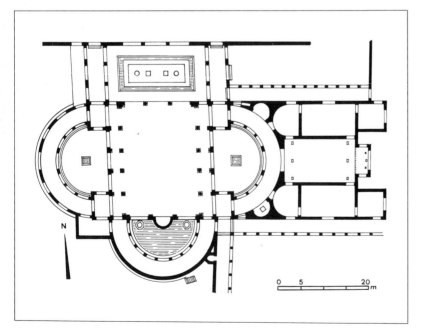

184, 185. *Tibur (Tivoli), Hadrian's Villa, vestibule of the Piazza d'Oro*

186. *Tibur (Tivoli), Hadrian's Villa, vestibule of the Piazza d'Oro, detail of the vault*

187, 188, 189. *Tibur (Tivoli), Hadrian's Villa, the Lesser Baths* ▷

190. *Tibur (Tivoli), Hadrian's Villa, the Large Baths, with remains of stuccoed vaulting. The walls were faced with marble*

191. *Tibur (Tivoli), Hadrian's Villa, exterior of the Sala dei Filosofi and end of the Stoa Poikile (Pecile)*

192. *Tibur (Tivoli), Hadrian's Villa, central wall of the Stoa Poikile (Pecile), a double portico for all-weather exercise. The horizontal grooves are due to the robbing out of the brick courses of the* opus mixtum *masonry*

193. *Tibur (Tivoli), Hadrian's Villa,* caldarium *of the Heliocaminus Baths*

194, 195. *Tibur (Tivoli), Hadrian's Villa, Piazza d'Oro, details of the pavilion wing*

196. *Tibur (Tivoli), Hadrian's Villa, Piazza d'Oro, looking northeast across the pavilion* ▷

197. *Ostia, Capitolium, east wall of the cella. The relieving arches mark the recesses of the interior*

joying the countryside while surrounded by all the comforts that an urban civilization could provide. In Hadrian's Villa the paradox was compounded by the contradictions of the emperor's artistic personality, which contrived to reconcile the dilettante eclecticism of a passion for all things Greek with a feeling for architecture which, even at its most whimsical, was a highly professional expression of contemporary architectural thought. The Canopus *(Plates 172–174)*, for example (so named after the great sanctuary of Serapis near Alexandria), was an elaborately landscaped cascade mirrored in the waters of an artificial canal, and the construction and detail of its buildings —including a huge mosaic-ornamented "melon" or "pumpkin" vault whose nine segments were alternately flat and concave—was the last word in modernity. The sculpture, on the other hand, seems to have consisted exclusively of old master copies of Greek and Egyptianizing Hellenistic works, among them a set of meticulously correct reproductions of the caryatids of the Erechtheum (whose last recorded appearance in Roman art was in the flanking porticoes of the Forum Augustum). Here and throughout the villa the buildings and the sculpture which adorned them belonged to two different worlds: the latter the product of an arid, eclectic academicism which had advanced little since the days of the omnivorous collectors of the late Republic; the former brimming over with the vitality and inventiveness of an avant-garde style which had broken out of the barren circle of a borrowed classicism, carrying with it such related decorative arts as mosaic, stucco, and polychrome marble work. Among educated Romans of the early second century, architecture and "art" were still operating on two quite separate levels.

Architecturally, it is the avant-garde aspect of these buildings which most precisely defines—and for our purpose also limits—their significance. It was an avant-garde movement which had reached the end of the road. For more than a century past the villas of wealthy Romans had been a hotbed of new ideas. Nero's plans for the Domus Aurea had unquestionably been shaped by his own previous work in his villas at Anzio and Subiaco. But by Hadrian's day the new architectural concepts had already won acceptance everywhere. The future lay not with fresh experiment, but with the long, prosaic processes of assimilation and consolidation.

It is, then, as the ultimate expression of the experimental thinking which had shaped the Roman Architectural Revolution that we must view the buildings of Hadrian's Villa—their intoxicating technical virtuosity, their lively interest in the properties of space and color, their preoccupation with the use of curvilinear forms. It is this last aspect that is the most readily illustrated. Already in the first phase of the villa, between A.D. 118 and 125, we see it in the bewildering in-

198. *Ostia, a predominantly domestic quarter in the western part of the city (Regio III). 1) House of the Triple Windows; 2) House of the Painted Vaults; 3) Insula of the Muses; 4) part of a group of standardized apartments set in a garden; 5) shops* (tabernae) *with apartments above them; 6) warehouses* (horrea); *7) shops* (taber-nae)

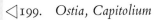

199.   *Ostia, Capitolium*
200.   *Ostia, House of Cupid and Psyche, pavement of polychrome marble*
201.   *Ostia, House of Cupid and Psyche, plan. A small but luxurious private house, c. A.D. 300*

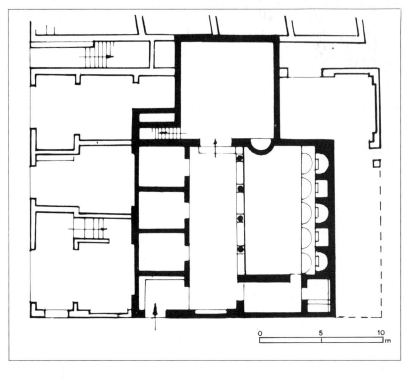

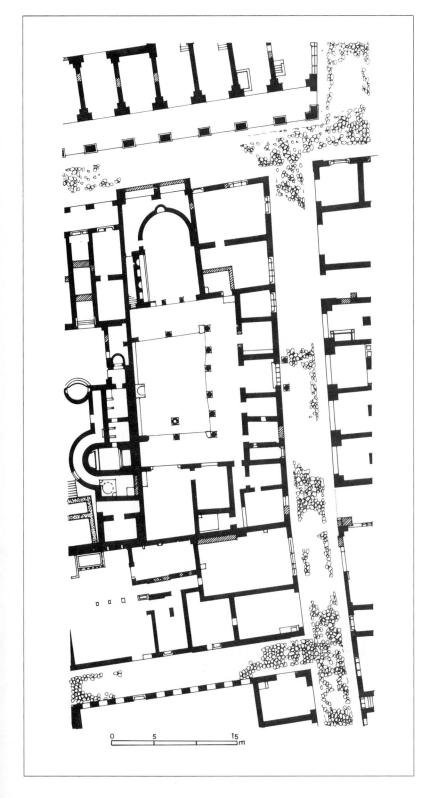

202. *Ostia, House of the Fortuna Annonaria*

203. *Ostia, House of the Fortuna Annonaria, plan. Late second century* A.D., *remodeled in the fourth century*

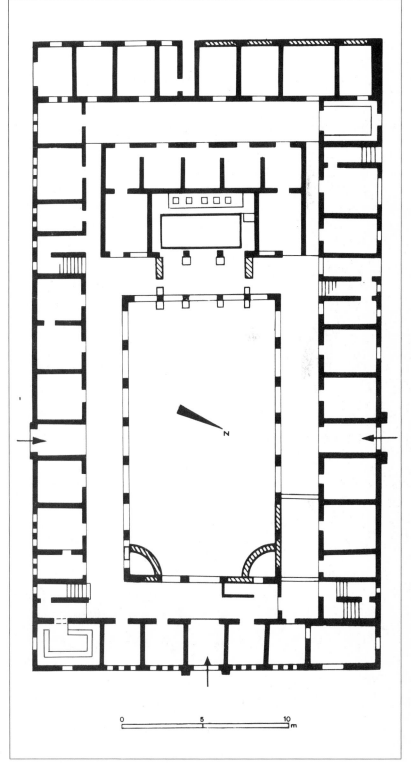

204. *Ostia, headquarters of the Fire Brigade (Vigiles), plan*

205. *Ostia, part of the commercial quarter near the river (Regio I). 1) public warehouses; 2) Horrea Epagathiana et Hilariana, a private multi-storied warehouse; 3) shops* (tabernae) *and stairs leading to apartments; 4) pòrtico overlooking street*

206. *Ostia, Horrea Epagathiana et Hilariana (right) and portico overlooking street (left)* ▷

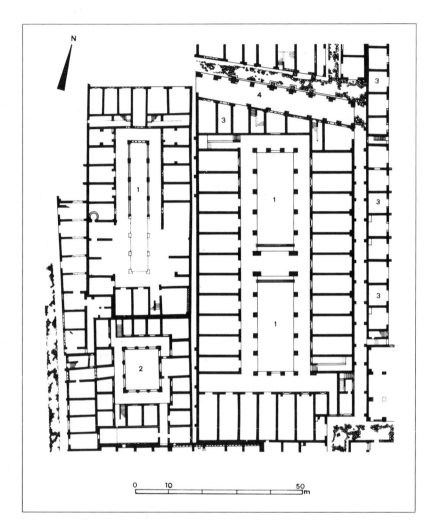

tricacies of the emperor's island retreat, the so-called Teatro Marittimo *(Plates 175–180),* and again a decade later (125–133) in rather more sophisticated form in the central pavilions of the Piazza d'Oro *(Plates 181, 194–196)* and of the West Palace, or Academy. These pavilions can never have been vaulted, but they may well have carried some form of superstructure in light materials. The Piazza d'Oro pavilion stood at the intersection of two long axes, framed on three sides by small fountain courts, and the resulting play of alternating light and shade and of curve and countercurve would have been all the more effective for the sober lines of the colonnaded peristyle of which it was the visual focus.

At the opposite end of the peristyle stood a vestibule *(Plates 183–185).* Its internal plan is one that was already familiar—in Domitian's palace, for example: an octagon inscribed within a square, with eight alternately rectangular and curved recesses, above which the ribs of the "pumpkin" vault merge into the uniform curvature of a dome with a central oculus. The novelty of the vestibule is that parts of the outer square frame have been stripped away, exposing in reverse the curvature of the angle-recesses. This was something quite new. We are still a long way from the achievement of an external architecture genuinely expressive of the new spatial forms within, but at least a tentative step had been taken in that direction.

Rome's harbor town, Ostia, lay at the opposite end of the social scale from Hadrian's Villa. The domestic and commercial quarters of Rome itself have largely been swept away by later building; but Ostia was already virtually abandoned by late antiquity. The streets and apartment houses, the offices and warehouses, excavated and restored, have survived to convey an impression of the new Roman urban architecture which is in its own way quite as vivid and compelling as that of Pompeii and Herculaneum, the representatives of the older Italic urban architecture which it replaced.

One of the most powerful factors at work was the steady rise in land values. Urban populations were rapidly growing, and there was no longer room for the relaxed, single-story planning of the older Roman tradition. Even in provincial Italy, at Pompeii and Herculaneum, we can already detect a marked tendency to build upward, renting out profitable street frontages for shops, and incorporating or adding upper stories around the atrium. In the capital the pressures were greater. Old Rome had long been notorious for its congestion, its narrow, winding streets and its ramshackle multi-storied tenement houses. The fire of A.D. 64 swept much of this away, and it is to the credit of Nero's erratic genius that he saw and grasped his opportunity. A new Rome rose from the ashes, and it was in essence a town built of brick-faced concrete.

209. *Ostia, House of the Charioteers, inner courtyard*
210. *Ostia, Baths of the Seven Sages* ▷

215. *Ostia, entrance to the Horrea Epagathiana et Hilariana. Foreground,*
remains of portico overlooking street

Apart from a certain number of individual buildings remodeled in later antiquity, when the main activity of the port of Rome had moved to a new site two miles to the north, the Ostia which one sees today is substantially the city as it was in the late first and second centuries A.D. Both its planning and its architecture closely reflect the regulations introduced in the capital after the fire of A.D. 64. The new Rome was to have broad, regular streets, flanked by street-side porticoes; the use of inflammable materials was strictly controlled; each building was to be structurally independent of its neighbors, and none was to be taller than 70 feet (20.8 meters). In Rome itself it seems that vested interests—not for the first or last time in history—were too strong for the planning aspects of these admirable regulations to be applied fully; in the marble plan of Rome drawn up soon after A.D. 200 tidy, regular quarters are the exception. But large areas of Ostia do reflect just such a pattern *(Plates 198, 205)*; and the buildings that accompany the pattern display precisely the broad unity of treatment that one would expect of an architecture which took shape within such a framework of formal planning.

The essential components of this new urban architecture were three: the *taberna,* a contemporary version of the timeless Mediterranean type of one-room shop or workroom opening directly off the street; an up-to-date masonry version of the timber street porticoes of Republican Rome *(Plate 215)*; and a residential unit which may be compared with the modern single-storied apartment. Out of these simple elements, variously combined, it was possible to meet all but the most specialized domestic and utilitarian requirements of a busy commercial community.

The *taberna* is a type we have already met in the Markets of Trajan, opening directly off the street or facing inward onto a courtyard or covered hall. It commonly incorporated a wooden loft, lit by a separate window and accessible by wooden steps, and a great many of the artisans and small tradesmen must have lived above their place of work. At the other end of the social scale there were still a few examples of the single-family house *(domus)* of the old type; but the great majority of the middle-class citizens lived in apartments. Some of these were situated over rows of shops, with separate entrance stairways from the street. Many of them were grouped together in multi-storied apartment blocks *(insulae),* with shops at street level and a central courtyard from which one or more flights of stairs led up to several floors of self-contained apartments. Superficially these *insulae* bear a strong resemblance to the medieval Italian *palazzo,* but there were in fact important differences. They were not occupied by a single family but by a number of families; there was consequently no *piano nobile,* and instead of stables and storerooms the ground floor was rented out for commercial use. The *insulae* resemble far more closely the modern Italian *palazzo.*

The same models could be applied with remarkably little modification to meet many of the city's other needs. Market buildings, warehouses *(horrea),* the offices of one of the merchant guilds, the headquarters of the fire brigade *(Vigiles)*—all of these could be expressed in very similar terms *(Plates 204, 206)*. There were still a few venerable monuments in an older style, and there were still sectors of public building in which the traditional classical proprieties had to be observed. But even here appearance and reality were fast parting company. In a building such as the Capitolium (c. A.D. 120; *Plates 197, 199*) only the columns of the porch, the entablature, and the massive door-frame were of solid marble. All the rest, though superficially encased in white marble, was in reality built of brick-faced concrete, as we see it today. A Roman passer-by would have seen nothing of the brickwork or of the relieving arches which, as in the Pantheon, are now such a prominent feature, but which are in fact no more than a constructional by-product of the statue recesses of the interior.

The result was an essentially contemporary architecture, shaped by function rather than tradition and relying for its effect less on artifice than on the use of standard materials, on simplicity of design, and on sound planning. Ornament was sparing: here and there a doorway or a recess of decorative brickwork *(Plate 215),* or an occasional string-course to frame an arch or to articulate a facade. As in the Markets of Trajan, the most conspicuous elements of the facades were now the doors and windows and shallow projecting balconies *(maeniana).* The windows in particular, a product of more settled times, were a notable innovation. Instead of the blank outer walls and inward-facing rooms of the old single-story Pompeian house, the apartments of Ostia could look outward, their windows closed by shutters or, increasingly, by panes of glass *(Plates 207, 208, 211, 214, 216, 218)*. They give these buildings a surprisingly modern look, an impression which is heightened by the fact that the rigid alternation of solids and voids characteristic of the older classical tradition has had to give place to a freer grouping reflecting the dispositions of the rooms on the interior. Another important forward-looking trend was the increasing use of brick arcades, as in the courtyard of the House of the Charioteers *(Plates 209, 212, 213)* and other examples *(Plates 210, 217)*. By the middle of the second century the domestic architecture of Ostia was already foreshadowing many of the orthodoxies of late antique building.

So far we have been discussing almost exclusively the architecture of Rome itself and of the adjoining areas of Central Italy. But Rome was also the capital of an empire that stretched from the Atlantic to the Euphrates; and although the principal object of this book is to single out the specifically Roman contribution to the architectural heritage of classical antiquity, it would be misleading to omit all consideration of the manifold Roman provincial architectures which in varying degrees reflected, or were themselves reflected by, the main currents of metropolitan Roman development.

It is not easy to present succinctly but meaningfully a story of such inherent complexity. Should one's approach be chronological or geographic? There is much to be said for the former method, since the Roman Empire was an evolving institution, and many aspects of its architecture inevitably reflect that evolution. From this viewpoint one may conveniently distinguish three main phases of development. The first of these (to set arbitrary limits to the successive stages of what was actually a continuing phenomenon) may be said to run from the effective accession of Augustus in 31 B.C. to the death of Trajan in A.D. 117. This was the period of military and political expansion and consolidation, the period when Rome was not only the center of power, but was also in many parts of the Mediterranean (and particularly in the West) still by far the more influential member of the resulting Romano-provincial cultural dialogue. The second phase, beginning with the accession of Hadrian and ending in the anarchy of the mid-third century A.D., was largely one of achievement, a time when, despite military pressures on the northern frontiers, many parts of the Mediterranean world enjoyed a hitherto unparalleled prosperity and sophistication of material culture. During this second phase Italy was still the center of authority, but it had already lost all claim to economic preeminence, and in many cultural fields too it was rapidly being overtaken by the more advanced of the western provinces. The third and final period was one of military and political recovery under the strong rule of Diocletian (A.D. 284–305) and his fellow-rulers of the Tetrarchy. This was a time when Rome was the capital of the Empire in name only, the effective center of power having shifted northward and eastward to a series of regional capitals: Trier, Milan, Sirmium, Thessalonica, Nicomedia, and Antioch. For a brief time the cultural trend was away from the old provincial groupings toward an ever-closer unity of forms and ideals. But after the brief reunification of political authority under Constantine, the Empire was once more divided into East and West, this time finally and irrevocably.

It is against this chronologically developing background that we must view the history of Roman Imperial architecture in the provinces. Whereas in the political and economic fields Italy's importance relative to the provinces steadily dwindled, this was not true of architecture. Not only did Rome remain the single most important recipient of imperial patronage, but—as we have seen in the previous chapter—it was also the birthplace of a lively, forward-looking school of contemporary architecture, the lessons of which had still to be assimilated by even the most advanced of the older provinces. To this consideration we must add the cultural gulf which at the time of Augustus still separated the former Hellenistic kingdoms of the East from all but a few privileged areas of the Roman West. Whatever the change wrought by nearly four centuries of growth, the story of Roman provincial architecture has still to be told in terms of the elementary facts of imperial geography—Italy and the western provinces on the one hand, and Rome and the eastern provinces on the other.

In the European provinces of the West, except for certain limited coastal areas that had been under Greek or Carthaginian rule, the expanding power of Rome found itself in contact with peoples whose native levels of material culture were notably inferior to her own. Republican Rome had been content to leave things much as it found them: apart from the basic requirements of security and communications, there is very little evidence of any systematic building activity prior to Caesar's conquest of the Three Gauls in 58–51 B.C. It was his establishment of several colonies of military veterans in Provence, followed in 44 B.C. by similar foundations at Lugdunum (Lyon) and Augusta Raurica (Augst, near Basel), that marked the beginning of a new and more enlightened policy. Instead of being treated as mere objects for exploitation, the provinces were to be developed and assimilated to Roman ways, and one of the principal instruments of this policy was the establishment of an urban civilization based on familiar Mediterranean models. The policy was taken up and systematically developed by Augustus and his successors, and it was a success from the start. Within a single generation many of the new foundations had taken firm root, and structures such as the Pont du Gard and the Maison Carrée (both first-generation buildings) attest to their architectural sophistication. By the second generation, Roman citizens from Gaul and Spain were sitting in the Senate. The first non-Italian emperor, Trajan (A.D. 98–117), came from Spain, and his adoptive grandson, Antoninus Pius, had close Gallic family connections. By the second century these provinces were already as much integral parts of the Roman Empire as Italy itself.

Brixia (Brescia), a) four Republican temples at the head of the Forum, on the site of the later Capitolium; b) Capitolium, built in A.D. 73–74 on the site of the earlier temples

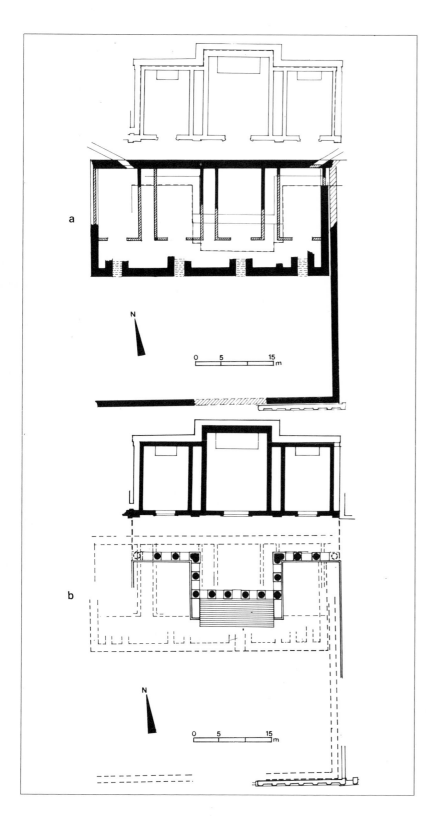

What was the secret of this spectacular success story? The answer is simple enough. However indifferent Republican Rome may have been to the welfare of the provinces overseas, the history of the last two centuries of the Republic in Italy itself, and in North Italy in particular (at that time still formally the province of Gallia Cisalpina), proved in retrospect to have been largely one of unconscious preparation for the tasks of empire. In North Italy, as later in the provinces, the chosen instrument of Romanization had been the establishment of urban life in areas where previously it had had only a very precarious hold, by the foundation of military colonies and by the refoundation of existing native centers on Roman lines and with Roman franchise. It was in these new cities of the Po Valley that Roman planners learned the lessons which they were to apply with such success in the new provinces beyond the Alps.

Of the contemporary Republican buildings of these North Italian towns we have only tantalizing fragments—traces of the pre-Imperial forum at Brixia (Brescia; *Plate 221*), part of an early gate at Verona, and traces of another at Comum (Como). But their plans have in many cases left an indelible mark on the street plans of their Imperial and medieval successors; including those of Pavia *(Plate 228)*, Rimini, Piacenza, Cremona, Padua, Verona *(Plate 227)*, Como, and (south of the Apennines) Florence, Lucca, and Luni (Carrara). All of these were regularly laid out around a grid of streets intersecting at right angles in accordance with the models which (as we saw in Chapter One) the Romans had derived and adapted from the Greek cities of South Italy. These were meticulously planned cities, and it is quite evident that the planning extended to making provision for certain clearly defined building types. When from the time of Augustus onward we finally begin to get a substantial body of surviving buildings, these demonstrate a broad uniformity of treatment which is explicable only as the result of a well-established local tradition, one moreover in which architecture and planning were regarded as two aspects of a single problem.

The fact that the models which shaped so much of the later architecture of the western provinces were conceived and first developed within the framework of an orderly planning tradition is cardinal to our understanding of them. True, the individual building types were in practice interpreted with the same flexibility as were the planning formulas themselves. No two temples, no two basilicas were identical, any more than the average town observed a rigid, four-square drawing-board regularity of plan. Towns such as Augusta Praetoria (Aosta) or Thamugadi (Timgad) in North Africa *(Plate 232)* were quite exceptional in this respect. But the familiar planning conventions and the established patterns of public architecture did

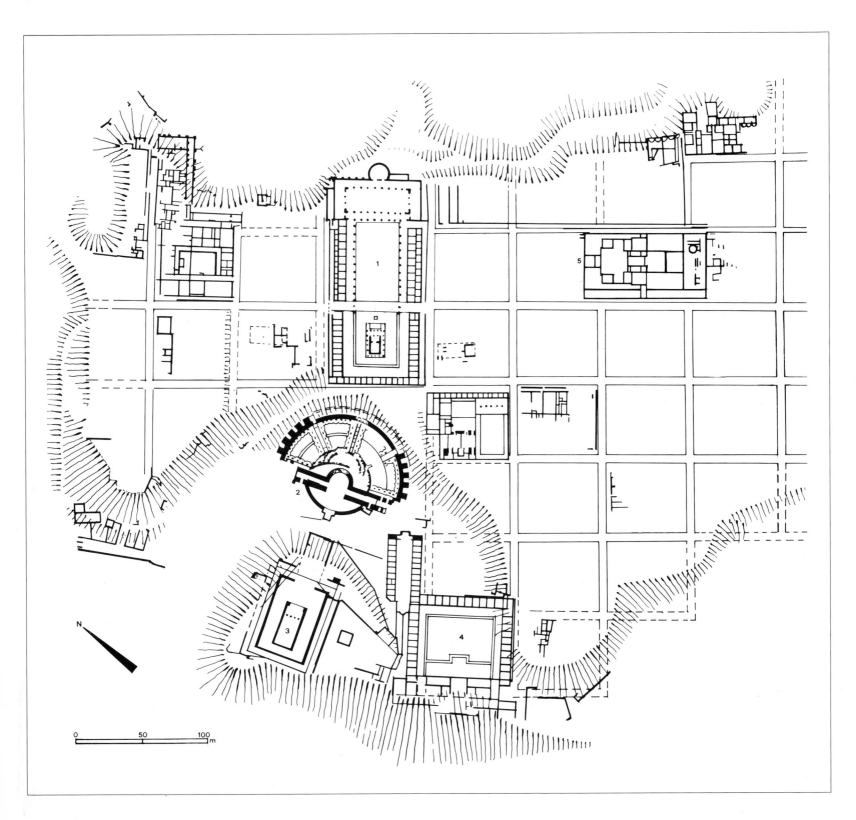

222. *Augusta Raurica (Augst, Germany), plan. 1) basilica-forum-temple complex; 2) theater; 3) temple; 4) market; 5) baths*

N

0   50   100
m

223. *Plans of basilica-forum-temple complexes at 1) Velleia; 2) Lugdunum Convenarum (Saint-Bertrand-de-Comminges, France); 3) Iader (Zadar, Yugoslavia)*

224. *Thamugadi (Timgad, Algeria), plan of the forum. 1) Curia (Senate); 2) temple; 3) entrance from main street; 4) basilica; 5) public lavatory at street level; 6) house at street level*

225. *Herdoniae (Ordona), plan of the forum at the time of Augustus (above) and in the early second century (below). 1) basilica; 2) temple; 3) temple; 4) market*

226. *Brixia (Brescia), Capitolium* ▷

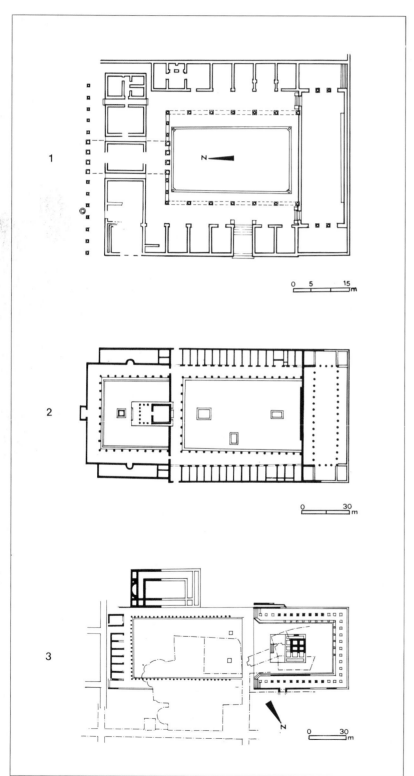

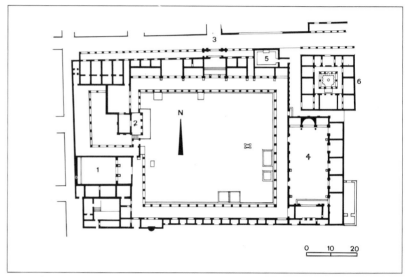

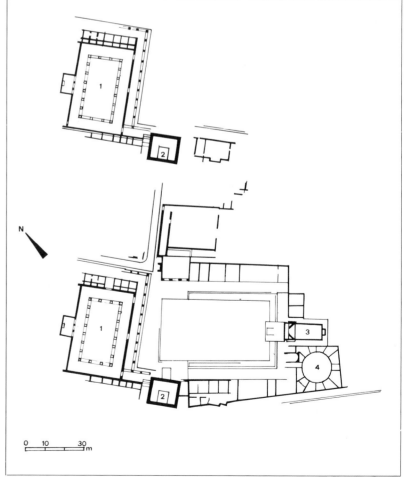

228. *Ticiunm (Pavia), aerial photograph showing survival of the Roman orthogonal street plan*

afford a well-tried framework within which, confronted by particular situations, planners and architects could develop their own variations upon the same basic themes. Moreover, once the urgent necessities of roads, defense, water supply, and housing had been satisfied, a town was able to develop its other amenities over the years, as funds and circumstances permitted, without ever losing its identity as a coherent organism. To cite a single example which happens to be well documented, we know that at Nemausus (Nîmes) in Provence the walls and gates *(Plates 235, 239)* and the aqueduct belong to the first years of the city's establishment, as does the Maison Carrée *(Plate 219)*, a state temple evidently designed to impress the population of what had been a flourishing native settlement. The amphitheater *(Plate 229)*, on the other hand, may well have been built as much as a century later. In this case the street plan contained anomalies taken over from the pre-existing settlement; but the central area was remodeled on conventionally orthogonal lines, with the forum sited beside the intersection of the two main streets.

As an example of a military colony founded on ground unencumbered by prior settlement we may take Augusta Raurica *(Plate 222)*, modern Augst. The site chosen was a plateau-like promontory on high ground, whose defenses followed its irregular outline. The theater, a relative newcomer to the architectural repertory and always an awkward component of any orthogonal scheme, was built into the slopes outside the walls. Inside, however, apart from such adjustments as running together two blocks to provide space for a large bath building, the grid of streets, once established, shaped all future development. The site of the forum was reserved from the outset; and although the buildings revealed by excavation date from the second century A.D., they follow a model established two hundred years before, almost certainly replacing an earlier version built in less durable materials. They consist of a colonnaded forum with shops facing both inward and outward; near one end, facing down the central space, stood an impressive state temple of Italic type, and across the opposite end a basilica. The main street of the town crosses the piazza, dividing it formally into halves, but only as a pedestrian thoroughfare. Wheeled traffic was excluded.

This composite basilica-forum-temple plan is a commonplace of early Imperial Roman architecture in the West. The details vary: the temple may be omitted altogether, or either it or the basilica may be displaced for reasons of local topography at which we can often only guess. At Iader (Zadar) in Dalmatia, the basilica lay along one of the long sides of the forum enclosure *(Plate 223)*, while at Glanum (Saint-Rémy-de-Provence) the temple (in this case a pair of twin temples) lay just outside the enclosure, on a different axis. At

Lugdunum Convenarum (Saint-Bertrand-de-Comminges in Aquitaine) the temple faced in the opposite direction *(Plate 223)*. In Britain it was usual to omit the temple, but not invariably so, as we see—albeit in somewhat eccentric form—at Verulamium. Frequently, as at Nîmes, we have only part of the plan and can only guess at its completion; in this instance there was no room for a basilica in the conventional position, which would have been opposite the Maison Carrée. Despite all these individual interpretations the solid authority of the accepted basic pattern appears in almost all the European provinces from the Iberian Peninsula (Conimbriga and Aeminium in Portugal) to Carinthia in Austria (Virunum, the capital of Noricum, re-founded in the mid-first century A.D.) and Dalmatia. Lutetia (Paris) is one of half a dozen Gaulish examples.

In North Italy early examples of the basilica-forum-temple complex are known at Angusta Bagiennorum (Benevagenna in Piedmont, an Augustan foundation) and at Velleia, in the foothills south of Parma, the latter a compact mini-version in which the temple has been compressed within the portico opposite the basilica *(Plates 223, 230)*, which is well dated by its statuary to the Augustan period. Despite the almost total lack of North Italian archaeological remains datable to the immediately preceding period, there can be little doubt that it was here, in the new towns of the second and first centuries B.C., that Roman architects and planners evolved this and the other stereotypes which they were to put to such good use in the western provinces. The constituent elements were already familiar features of the Central Italian architectural scene—at Cosa, at Pompeii, in the Forum Romanum itself. What was new was their integration into more or less standardized planning units. In this integrated form the basilica-forum complex in due course found its way southward, where we find it in such reconstructed Augustan city centers as Alba Fucens and Herdoniae (Ordona; *Plate 225)*. Rome itself was as usual more conservative, and it was another century before the type finally won resounding acceptance in the Forum of Trajan. In Africa, which as we shall see depended more closely on South Italy, the type was slower to establish itself: hesitantly in the mid-first century additions to the Old Forum at Leptis Magna, with more assurance in the Trajanic colonies of Thamugadi (Timgad; *Plates 224, 232)* and Cuicul (Djemila; *Plate 231)*, and finally and triumphantly in the new Severan Forum and Basilica at Leptis Magna *(Plate 300)*.

The municipal architecture of North Italy and the western provinces is very unevenly represented in the surviving remains. Some buildings continued to serve their original purpose: bridges, city walls and gates, or arches converted into gates. Others, such as amphitheaters and theaters, could easily be converted into fortresses. On the other hand, as the standards of urban life dropped in the early Middle Ages, basilicas, porticoes, markets, apartment houses, and warehouses one by one fell into disrepair and became quarries for building materials. Survival has been a selective process, and except on excavated sites one's choice of monuments for illustration is almost bound to reflect the bias of that process. The discussion that follows must therefore be read as a commentary on what can now be illustrated rather than as a survey of what once existed.

The city gates of North Italy repeat, in a variety of related forms, a type whose essential elements were a pair of towers projecting to frame a carriageway, or twin carriageways, which might be flanked by smaller arched footpaths; a sentry path with smaller arched windows, which also served the portcullis mechanism; and frequently an enclosed inner courtyard. As we saw in an earlier chapter, this type had its roots in the architecture of Republican Central Italy; the Porta dei Leoni at Verona *(Plate 29)* shows it already established in the North by the mid-first century B.C. Among the Augustan gateways of this type are those at Augusta Praetoria (Aosta, 25 B.C.; *Plate 238)*, Fanum Fortunae (Fano, 9 B.C.; *Plate 234)*, Hispellum (Spello; *Plate 237)*, Augusta Taurinorum (Turin; *Plate 236)*, and—in Gaul—Nemausus (Nîmes; *Plate 239)* and Augustodunum (Autun), both erected in or soon after 16 B.C. Though often built to impress, the type was essentially functional and remained the standard Western model down to late antiquity. The original gates of the Aurelianic Walls of Rome were of this type, and the late third-century Porta Nigra at Augusta Treverorum (Trier; *Plates 240, 403–405)* is still in essence an elaborate variation of the same theme.

Closely allied to the city gate was another very common type of monument, the commemorative arch. Representations of such arches on coins show that they were regularly crowned with sculpture, and private family monuments of this form, usually celebrating some military success, are attested well back into the Republic. None of these Republican arches *(fornices)* have survived, but it is a reasonable guess that the very simple architectural type found in such early surviving public arches as that erected in 8 B.C. at Susa in honor of Augustus was derived from Republican models.

Under the Empire one can distinguish two broad lines of development from this basic type. Many of the later arches continued to be victory monuments, triumphal arches in the literal sense of the term. But by a simple extension of meaning arches began also to be used to commemorate other noteworthy events, most commonly in the person of the reigning emperor or—as in the case of the Arch of Titus *(Plate 241)*—to commemorate the victories and apotheosis of an

234. *Fanum Fortunae (Fano), Gate of Augustus (left) adjoining the facade of the church of San Michele (A.D. 1504), with a relief showing the gate with its upper story still intact*

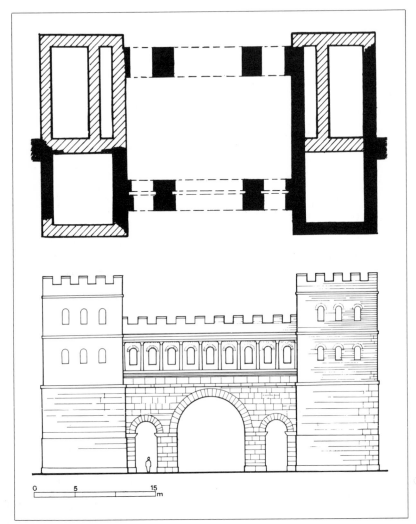

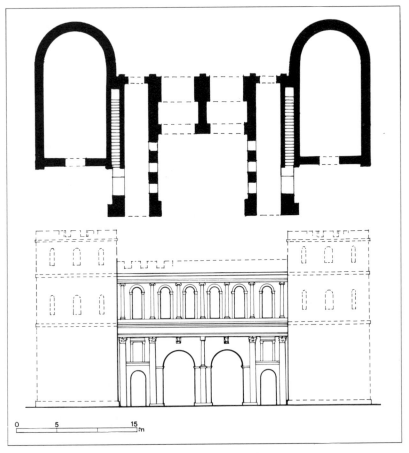

emperor recently deceased. As city gates too began to be used for much the same purposes, the formal distinction between arch and gate became increasingly blurred. An early and striking instance of this trend is the Arch of Augustus at Rimini *(Plates 242, 243)*, which is in reality the carriageway of a gate in the Roman and medieval city wall. It was also, however, one of a pair of monuments, erected in 27 B.C. at the two ends of the Via Flaminia to record its restoration by Augustus. Its Roman counterpart, which stood near the Pons Mulvius, may well have been a free-standing arch, and the decorative scheme of the Rimini gateway is itself that of an arch rather incongruously adapted to the flat wall space available between the two gateway towers. Such interchanges of motifs between city gates and arches are a regular feature of the subsequent development of both types. An outstanding example was the now destroyed mid-first century Porta Aurea at Ravenna.

The other line of development consisted of the formal elaboration of the prototype represented by the Arch of Augustus at Susa by means of such varied expedients as the doubling of the framing pilasters, the introduction of a continuous plinth, the elaboration of the wall surfaces by means of decorative aediculae or sculptured panels, the introduction of small flanking passageways (as in city gates), and the articulation in depth of the vertical faces of both archway and attic in conformity with the main vertical architectural members. Typologically this development was from simple to ever more complex forms, but it would be a mistake to use this as a criterion of date. The arch at Arausio (Orange; *Plate 244*), built shortly after A.D. 21, is formally an extraordinarily precocious monument for its date, whereas the twin arches of another Provençal monument, the bridge at Saint-Chamas, though some half a century later, still retain the simple basic form, which continued to be used in provincial Spain and North Africa until an even later date. The immediate models were not always local: Trajan's two arches at Benevento (A.D. 114) and Ancona (A.D. 115) derive very closely from the Arch of Titus in Rome and were in effect metropolitan monuments in provincial Italy. The late second-century "Arch of Trajan" at Thamugadi (Timgad) in North Africa is, on the other hand, a monument typical of its own time and place *(Plate 245)*. The story is a tangled one, defying tidy synthesis and reflecting to the full the wealth of variety which Roman provincial architects were able to extract from the basic themes which were their stock in trade.

Aqueducts and bridges *(Plates 246–248)* call for little comment. It is perhaps worth remarking that an aqueduct bridge such as the Pont du Gard was a product neither of megalomania nor of ignorance of the fact that water in a sealed pipe will find its own level. It was a

product of shrewd calculation, based on highly skilled surveying. The Romans could and did use the reverse syphon in certain situations. There were several in the aqueducts which served Lyon; another was that which carried water across the bed of the Rhone to Arles in a battery of lead pipes. But such pressure piping was expensive both in materials and in maintenance. A gravity flow was far cheaper, and the Pont du Gard makes excellent sense when one recalls that thanks to this single great bridge the remaining 31 miles, or 50 kilometers, of conduit could be carried almost exclusively below ground. As recently as 1842, when it was decided to carry the water of the Durance to Marseille, the model chosen for the aqueduct at Roquefavour, near Aix-en-Provence, was none other than the Pont du Gard.

Another group of buildings that calls for little comment is that of theaters and amphitheaters. Many were first built, and indeed continued to be built, of timber on masonry substructures. This was common enough building practice wherever timber was abundant. The great bridge which Apollodorus built across the Danube was of timber on masonry piers. Already in Augustan times, however, we begin to get theaters built entirely of masonry like those of Rome: at Arles, for example, at Lyon, and at Orange. The great masonry-built amphitheaters of the provinces—at Verona *(Plate 249)*, at Pola in

247. *Augusta Emerita (Merida, Spain), bridge over the Guadiana River*
248. *Augusta Emerita (Merida, Spain), aqueduct of Los Milagros*

250. *Augusta Emerita (Merida, Spain), stage and stage building (scaena) of the theater*

251. *Sabratha (Tripolitania, Libya), stage and stage building of the theater* ▷

252. *Arausio (Orange, France), stage building of the theater* ▷

253. *Arausio (Orange, France), theater*
254. *Leptis Magna (Tripolitania, Libya), theater* ▷

256. *Thysdrus (El-Djem), amphitheater*

257, 258, 259.   *Thysdrus (El–Djem), amphitheater*

Istria, at Arles and Nîmes in Provence, and in North Africa at Leptis Magna—are later, none of them demonstrably earlier than the Colosseum, which may have set the fashion. Allowing for differences of terrain and for unique local building traditions, these all follow closely the models first developed in Campania, where the great amphitheater at Pozzuoli (Puteoli) is of roughly the same date (*Plates 260, 261*). In Gaul and Britain we meet a type that was more specifically provincial (in both senses of the word), a small arena combining the function and the form of both theater and amphitheater. In the eastern provinces, where most cities already possessed a theater, the same shift of taste was met by converting into a miniature arena the semicircular space (*orchaestra*) between the seating area (*cavea*) and the stage (*proscaenium*).

North Africa is unusually rich in fine theaters. A magnificent early example (A.D 1; *Plate 254*) is that at Leptis Magna. At Sabratha (c. A.D. 180; *Plate 251*) the stage building has been restored, offering a vivid picture of the sort of three-dimensional columnar backdrop (*scaenae frons*) with which in antiquity all these buildings were equipped. Other fine examples are at Augusta Emerita (Merida) in Spain (*Plate 250*) and Cuicul (Djemila) in Algeria (*Plate 255*). Stripped of its columns, the framework of such a scheme is seen at

Orange in Provence *(Plates 252, 253)*. The finest of the North African amphitheaters, at Thysdrus (El-Djem), is a relatively late building, dating from the third century *(Plates 256–259)*.

Wherever the Romans went they brought with them the bath building. One might have expected so essentially functional a structure to conform to a single, standardized architectural model, but in fact the basic type lent itself to a bewildering number of variations. Just as in Rome, the earliest examples outside Italy, as at Glanum (Saint-Rémy-de-Provence; *Plate 262*), still indicate a close derivation from Campanian prototypes; but within a very short time each province was producing its own particular versions. From this profusion of local types we must be content to single out three for brief mention.

One of these is the ancestor of the modern spa. In this type the actual bathing establishment is characterized by the number and size of the plunge baths. Though particularly common in Gaul, it is in fact found wherever there were mineral springs: in Britain at Bath (Aquae Sulis), in Germany at Badenweiler *(Plate 263)*, in Bulgaria near Stara Zagora (Augusta Traiana; *Plate 264*), in Tunisia at Bulla Regia *(Plate 267)*, and in Algeria at El-Hammam (Aquae Flavianae; *Plate 265*). Like their modern equivalents, such medicinal baths were often the centers of flourishing communities.

The other two types of bath buildings both derive from Italian models that were themselves not fully developed before the second century A.D. The huge, symmetrically planned "Imperial" baths were obviously emulating buildings like the Baths of Trajan and of Caracalla in Rome: the Hadrianic Baths at Leptis Magna (A.D. 123) are a large but by no means exceptional example of the type *(Plate 266)*. Formally nothing could be more different than the early third-century Hunting Baths in the same city, and yet both derive from the contemporary concrete-vaulted architecture of the capital *(Plates 266, 298)*, the former from the great public *thermae (Plates 389, 390)*, the latter from the more intimate, domestic versions *(balnea)* represented, for example, by the Lesser Baths of Hadrian's Villa. Such startlingly anti-classical buildings were far commoner than is usually realized. Their candid acceptance of the dominating role of the interior spatial forms represents the logical outcome of the ideas inherent in the new contemporary school of Roman architecture, and it was bath buildings of this type which played a predominant role in the spread of such ideas in East and West alike.

The principal secular monument of most cities was the basilica. As we have seen, the type was created in Republican Central Italy, from which it was copied throughout the provinces of the Roman West. No two basilicas were exactly alike, but all were large, timber-roofed halls, almost always opening off the forum, usually colonnaded internally and often incorporating secondary rooms that could be used for such purposes as shrines for the imperial cult, law courts, municipal archives, secretarial offices, and the display of public notices. An interesting aspect of these buildings is the evidence they afford of the interplay of civilian and military architecture, particularly during the period (under the early Empire) when the frontiers were being stabilized and when the legionary encampments were beginning to take on a permanent character. In the provinces military architects were often the best available. When as civilian governor of Bithynia Pliny the Younger required the services of an expert surveyor of levels, he was advised by Trajan to apply to the governor of the nearest military province, Moesia, on the lower Danube. The reverse was also true: an army accustomed to building temporary encampments in temporary materials naturally looked to civilian architecture for a rich store of building practices and models. The close resemblance between certain civil basilicas and military headquarters *(principia)* was no accident. It is not unlikely that the apses at the two ends of Trajan's Basilica Ulpia reflect this relationship. It does not follow, however (as has been claimed), that the Basilica Ulpia is simply an adaptation to civilian use of an essentially military building type. It is rather the product of a long-established urban tradition, upon which the military architects of the frontier towns and camps had themselves drawn.

Every province had its own religious traditions and practices, and except where, as in the case of Christianity, these were thought to be subversive of authority, they enjoyed full liberty of expression. Roman provincial architecture reflects this circumstance to the full. Side by side with the ostentatiously classical temples of the official state cults *(Plate 220)* there were innumerable sanctuaries of local divinities, built in the local manner and ranging from rustic wayside shrines to large monumental complexes. In Gaul, for example, and in the neighboring Celtic countries, the common native form was a square (sometimes circular or octagonal) hall or low tower, usually surrounded on all four sides by an outward-facing, verandah-like ambulatory *(Plate 272)*. This might simply be monumentalized in permanent materials, as were the circular Temple of Vesunna at Périgueux *(Plates 270, 271)* and the square Temple of Janus at Autun; or it might take on such classicizing attributes as a pedimental entrance porch, or be set within a conventionally classical peristyle. But the basic type remained in use right down to late antiquity, and some of these native sanctuaries, notably in Gaul, were flourishing centers for pilgrimages or seasonal fairs, around which grew up small townships, with inns, bath buildings, shops, porticoes, and theaters. Such

262. *Glanum (Saint-Rémy-de-Provence, France), plan of the baths, second half of the first century B.C. 1) caldarium; 2) tepidarium; 3) frigidarium; 4) palaestra; 5) natatio*

263. *Badenweiler (Germany), plan of the thermal baths*

264. *Augusta Traiana (Stara Zagora, Bulgaria), plan of the thermal baths*

265. *Aquae Flavianae (El-Hammam, Algeria), plan of the thermal baths*

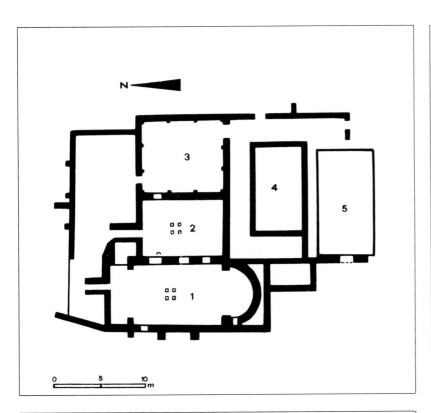

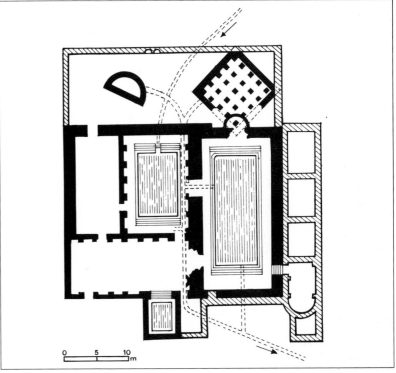

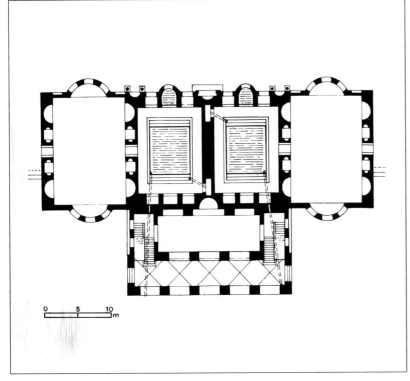

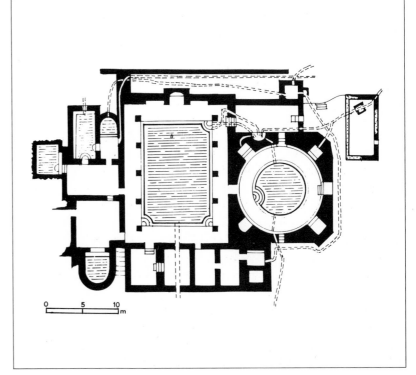

were Sanxay (Vienne) and Champlieu in the Forest of Compiègne and Lydney in Gloucestershire.

The story varies from one region to another. In the territories ruled by Carthage many places of worship seem to have consisted simply of an altar or an open place of sacrifice with perhaps, adjoining it, a small reserved "Holy of Holies." This could easily be expressed in classical architectural terms, as in Tunisia, for example—at Sufetula (Sbeitla), Thugga (Dougga; *Plates 275, 279*), and Thuburbo Maius. In this case, however, the precise architectural form seems to have meant less to its users than that of the Celtic temple did to the Gauls, and already by the second century A.D. they had almost everywhere given place to temples of conventional Italic type. The divinities worshiped remained the same, but they now went under a classical name and were housed in a classical building. One very common North African type resembles a miniature Imperial Forum, with an Italic temple set against the rear wall of a rectangular precinct, which was usually colonnaded on three sides. Such were the *capitolia* at Thamugadi and Thuburbo Maius *(Plates 273, 274)* and at least half of the independently located temples at Leptis Magna and Sabratha. At the other extreme we have cults such as Mithraism, in which the architecture and ritual were so inextricably linked that wherever its devotees went they carried with them their own specialized places of worship.

The Roman passion for grandiloquent self-commemoration found expression in a funerary architecture so rich and varied as to defy summary analysis in Italy alone, much less throughout the provinces. There were, it is true, certain widely recurrent types—the monumentalized tumulus, the rock-cut hypogeum with an architectural facade, the funerary temple, the tower-tomb, the commemorative column—and many of these did find local expression in more or less consistent local types, of which one can usually trace the main lines of the pedigree. To take a single rather exotic example, the needle-thin pyramidal towers of the Libyan desert *(Plate 281)* can be seen to be an extreme expression of the Semitic tower-tomb, derived through Carthage—Mactar, Thugga *(Plate 278),* Sabratha—from the same ultimate source as the tower-tombs of northern Syria— Hermel, Emesa *(Plate 280),* Palmyra, Assar in Commagene, Diokaisareia in Cilicia *(Plate 282).* More distantly the network of architectural associations leads us to the Monument of the Julii at Glanum in Provence *(Plate 12),* to the tomb of A. Murcius Obulaccus at Sarsina in the Marches, to the richly baroque tombs of Campania *(Plate 283),* to the tower-tomb of the Secundini at Igel, near Trier (c. A.D. 245; *Plate 276*), perhaps even to the great monument of Mausolus himself; or again, in another direction, to the victory

268. *Sabratha (Tripolitania, Libya), plan of the basilica in the third quarter of the first century A.D.*

269. *Leptis Magna (Tripolitania, Libya), the Old Forum (Forum Vetus). 1) temples; 2) temple, later a Christian church; 3) basilica; 4) Curia (Senate)*

monuments of La Turbie above Monte Carlo (7–6 B.C.) and of Tropaeum Traiani in the Dobrudja and to the great imperial mausoleums of Rome itself; possibly to the enigmatic Augustan Tourmagne on the hilltop overlooking Nîmes *(Plate 277)*. We are reminded that although Roman architects liked to think in terms of accepted categories, they also moved in a world so full of inherited meanings and associations that the transition from one category to another must often have been quite imperceptible. It is at once the delight and the despair of the architectural historian that, to appreciate the full significance of any given Roman monument, we must almost literally review the monuments of half the Roman world.

To conclude this summary account of the more common types of buildings to be found in the provinces of the Roman West, let us glance at the domestic architecture of town and countryside. This was another field in which one would expect to find considerable differences from one province to another in accordance with local traditions and materials, social habits and climate. In the Mediterranean coastlands the Romans inherited an urban tradition of which the standard well-to-do residence seems to have been the Hellenistic peristyle house, but elsewhere pre-Roman urbanization had been too rudimentary to have left much mark on later practice. Although Roman Silchester (Calleva Atrebatum) was the market town and administrative center for a considerable tribal territory, architecturally it was little more than a backwoods version of a model imported by the Romans *(Plate 284)*.

The late Republican peristyle houses of Utica in Tunisia, like those of Glanum *(Plates 285, 286)* and of Aquae Sextiae (Aix-en-Provence), represent a far more sophisticated tradition, and in many North African towns—Althiburos, Thysdrus, Tipasa, and Volubilis *(Plate 287)*, for example—peristyle houses continued to be the typical residence of the wealthy citizen. In others, such as Sabratha, population pressures dictated the developement of more compact town houses, two-storied and lit by small courtyards, and it is these more compact types which one finds in such new foundations as Thamugadi (Timgad) and Cuicul (Djemila), both established in the closing years of the first century A.D. The houses at Bulla Regia *(Plate 288)* in northwestern Tunisia, with their living rooms grouped around a central courtyard at two distinct levels, one above and one below ground (presumably for climatic reasons), appear to be a local creation unparalleled elsewhere.

About the country houses of North Africa *(Plates 291, 292)* it is, given our present state of knowledge, difficult to generalize. Along the coasts, near the cities, there are a number of wealthy residential villas built in more or less direct imitation of those of Latium

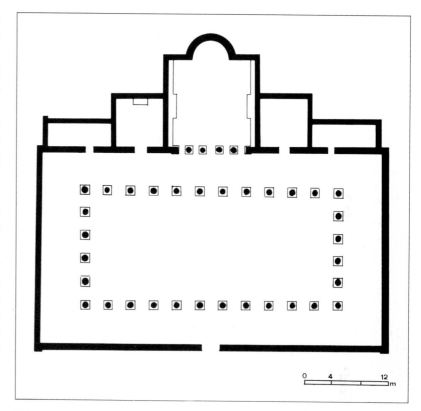

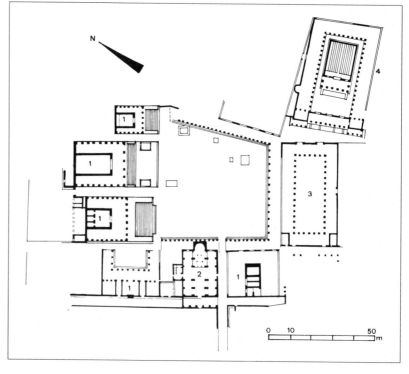

270, 271. *Vesunna Petricoriorum (Périgueux, France), Temple of Vesunna*

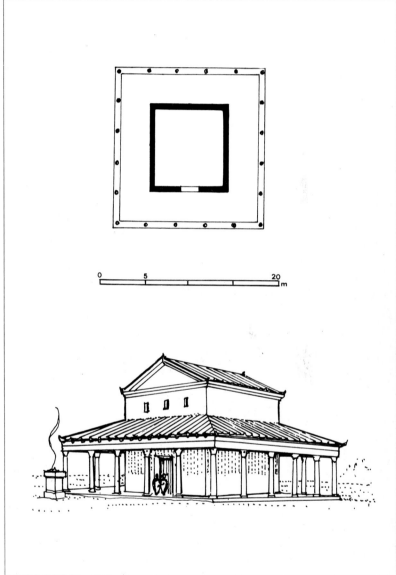

272. *Augusta Treverorum (Trier, Germany), plan and reconstruction of one of the temples in the Altbachtal sanctuary*

273.   *Thuburbo Maius (Tunisia), plan of the forum. 1) Capitolium; 2)   274.   *Thuburbo Maius (Tunisia), Capitolium* ▷
Curia (Senate); 3) markets*

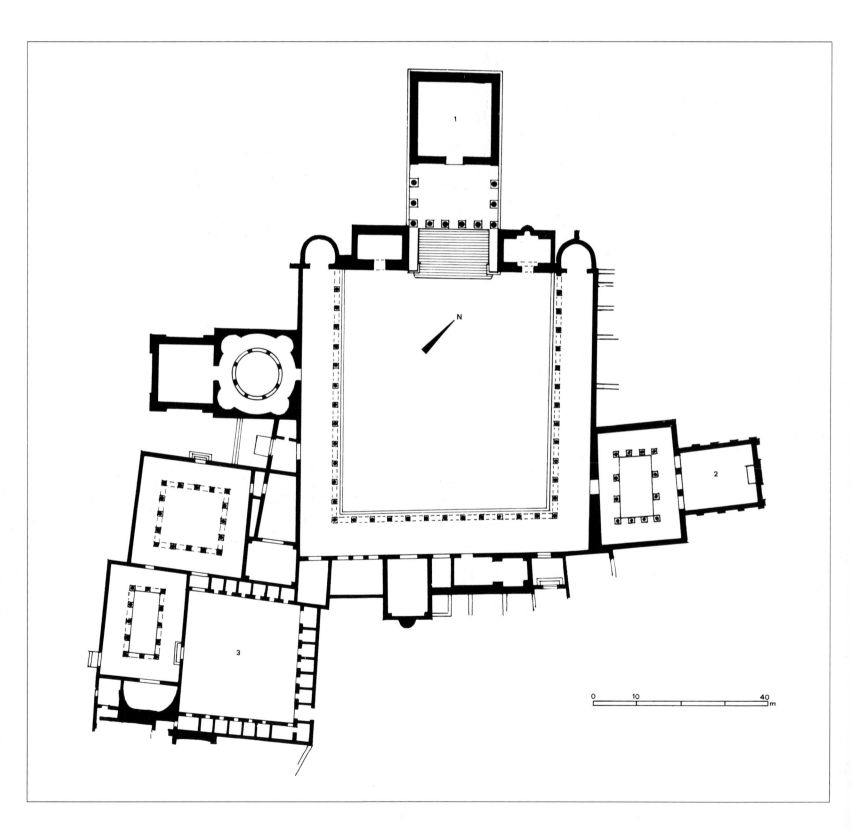

275. *Thugga (Dougga, Tunisia), Capitolium*
276. *Igel (near Trier, Germany), tower-tomb of the Secundini*

277. *Nemausus (Nimes, France), Tourmagne*

278. *Thugga (Dougga, Tunisia), Numidian tower-tomb*

280. *Emesa (Homs, Syria), tower-tomb of Caius Julius Samsigeramos*
(A.D. 78–79)

279. *Thugga (Dougga, Tunisia), Romano-Punic Temple of Saturn, plan*

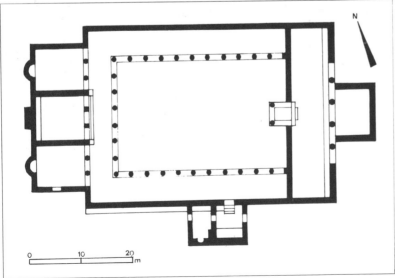

281. *El-Mselleten (Tripolitania, Libya), Romano-Libyan tower-tombs* 282. *Diokaisareia (Uzuncaburç, Cilicia), tower-tomb*

283. *Capua (Santa Maria Capua Vetere), mausoleum, axonometric reconstruction*

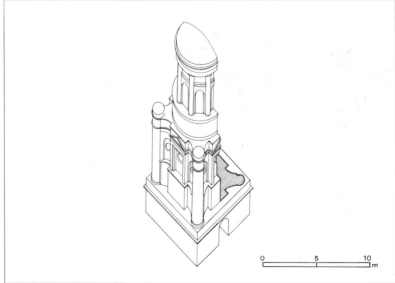

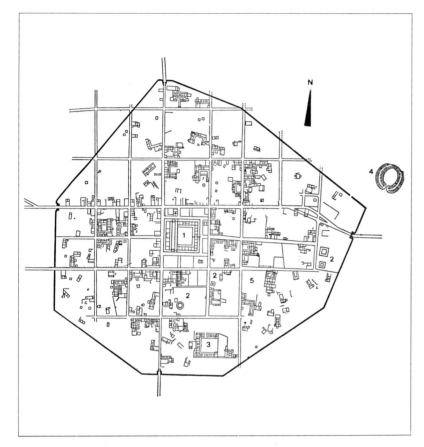

and Campania, but most of what has been recorded inland represents the remains of working farmhouses or the centers of large agricultural estates. Plates 289 and 290 illustrate a building which housed the oil-presses of such an estate, not far from Theveste (Tébessa). The structural skeleton of dressed stone, framing panels of mortared rubble, is typically North African—the local equivalent of the timber framing characteristic of the forested provinces of central and northwestern Europe.

In the countryside of Gaul, Britain, and the Rhineland we are better served by excavation, and we know that in many areas the Romans did find the nucleus of a system of independent farms which, expanded and enriched, were to become the familiar villas of Roman times. A few of these, such as Chiragan and Montmaurin *(Plate 293)* in southwestern Gaul, were luxury residences on the Italian model, but the great majority were both residences and the centers of working estates. Architecturally they can be seen to represent a broadly consistent evolution from the simple, barnlike, timber-framed farmhouses of the earliest settlers—at first by the addition of a corridor or portico along one long side and the relegation of storage and stabling to separate buildings (the "corridor" villa) and subsequently by the addition of projecting wings and the regrouping of the farm buildings and annexes around one or more courtyards (the "courtyard" villa). With the spread of such luxuries as window glass, painted wall plaster, mosaic pavements, and central heating there was also an ever-increasing assimilation of classical architectural forms. But the villas of northern France, Britain, Belgium, and Germany remained a Romano-provincial phenomenon. However Roman their externals, they were basically shaped by social and environmental factors that were peculiar to this part of the Empire. Much the same could be said of the patterns of rural architecture throughout the Empire.

This rapid survey of the architecture of the western provinces has been concerned principally with the working out of forms and ideas which were imported from Italy or which, in some cases, were already present in the provinces themselves. Right through Roman times these were to remain the essential basis of Roman provincial architecture in the West. From the second century onward, however, many of the cities of the West did find themselves in more and more direct contact with the contemporary architecture of the eastern provinces, and the city of Leptis (Lepcis) Magna in Tripolitania—by reason both of its geographic situation and of the extent and representative character of its excavated remains—will serve very well as an illustration of what such contacts might mean in terms of architectural change.

286. *Glanum (Saint-Rémy-de-Provence, France), plan of peristyle houses*

287. *Volubilis (Morocco), plans of peristyle houses. a) House of Venus, a luxury residence with many mosaics and a private bath suite; b)House of the Bronze Bust, residence of a businessman: 1. living quarters; 2. oil-pressing establishment; 3. bakery; 4. shops*

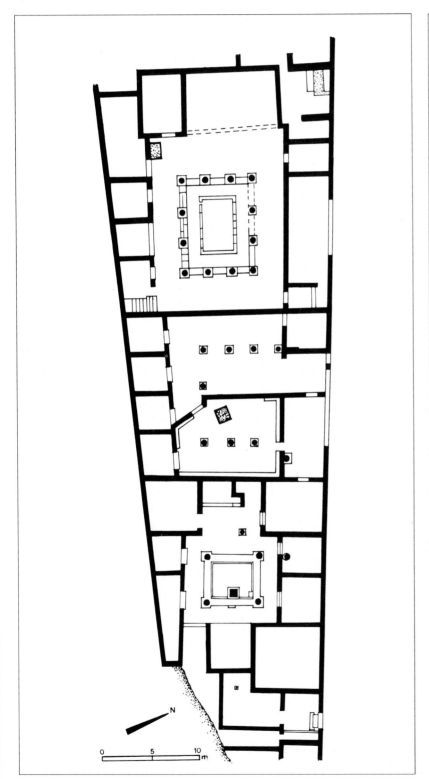

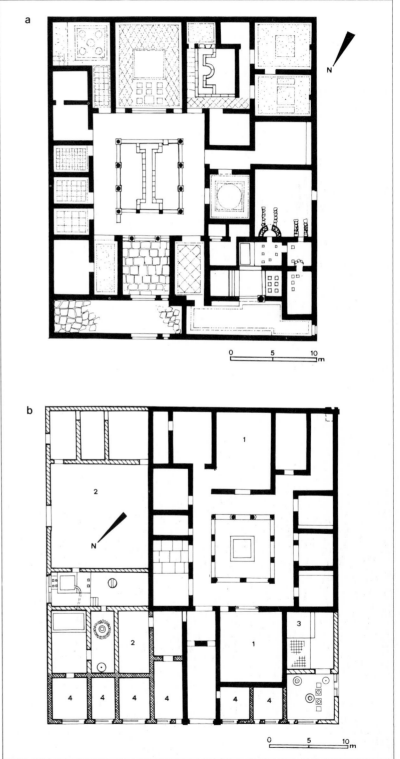

293. *Montmaurin (Haute-Garonne, France), luxury residential villa of the mid-fourth century* A.D., *plan*

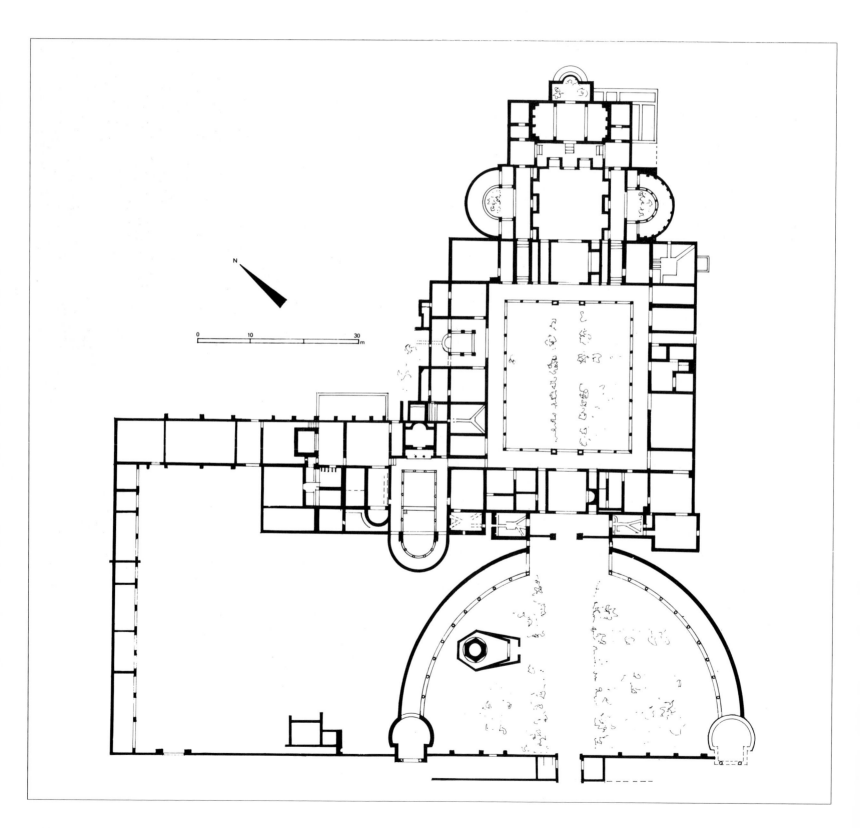

Leptis was a Carthaginian (Punic) commercial foundation, and the builders of the early Imperial city were wealthy merchants whose native culture and language were Punic, not Latin. This was not an expatriate colonial society, but an established provincial society under Roman rule; and although the parallels for such early surviving buildings as the Market (8 B.C.; *Plates 294, 295*), the Theater (A.D. 1), and the temples and basilica beside the Old Forum (Augustan to Claudian period) are all to be sought in South Italy, these links reflect a situation that was already prevailing in the Republican province of Africa and to some extent even earlier, during the last century of Carthaginian rule. The earliest known market of the Leptis type, with a circular central pavilion, is at Morgantina in central Sicily and dates from the second century B.C. Other well-known examples are at Pompeii *(Plate 20)* and Puteoli (Pozzuoli), and in Africa at Hippo Regius, Cuicul *(Plate 297),* and Thamugadi *(Plate 296).* Despite its classical roots and continuing classical links, this was an architecture thoroughly acclimatized to local needs, skills, and materials, and throughout the first century A.D. it retained this distinctively Romano-Tripolitanian character.

This situation changed dramatically during the middle years of the second century A.D. when, under Hadrian and Antoninus Pius, the marble of the Aegean—long the accepted prestige building material in Rome—was suddenly made available in quantity to the provinces. The phenomenon will be discussed more fully in the next chapter; suffice it to say that, as had happened in Augustan Rome, the new material was accompanied by craftsmen trained in its use. In Tripolitania the result was the destruction within a single generation of the lively but less sophisticated local school. Imported architectural marbles made their first appearance at Leptis in the Hadrianic Baths (A.D. 123; *Plates 298, 305*), and thereafter there is hardly a building of importance in Leptis or Sabratha which was not at least partially rebuilt in the new material. In place of the individuality conferred by local materials, techniques, and decorative traditions, buildings took on the materials and outward forms of an architectural style which was rapidly acquiring international status all over the coastal provinces of the central and eastern Mediterranean and the Black Sea.

In A.D. 193 the Leptis-born Septimius Severus ascended the imperial throne. The following twenty-five years were a time of unparalleled building activity in his native town, the central features being a colonnaded street leading from a piazza alongside the Hadrianic Baths down to a new, artificial harbor basin and, beside the street, a magnificent new forum and basilica *(Plates 300–303).* The forum was dominated at one end by a temple set on a very tall podium, and at the other by the transverse bulk of the basilica, whose

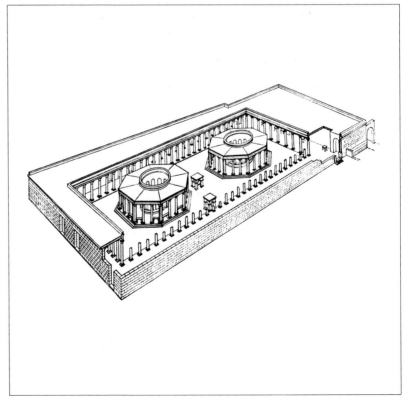

298. *Leptis Magna (Tripolitania, Libya), aerial view of the Hadrianic Baths (foreground); beyond them is the Severan complex*

299. *Leptis Magna (Tripolitania, Libya), Severan fountain building (Nymphaeum)* ▷

300. *Leptis Magna (Tripolitania, Libya), plan of the Severan Basilica-forum-temple complex*

301. *Leptis Magna (Tripolitania, Libya), Severan Basilica*

302. *Leptis Magna (Tripolitania, Libya), Severan Forum, doorway to a shop or office*

303. *Leptis Magna (Tripolitania, Libya), Severan Forum, capital*

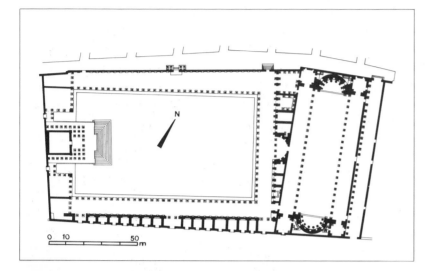

central hall—measuring more than 100 feet (over 30 m.) from floor to coffered ceiling—was closed at each end by an apse and flanked by lateral aisles with galleries over them. Though not a direct copy, this basilica-forum-temple complex was unquestionably based on the model of the Imperial Forums in Rome, and the basilica specifically on that of the Basilica Ulpia. But the actual execution of the work, from the architect on down, was unmistakably a product of the East Roman "marble style" workshops described above: the white marble came from Proconnesus (Marmara) and Attica, the red granite columns of the basilica and temple from Aswan, the green marble columns of the forum and colonnaded street from Karystos in Euboea; the master-masons and sculptors signed their names in Greek; and such features as the colonnaded street, the huge fountain building, or Nymphaeum *(Plate 299)*, dominating the piazza, and even the masonry conventions proclaimed that the architect himself had been trained in the eastern provinces, possibly in Bithynia.

The Severan complex at Leptis was, in sum, metropolitan Roman in conception, East Roman in execution, and built under the patronage of an African-born emperor, in a provincial city where even the educated classes spoke a Neo-Punic Semitic dialect as well as Latin. This was what the Roman Empire had come to mean by the end of the second century. Although in themselves these buildings were the product of a unique situation, they were also an eloquent expression of the directions in which the monumental architecture of the age was moving. In this they foreshadow the creations of the Tetrarchy a century later.

307. *Cuicul (Djemila, Algeria), temple of the Severan family (Gens Septimia)*

308. *Cuicul (Djemila, Algeria), temple of the Severan family and arches of Antoninus Pius (A.D. 161) and of Caracalla (A.D. 216)* ▷

309. *Cuicul (Djemila, Algeria), temple of the Severan family*

In the eastern Mediterranean the situation faced by the conquering armies of Rome was altogether different. Here Rome found herself everywhere the political master of peoples whose cultural traditions were far older and richer than her own—in Greece, Asia Minor, and Cyrenaica that tradition was predominantly Greek, and in Syria and Egypt it was Greek variously mingled with even older traditions of the ancient East. In Chapter One we saw something of the dramatic impact upon Republican Rome of the confrontation with the sophisticated arts of the Hellenistic East. It is true that Roman architecture had been more successful than the visual arts in maintaining something of its Italic identity, but this was a battle that had had to be fought out on Italian soil. The resulting Italo-Hellenistic architecture of the late Republic might be suitable for export to the western provinces, but it had little or nothing to offer to many parts of the Greek-speaking East.

With the reunification of the Mediterranean world under Augustus the conditions were established for a more fruitful dialogue between East and West. The extent and character of the Roman contribution was bound to vary greatly according to local circumstance. The older centers of Greek and Hellenistic culture, with their own rich traditions, were naturally slow to accept innovations from the West, particularly in the field of monumental public architecture. The Odeion of Agrippa at Athens (c. 15 B.C.; *Plate 310*), with its clear indications of Campanian influence, was quite exceptional in this respect. Roman rule everywhere furnished the conditions of peace and prosperity which favored architectural development; and it might also on occasion provide the funds for it, as when Tiberius helped the cities in the province of Asia after a disastrous earthquake in A.D. 17. But otherwise towns such as Ephesus or Pergamon continued to go their own way, little influenced by contemporary developments in the West. Their public architecture of the first century can be considered Roman in the sense that it was the product of the conditions created by Roman rule, but (with a few notable exceptions which we shall be examining shortly) there was little about it that was actually derived from Italy.

For Roman influence in this narrower sense of the word we must look elsewhere. Not surprisingly, we find it in those fields of architecture and in those regions where the Hellenistic tradition was less massively entrenched. One such field is that of engineering and building technology. Another is that of the building types for which there were no established local precedents and thus fewer prejudices to be overcome. (There is a clear analogy here with the position of the "new" architecture in late Republican and early Imperial society in Rome itself.) A third field open to western innovations was in those

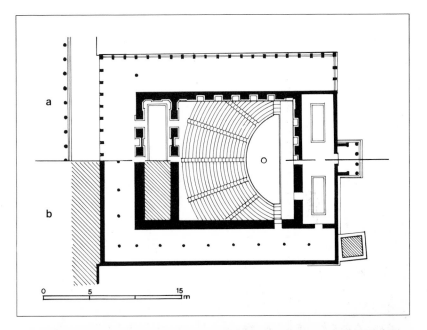

310. *Athens, Odeion of Agrippa, plan at gallery level (a) and at ground level (b)*

311. *Ephesus, aqueduct of C. Sextilius Pollio*

areas of Asia Minor, Syria, and Egypt where Hellenism was itself a relative newcomer. In the paragraphs that follow we shall glance at each of these fields in turn.

It is a commonplace that the Romans were good engineers. However, they were not by nature inventors. They were not the first to use the arch or the vault; their precision implements were mostly derived from the Greeks of Alexandria, and a great deal of their knowledge of road-building, water supply, and drainage was directly inherited from the Etruscans. What they did have was the temperament, the resources, and the organizational skills to put such knowledge to systematic and effective use. One of Augustus's first aims had been the modernization of the road system in Italy; and in Rome itself the building of new aqueducts and a complete overhaul of the drainage system were among the first tasks assigned to his close friend and colleague, Agrippa. Rome's attitudes toward such matters are neatly summed up in the dedicatory inscription of the first Porta dei Leoni at Verona *(Plate 29)*, in which the four founding magistrates of the new town recorded their task as the construction of "the wall, the gates and the drains" *(murum portas cluacas fecerunt)*.

Here, then, was a field in which Rome did have a great deal to offer even in Greek lands. Roads, bridges, harborworks, warehouses, aqueducts, drainage schemes—throughout the Empire these were among the first fruits of Roman rule. The aqueduct built at Ephesus by C. Sextilius Pollio in the last years of Augustus's reign is a less ambitious structure than the Pont du Gard, but it is no less symbolic of the solid material benefits of the new regime *(Plate 311)*. It also marks the first tentative introduction of Roman building methods to Asia Minor. It will be recalled that in Rome it was utilitarian architecture of this sort which had furnished one of the main fields for the exploration of the formal implications of the new building material, Roman concrete. The architects of the eastern provinces were slow to adopt the new medium, not only because of temperament and tradition but also because they mostly lacked the volcanic sands which gave the concrete of Central Italy its unique strength. Their mortar fell short of the quality of its Italian counterparts, and in many areas of the East dressed stone remained the preferred medium for the walls and even the vaults of such buildings as theaters *(Plate 312)*, stadiums *(Plate 116)*, and bath buildings long after it had gone out of use in Rome in such contexts. A glance at two formally similar buildings— the large vaulted *frigidarium* of one of the bath buildings at Hierapolis *(Plate 313)* and the Basilica of Maxentius in Rome *(Plates 381, 382)*— shows how differently the architects of Asia Minor and Italy could approach the same task. Nevertheless, the new medium did make slow but steady headway, and it was in buildings such as Pollio's aqueduct

314. *Ephesus, plan of the original Hellenistic theater*

315. *Ephesus, facade of the Roman stage building. The two lower stories date from the mid-first century A.D., and the upper story is an early third-century addition*

316. *Ephesus, plan of the enlarged Roman theater*

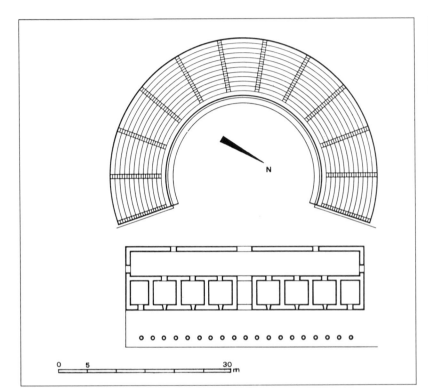

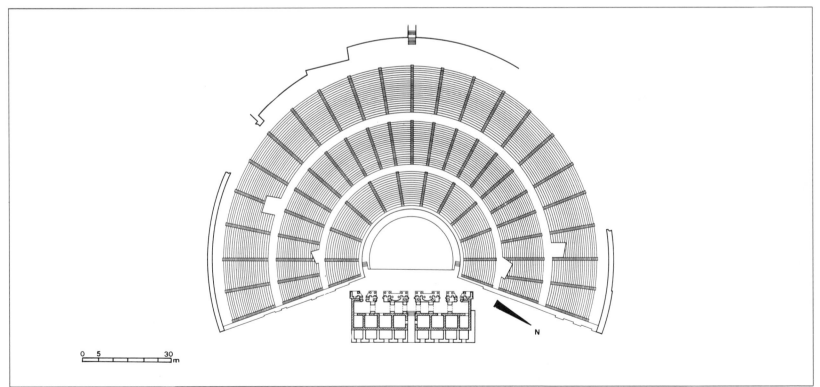

317. *Philippopolis (Syria), axonometric reconstuction of the theater, mid-third century* A.D.

318. *Miletus, theater*

319. *Miletus, theater, seating area, and part of the stage* ▷

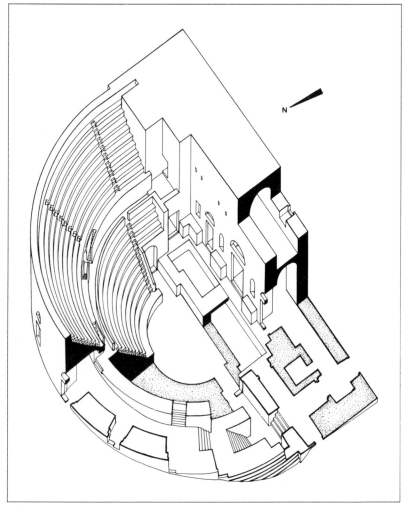

321. *Ephesus, view of the theater and colonnaded street, looking toward the harbor and the Harbor Baths*

322. *Aspendos (Pamphylia), theater*
323. *Aphrodisias (Asia Minor), hippodrome*

324. *Miletus, plan of the Hellenistic* gymnasium *and Roman Baths of Cnaeus Vergilius Capito.* 1) gymnasium; 2) baths; 3) Roman palaestra; 4) Ionic portico

325. *Miletus, Humeitepe Baths*

the side that faced out onto the porticoed *gymnasium* square, as did the so-called Marble Court at Sardis *(Plate 335)*. This was an adaptation of a feature which was already present in the Hellenistic *gymnasium*, and which did in fact undergo a similar development in the relatively rare instances of *gymnasia* that were not converted into bath buildings. There is a good example of the latter at Side in Pamphylia *(Plate 336)*.

As had previously been the case in Rome, so rapid an assimilation of the western type of bath building can only have taken place in response to a strongly felt social need; and because (again as in Rome) there were no established architectural precedents, bath buildings in the East imitated the vaulting practices and the constructional methods which had been developed in Italy *(Plates 327, 330, 331)*. The outward appearance of this concrete work varied greatly in accordance with the facing materials available locally: at Ephesus *(Plates 328, 337)* and Pergamon, for example, courses of small, neatly squared blocks of limestone, and at Miletus *(Plates 325, 327)* splintered stone and that it did so first. In this respect engineering and the new building technology were two faces of the same coin.

As regards the introduction of new building forms, the Hellenistic world had its own traditional models, sanctioned by custom and long use. Temples, colonnaded squares, porticoed stoas, roofed theater-like council halls—these were all products of a way of life which felt little need for change. Even so outstandingly successful a western building type as the basilica had to fight for acceptance in the East; the earliest known example in metropolitan Asia Minor, at Smyrna, dates from the second century. As for places of public entertainment, the hippodrome *(Plate 323)* and the stadium were themselves both Greek exports to the West; existing Greek theaters could easily be remodeled to suit the new Roman fashion *(Plates 314–319)*, while the amphitheater, an essentially Italian creation, never won wide acceptance in the East.

The only conspicuous newcomer to the accepted canon of monumental public architecture was, as in the West, the bath building. In a form that clearly derives from Italy we find it already accepted at Ephesus and at Miletus *(Plate 324)* in the first century A.D., in both cases occupying one wing of a *gymnasium* of otherwise traditional Greek type. By the second century bath building and *gymnasium* had been integrated into a single architectural unit of which the bathing establishment was by now the dominant element. Huge complexes such as the baths at Sardis *(Plate 326)* and Ancyra (Ankara), of late Antonine and Severan date, respectively, mark the culmination of this trend. These buildings did, of course, take on many features derived from local usage. One that was typical of Asia Minor was the elaborately ornamented hall which regularly occupied the middle of

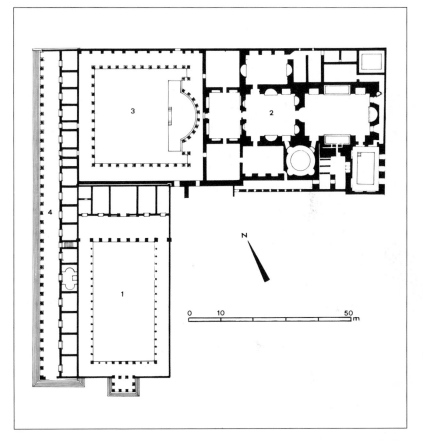

326. *Sardis (Asia Minor), plan of the bath building and gymnasium of the second century* A.D., *partly remodeled under Septimius Severus. The building at the southeast corner is a synagogue*

327. *Miletus, Baths of Faustina*

328. *Ephesus, Baths of Vedius, detail of masonry*

329. *Ephesus, Harbor Baths, detail showing marble piers with brick superstructure*

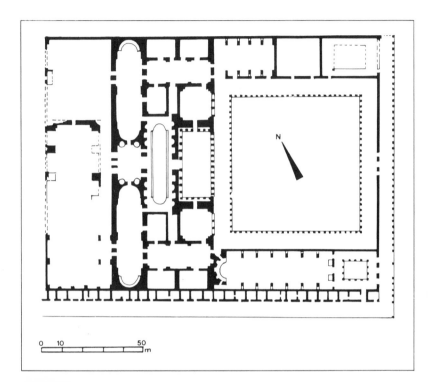

330, 331. *Aspendos (Pamphylia), bath buildings with brick vaults*

332. *Aphrodisias (Asia Minor), bath building. Room with floor of marble tiles*

333. *Aphrodisias (Asia Minor), bath building. Room with* natatio

334. *Aphrodisias (Asia Minor), bath building. Carved bracket*

335. *Sardis (Asia Minor), so-called Marble Court, a colonnaded hall between the* gymnasium *and the bath building*

336. *Side (Pamphylia), colonnaded hall of the* gymnasium

small river boulders. Such work looked very different from the neat reticulate work or brickwork of Rome, but the difference was purely superficial. This was the local equivalent of the *opus caementicium* of Rome.

As we have already remarked, the readiness of the eastern provinces to accept Roman innovations was in almost precisely inverse proportion to the strength of the hold which Hellenism had taken upon them. By the end of the Roman Republic Greece itself was rapidly becoming a cultural backwater. Athens continued to be a source of retrospective inspiration, in much the same way as Rome was to the architects of Renaissance Italy; but it was no longer a creative center. The heart of a living Hellenistic tradition was to be found in western Asia Minor, in Alexandria, and in a few of the cities of northern Syria, notably Antioch on the Orontes (today Antakya in Turkey). Outside these cities, however, there were vast areas where Alexander's conquests had done little more than spread a thin veneer of Hellenism over the time-honored ways of the ancient East. Here Rome was only the most recent of a long succession of conquering powers, but at least it did not have to contend with the prejudices of an established Hellenistic tradition. We see this very well in the case of a classical building type, the theater, for which there were no Oriental precedents, nor for that matter (it seems) many actual theaters of Hellenistic date outside Antioch. The known Roman-period theaters of Syria all derive from the form already established in late Republican Italy—at Pompeii, for example, and in Rome in the theaters of Pompey and of Marcellus.

In this particular instance we can perhaps be even more explicit. The recently excavated theater at Caesarea Marittima in Judaea, a building of this Italo-Hellenistic type, was begun by Herod the Great (d. 4 B.C.). Herod, the ruler of a Roman protectorate, was not only a prodigious builder; he was also a man of cosmopolitan tastes who knew Rome well. As one would expect, many of his known works were typically Hellenistic Greek buildings—agoras, stoas, *gymnasia*—but others were no less distinctively Roman. These included an aqueduct at Laodicea, bath buildings at Ascalon and at Masada, a temple of Italic type at Samaria, and even an amphitheater at Caesarea; the theater at Caesarea used Roman concrete in its substructures, and the terraces of his country villa near Jericho were built in *opus reticulatum*. A roughly contemporary example of this last, in the walls of Samosata on the Euphrates, was the work of another client-prince with Roman connections. The principalities along the frontier were a natural setting for such western exotica. Herod's building program, though based on Hellenistic practice, had strong contemporary Roman overtones, and it left an indelible mark on the subsequent architecture of Roman Syria. It is quite possible that the colonnaded street he had built at Antioch was the first of its kind, a monumentalization in Hellenistic terms of the street-side porticoes *(viae porticatae)* of late Republican Rome. If this is so, one of the most characteristic features of eastern Roman architecture was a Romano-provincial creation of the Augustan age.

In the East, as in the West, a powerful instrument of Romani-

337. *Ephesus, monumental staircase leading to the Temple of Domitian*

338. *Ancyra (Ankara, Turkey), Temple of Rome and Augustus*

339. *Heliopolis (Baalbek, Lebanon), plan of the Sanctuary of Jupiter Heliopolitanus. 1) Temple of Jupiter, first century A.D.; 2) forecourt, second century; 3) sacrificial altars, first century; 4) hexagonal forecourt and propylaea, early third century; 5) Temple of Dionysus (Bacchus), second century*

340. *Heliopolis (Baalbek, Lebanon), Temple of Jupiter, looking toward the Temple of Dionysus (Bacchus)* ▷

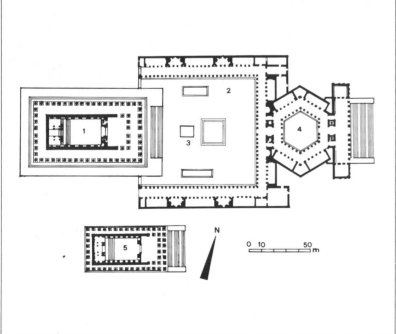

zation was the establishment of Roman military colonies. Corinth (resettled in 44 B.C.), though still essentially a Greek town, embodies many features that derive directly from Italy—temples of Italic type, no less than three basilicas, certain typically Italian moldings, sporadic early examples of Roman concrete, and so on. If this could happen in metropolitan Greece, how much more so in a city such as the Augustan colony of Antioch in Pisidia, in the untamed mountain region of south-central Asia Minor. The building that dominated this site was a state temple, probably dedicated to Rome and Augustus. It stood on a podium at the head of a flight of steps, near the rear of a monumental platform from which it faced axially outward down a long approach avenue. The program, the planning, the actual form of the temple are purely Roman. For another hundred years and more one would have looked in vain for anything comparable in the great Hellenistic cities. The Temple of Rome and Augustus *(Plate 338)* at Ancyra (Ankara), for example—a building identical in purpose and almost exactly contemporary with the temple at Antioch—is so faithful to the traditions established by the second-century B.C. Asiatic Greek architect, Hermogenes, that it has even been thought to be itself of Hellenistic date. Such were the preferred models in Asia Minor right down to the time of Hadrian and Antoninus Pius. Not until the mid-second century A.D., in the Sanctuary of Aesculapius at Pergamon *(Plate 359),* do we find a temple based directly on a Roman model, that of Hadrian's Pantheon.

In this respect things could be very different in Syria. The great Sanctuary of Jupiter Heliopolitanus *(Plate 339)* at Baalbek in Lebanon had long been the center of an important native cult, and the decision to give this cult a grandiose classical setting must have been taken quite soon after the establishment of the adjoining Roman military colony in about 16 B.C. The liturgical focus of the sanctuary retained its native Semitic form, a pair of tower-like sacrificial altars in the center of a great open courtyard *(Plate 341)*; but around it the rest of the complex was remodeled along classical lines, with the altar court framed on three sides by porticoes and dominated from the fourth side by the towering bulk of the Temple of Jupiter *(Plate 340)*. The latter, with its facade of ten huge columns, was a very large building indeed, and it was made to seem even larger by being raised up on a massive platform, at the head of a monumental flight of steps. It is this very Roman emphasis on the element of height which immediately distinguishes it from the giants of classical Greece, the ground plans of several of which were in fact even larger than that of Baalbek. The Temple of Artemis at Ephesus, for example, measured $180\frac{1}{2} \times 374$ ft., or 55×114 m., and the Temple of Zeus Olympios at Akragas (Agrigento) 173×361 ft., or 52.75×110 m., as against the $157 \times$

343. *Pergamon, colonnaded avenue leading to the Sanctuary of Aesculapius.*
In the distance is the Acropolis   345. *Palmyra (Syria), colonnaded street*

344. *Perge (Pamphylia), colonnaded street*

◁349. *Ephesus, Temple of Hadrian*

350. *Ephesus, marble cornice in the Agora*
351. *Perge (Pamphylia), marble cornice in the theater*
352. *Side (Pamphylia), marble cornice near the north gate*

289 ft., or 48 × 88 m., of Baalbek. But the platform at Baalbek was already 44 ft., or 13.5 m., above the courtyard; the columns (65 ft., or 19.90 m., from floor to capital) were nearly half as tall again as those of the Pantheon; and the peak of the gable must have risen nearly 130 ft., or 40 m., above the pavement of the altar court. All of this was very Roman, and it comes as no surprise to learn that a study of the architectural detail suggests that some of the original workmen at Baalbek had actually worked on the state monuments of Augustan Rome.

Like many ancient sanctuaries, the complex at Baalbek was a long time building. The Temple of Bacchus was not added until the second century, and the monumental entrance complex (the flanking towers of which represent a concession to an older, non-classical, native architectural tradition) not for nearly a century after that. In these later buildings one can trace a steady development of taste: a greater variety and opulence of materials (the red and gray granite columns of the altar court came from Aswan and from near the Dardanelles, respectively), an increasingly baroque treatment of the architectural detail, and a growing tendency to minimize the solid qualities of the masonry in favor of freer, more illusionistic treatments. In the interior of the Temple of Bacchus, for example, which is the actual wall face? But these developments took place in terms of an architectural vocabulary which was firmly established from the outset. The resulting architectural style was every bit as much Romano-Syrian as that of early Imperial Gaul was Gallo-Roman.

During the first century A.D. it is still possible to characterize Rome's relationships with the individual eastern provinces or groups of provinces as in the nature of more or less independent dialogues. But, as we saw at the beginning of the last chapter, the situation was changing. Except as the seat of the political capital of the Empire, Italy was rapidly losing its dominant position and becoming merely one province among many; and as standards of prosperity everywhere rose there was an ever-increasing exchange of goods and ideas between one province and another. The colonnaded street may have been a Syrian invention in the first place, but by the second century it was also found throughout Asia Minor *(Plates 343–346)*. Another originally Syrian feature which was to have a long history in later Roman and Byzantine ceremonial architecture was the combination of a horizontal architrave and a central arch, as in the little Temple of Hadrian at Ephesus *(Plate 349)*, built soon after A.D. 117. The occupation of the imperial throne by a Spanish-born emperor, Trajan (A.D. 98–117), aptly symbolizes the emergence of a new order. What had been a series of more or less independent Romano-provincial dialogues now became a general exchange, within which Rome's was

353. *Leptis Magna (Tripolitania, Libya), Old Forum (Forum Vetus), Romano-Punic limestone capital of the Augustan era*

354. *Leptis Magna (Tripolitania, Libya), Severan Basilica, marble capital*

only one participating voice. The Empire was fast becoming a commonwealth.

An outstanding manifestation of this new situation was the diffusion over large parts of the eastern and central Mediterranean of a type of monumental architecture and of architectural ornament which was closely based on that of contemporary western Asia Minor *(Plates 350–352)*. The medium of this "marble style" or "Asiatic" architecture was marble, and it was the product of a highly organized commerce centered upon a limited number of imperially owned marble quarries situated in the northern Aegean, outstanding among them being the quarries of Proconnesus, in the island of Marmara. The models were those of the developed Romano-Hellenistic tradition of the cities of western Asia Minor; and because the systems of production and export envisaged not only a considerable degree of prefabrication at the quarries, but also the establishment of agencies overseas staffed by craftsmen who were trained in the techniques and styles of Asia Minor, this commerce represented a massive injection of fresh classicizing forms and ideas into the already existing architectures of the receiving provinces.

The impact of such a situation was varied. In Rome itself it was rather superficial. Even so, the building of Hadrian's Temple of Venus and Rome in Proconnesian marble, by an architect who may well have worked on the Trajaneum at Pergamon, left a clear mark on the current repertory of architectural ornament. We see this in the rather arid classicism of the Temple of Antoninus and Faustina in the Forum Romanum, much of the white marble for which came from Proconnesus and the colored columns from Karystos, in Euboea. By contrast, Tripolitania shows what could happen in a small outlying province. Here, as we have seen, the lively Romano-provincial architecture of the first century, though derived directly or at one remove from Italy, had drawn heavily on local needs, local building traditions, and local materials *(Plate 353),* and was quite unable to withstand the greater opulence and sophistication of the new second-century marble architecture *(Plate 354)*. Within little more than a generation it had been swept away, transforming the face of public architecture as drastically as Augustus and his successors had transformed the face of Rome. Where there was already an established Hellenistic tradition, as in the coastal cities of the Levant, the impact of the new style was less drastic. Even so (to take two well-documented instances), in the rich and extensively excavated Pamphylian cities of Perge and Side one hunts almost in vain for surviving buildings of the earlier Romano-Hellenistic period. The overwhelming majority of the monuments are Hadrianic, Antonine, or later; they are built in imported Aegean marbles and in a style which would have been

virtually interchangeable with that, say, of contemporary Tomis (Costanza) on the Black Sea, or of Leptis Magna.

There are two aspects of this commerce which call for brief comment in the broader context of the architecture of the later Roman Empire. One is the element of prefabrication at the quarry workshops. Columns in particular were regularly quarried to standard lengths before shipment *(Plate 355)*. The columns of the porch of the Pantheon were a product of this system, in this case standard 40-ft. (12.2 m.) monoliths from two different Egyptian quarries. Capitals, bases, pilasters, and other architectural elements might be similarly treated. Such practices obviously created problems as well as opportunities: the architect had somehow to make do with what he received from abroad, and later Roman buildings are full of the resulting adaptations and compromises. On the other hand, careful planning enabled construction time to be drastically cut by these mass-production techniques. Trajan's Forum took about fifteen years to build, the Baths of Diocletian less than ten. Many a Greek temple had taken centuries.

The other significant aspect of this interchange is the new vitality it gave to conservative classicism at a moment when in Rome itself architects were busily engaged in developing an architecture in which the classical orders represented at best a conventional top-dressing. In Asia Minor it is in no way surprising that the classical orders should have retained their authority down to late antiquity; but that they did so elsewhere, even in strictly contemporary architecture, was due in no small measure to the influence of this massive, state-organized commerce in marble—the prestige building material of the day.

The marble trade was predominantly, though not exclusively, based upon the quarries of the Aegean world and of Egypt. When we turn to the specifically Italian contribution to the architecture of the second and third centuries A.D. in the eastern provinces we find that, even if in many aspects of life Italy had lost its privileged position and was now little more than one province among many, its architecture was emphatically an exception. The builders of the Flavian Palace, the Baths of Trajan, and the Pantheon had created a new prestige architecture which no self-respecting province, however rich in monuments of its own, could afford to ignore. But although there was in consequence a growing demand in some of the eastern provinces for the architecture of contemporary Italy, the terms of the relationship between East and West had changed in more ways than one. So long as the architects of Asia Minor and Italy shared a vocabulary of architectural forms and an approach to the problems of structure and design both of which stemmed more or less directly from previous Hellenistic practice, any reluctance on the part of the former to adopt certain western monumental building types had been based on the belief—not altogether unjustified—that they already possessed local equivalents that were as good, if not better, than those of Italy. The problem was principally one of familiarity and of social acceptance, and with time some of these western types, notably the basilica, did in fact succeed in entering the East Roman canon.

356. *Thebes (Egypt), Ramesseum, diagram showing "pitched" brick vaulting of the Pharaonic period*

357. *Diagram showing "pitched" brick vaulting of the late Roman and Byzantine periods*

358. *Aspendos (Pamphylia), substructures of the basilica, "pitched" brick vaulting*

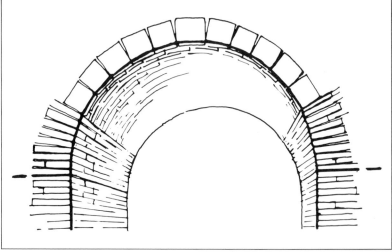

359. *Pergamon, plan of the east end of the Sanctuary of Aesculapius. 1) library; 2) monumental entrance courtyard; 3) Temple of Aesculapius; 4) lobed rotunda; 5) colonnaded processional avenue*

360. *Pergamon, Sanctuary of Aesculapius, vaulted undercroft of the rotunda*

The new Roman architecture presented a far more formidable problem in that it was dependent on materials that were neither available everywhere nor readily transportable over large distances. As a result—whereas the starting point for the late Republican and early Imperial architects of Rome had been a new building material and the finishing point the new architectural forms which had resulted from a systematic exploration of the properties of that material—the second-century architects of the Roman East had to face the reverse problem: given the new architectural forms, they had somehow or other to devise ways of expressing them in terms of whatever materials and technical resources happened to be locally available.

The logical starting point for their search was the local equivalent of the Roman *opus caementicium* which had already gained widespread acceptance in the bath buildings and the utilitarian architecture of the Roman East. The drawback to this material was the relatively poor quality of most local versions of the constituent mortar and the resulting impossibility of using it for any but rather small, simple forms of vaulting. The traditional local alternative, dressed stone, was cumbrous and costly. A substitute material had to be found, and the one which seemed to answer the architects' requirements best was brick.

Crude, sun-dried brick had had a long history in the ancient East, notably in Mesopotamia and Egypt, where stone and wood were either costly or in very short supply. Asia Minor, with its wealth of good building stone and timber, had less need to rely on such alternatives but, just as in a great many parts of Europe, crude brick was in fact widely used as a cheap secondary building material, with or without timber framing and in some contexts probably also for vaulting corridors and small rooms. There are two principal ways in which brick can be used to build a barrel vault: one is that invariably used in the West, where the bricks are laid radially as if they were the slender voussoirs of a stone arch *(Plate 217)*; the other is to "pitch" the bricks, that is, to lay them edge to edge across the vault, usually on shoulders that have been corbeled inward either radially or in horizontal courses so as to reduce the actual span to be vaulted. "Pitched" vaulting had been used since time immemorial in Mesopotamia and Egypt *(Plate 356)*. It is never found in the West, but it was the method preferred by early Byzantine architects *(Plates 357, 365)*, who may reasonably be assumed to have derived it from Asia Minor *(Plate 358* illustrates a rare surviving example of the Roman period in the substructures of the basilica at Aspendos).

The monument which tells the story most clearly is the Sanctuary of Aesculapius at Pergamon *(Plate 359)*. Built between about A.D. 140 and 175, it consisted of a sacred healing spring situated within a large

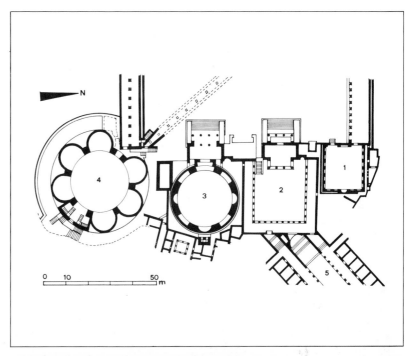

361. *Aspendos (Pamphylia), brick vaulting of the bath building*
362. *Aspendos (Pamphylia), aqueduct with pressure towers*

rectangular enclosure, framed on three sides by porticoes. It was approached from the city by a colonnaded avenue, and in addition to simple lodgings it was equipped with a theater and a library. Two buildings in particular attest to the influence of contemporary Roman design. One, at the southeast angle, was a lobed rotunda with a vaulted undercroft *(Plate 360)* built in the familiar local version of Roman concrete and an upper story which was presumably timber-roofed, possibly with a central oculus. The other building was the actual Temple of Aesculapius, which was designed in deliberate imitation of Hadrian's Pantheon: it was little more than half the size, but had the same pedimental porch leading to a rotunda which incorporated eight alternately rectangular and apsidal recesses. We do not know how it was lit, but the massive walls were of dressed stone and the excavators found substantial remains of the fallen dome—made of brick.

From the mid-second century onward brick vaulting *(Plate 361)* was in fact much commoner in Asia Minor than the number of recorded examples might seem to suggest. Many bath buildings (at Miletus, Perge, and Side, for example) can be seen to have been vaulted in mortared rubble *(opus caementicium)* laid over an inner framework of brick, and excavators' reports give details of a number of other buildings (mausoleums, markets, rotundas) that were similarly vaulted. Brick also began to be used in ordinary walling to give it added strength. One method was to alternate the mortared rubble with horizontal bands of brick. In appearance this resembles the *opus mixtum* of Central Italy *(Plate 162),* but unlike the latter the bricks do in fact run right through the body of the masonry, reinforcing it. Good Roman-period examples of this method can be seen in the baths at Sardis and at Ankara *(Plate 363),* in the walls at Nicaea (Iznik), and in the pressure towers of the aqueduct at Aspendos *(Plate 362).* Elsewhere we find walls built of brick alone. Here again there is a superficial resemblance to Italian practice; but whereas in Italy it was merely a facing over the concrete core, in Asia Minor brick was used as a building material in its own right—something which the Romans in the West never did before late antiquity. Notable examples of such brickwork are to be seen in the Kizil Avlu at Pergamon *(Plate 366),* the Harbor Baths at Ephesus *(Plate 329),* and—again—the aqueduct towers at Aspendos.

At this point, with the emergence of brick vaulting as an effective counterpart to the concrete vaulting of Italy, we may for a moment interrupt our survey of Roman architecture in Asia Minor. The stage was now set for the brief episode of the establishment of regional capitals at Nicomedia (Izmit) and Thessalonica (Salonica), followed in turn by the foundation of Constantinople *(Plates 364, 365),* which for over a millennium thereafter was to be the principal repository of

what Greece had once been. This was in essence a Romano-Hellenistic architecture and, after that of Rome itself, it was the most important single component in the elaborate complex of interconnected regional traditions which constituted the architecture of the Roman Empire.

We shall have very little to say about the regional traditions of Syria and its immediate neighbors. This is not because of any lack of intrinsic interest (that could hardly be said of an area which included the remains of Antioch on the Orontes, Apamea, Baalbek, Bostra, Damascus, Dura-Europos, Gerasa, Palmyra, Petra, the villages of the hill country near Aleppo, and the cities of the Hauran) but because, architecturally speaking, these cities lived a life somewhat apart. It is true that the early Imperial architecture of the Syrian provinces was heavily influenced by Rome, far more so than that of contemporary Asia Minor; but although it in turn inevitably exercised some reciprocal influence on its neighbors—the diffusion of the colonnaded street is a notable instance of such influence—Syria's direct architectural impact upon the larger Mediterranean scene was surprisingly slight. The influence of this area was mainly felt in other ways, through the medium of ideas (particularly religious ideas), through the visual arts, and in all matters where Syria was the natural intermediary between the Mediterranean world and the ancient East. With the establishment in Constantinople of a theocratic state, whose religion came from the East and whose holy places lay within Palestine, Syria's southern neighbor, the architectural links too became of the first importance. But that still lay in the future. In terms of Roman architecture as we have defined it, the Syrian provinces are not really central to our story.

Finally, a word about Athens. Long before the Romans conquered Greece the city had lost all political importance. But it had two valuable assets, its immense cultural prestige and its unrivaled tradition of sculptural craftsmanship. Already in the second century B.C. we hear of Hermodorus of Salamis working in Rome, while wealthy Romans, like the Hellenistic monarchs before them, were proud to be able to erect fine buildings in Athens. One of Cicero's correspondents, Appius Claudius Pulcher, had a monumental gateway built at Eleusis *(Plates 367, 368)*, the remains of which survive, and much of the earliest architectural marblework of Rome was executed by Attic craftsmen working at first with Attic, and later with Italian, marble. Among the imperial donors of buildings in Athens were Caesar, Augustus and his colleague Agrippa, Nero, Hadrian (who built a whole new city quarter), and Antoninus Pius. Attic workmen were busy adorning the Antonine Baths at Carthage in A.D. 143, and half a century later we find them working in the Severan Forum at Leptis Magna. The splendid series of carved Attic sarcophagi, exported all

classical culture in the eastern Mediterranean. We shall be returning to these events in the next chapter; suffice it here to stress once again the essential characteristic of the Roman-period architecture of Asia Minor, namely its enduring attachment to its own native heritage of Hellenistic forms and inspiration. Over the years this might be modified, and even on occasion transformed, by the acceptance of western ideas, but it always retained enough of its own essence to be the major vehicle for the transmission to Byzantium of a living sense of

367. *Eleusis (Attica), reconstruction drawing of the Inner (Lesser) Propylaea, built shortly after 50 B.C. The inner face of the doorway is flanked by caryatids*

369. *Athens, Tower of the Winds*

368. *Eleusis (Attica), Inner (Lesser) Propylaea, capital*

over the central and eastern Mediterranean, came to an end when Athens was sacked by the Heruli in 267.

The patronage, the material, the skills: one might well have expected a distinguished school of Roman provincial architecture in Athens, comparable to that of the cities of Asia Minor. But the dead weight of the past was overwhelming: just as Attic sculptors were too busy carving old master copies from every period to develop a contemporary style of their own, so too the architects of Attica were the victims of their own versatility. They were craftsmen, not creators, equally at home in transporting a fifth-century temple from the countryside of Attica to a new site in the Agora, in restoring the Erechtheum (an event promptly echoed in Rome, in the Forum of Augustus, perhaps also in Agrippa's Pantheon), or in erecting a new public monument to the specifications of a foreign patron. At least three of the major Roman buildings in Athens belong to this last category: the Odeion of Agrippa (c. 15 B.C.), the Forum of Caesar and Augustus (between 12 and 2 B.C.), and Hadrian's Library *(Plate 370)*. Of these, the first two were directly based on South Italian models, while the Hadrianic building was a close copy of Vespasian's Templum Pacis in Rome, a building which had itself owed much to South Italy. The architectural detail of all three buildings was exclusively Attic.

The nearest one gets to a genuine creativity in Athens is in minor monuments such as the Tower of the Winds *(Plate 369)* or the Arch of Hadrian *(Plates 371, 372),* erected to mark the boundary between the old city and Hadrian's new quarter. The Tower of the Winds was built to house the water clock of Andronicus of Cyrrhus, probably about the middle of the first century B.C., and it is a small masterpiece of its kind. The graceful lotus-leaf capitals which first appear here, in the porch, were copied again and again throughout antiquity; they may be seen, for example, carved by Attic workmen, in the porticoes of the Severan Forum at Leptis Magna *(Plate 303)*. The Arch of Hadrian suffers today from the loss of the pairs of columns which flanked the two faces of the arch, seeming to support the outer ends of the upper structure, and from the loss of the statues which carried the lines of the two end-pilasters upward. What now appears to be a rather meaningless discrepancy of dimension between the actual archway and the superstructure was in fact the product of an elaborately contrived superimposition of two contrasting architectural schemes. Although the vocabulary is traditional, its use is highly sophisticated, deliberately setting out to mislead the eye as to the real function of the (in themselves very familiar) constituent elements. In this case we may suspect the influence of contemporary Asia Minor, where the facade of the Library of Celsus is a product of the same baroque illusionism.

We left the story of Roman architecture in the capital at a point which may aptly be summarized by reference to Hadrian's four great state monuments within the city: the Temple of the Divus Traianus, a grandiose building of traditional Italic type, conceived in the spirit, and as a formal completion, of the Forum of Trajan; the new dynastic mausoleum (today the Castel Sant'Angelo), an updated and elaborated version of the Mausoleum of Augustus; the gigantic Temple of Venus and Rome, an eccentric reflection of Hadrian's own eclectic, philhellenic tastes, and important as the first state monument to be built in Greek (Proconnesian) marble by Greek workmen imported from Asia Minor for the purpose; and that masterpiece of the new concrete-vaulted architecture, the Pantheon. Roman architecture was still a stream consisting of many currents, but by the time of Hadrian's death in A.D. 138 the new concrete architecture may be said to have won unqualified acceptance. In Hadrian's Villa architects had explored to the limit the aesthetic refinements of the new medium; in the Baths of Trajan, in the Pantheon, and on the Palatine they had used it to achieve grandiose new spatial effects, and at Ostia and in the Markets of Trajan to evolve new settings for the activities of daily life. The years from Nero to Hadrian had been a time of headlong advance into new territory. The next two hundred years were to be spent largely in consolidating the ground so gained: following the Architectural Revolution came a time of cautious evolution.

The half-century that followed the accession of Antoninus Pius in A.D. 138 was a period in which there was little public building in Rome. Official attention was turning increasingly to the provinces—one thinks of buildings such as the huge Antonine Baths (A.D. 143) at Carthage—and in any case, after 150 years of almost continuous building activity, the capital was saturated with public monuments. A short period of renewed imperial patronage under Septimius Severus and his immediate successors saw the construction of the Baths of Caracalla, the now-lost Baths of Severus Alexander, and the enlargement of the palace on the Palatine. Then, during the anarchy of the mid-third century, there was another pause in construction until the reign of Aurelian (A.D. 270–275), which inaugurated the last great building phase of pagan Rome, under Diocletian (284–305) and Maxentius (306–312). The few public buildings that have survived from this intervening period are mainly conservative monuments: the Temple of the Divus Hadrianus, the Temple of Antoninus and Faustina, the Column of Marcus Aurelius, the Arch of Septimius Severus (Plates 373, 374). It is true that if one looks more closely at the sculpture of the last-named monuments one can see clear signs of the final breakdown of the canons of official classicizing taste established two centuries earlier by Augustus (Plates 377–379). But in the strictly

373.   *Rome, Arch of Septimius Severus*
374.   *Rome, coin showing the Arch of Septimius Severus crowned by a bronze triumphal chariot and other figures*

375, 376. Rome, Circus of Maxentius on the Via Appia

architectural field it is to the commercial and residential quarters of Ostia that one must turn for a clearer vision of how society was accommodating itself to the new standards of taste implicit in the new architecture.

What were these new standards? At the risk of over-simplification they may be said to represent a steadily increasing acceptance of the functional properties of the new concrete medium, an acceptance which found expression in various ways: internally through a greater sophistication in the suggestion of spatial relationships; externally through the evolution of architectural schemes which, while still responsive to the logic of interior space, might present a more coherent, self-sufficient face to the outer world; and in every field through the steady elimination of the classical orders from any but the few roles in which they had successfully come to terms with the new concrete architecture. Let us glance briefly at each of these aspects in turn.

After the extravaganzas of Hadrian's Villa, the sheer geometry of enclosed space might reasonably be felt to have been exhaustively explored, and the emphasis was now increasingly upon the suggestive relationships that might be established with whatever space or spaces lay beyond the immediately enveloping structure. The great *frigidarium* which stood at the center of the standard "Imperial" bath building could be regarded as a self-contained unit—three soaring, cross-vaulted bays, buttressed on either side by three pairs of barrel-vaulted side chambers—and it was so regarded by Maxentius when he borrowed the form for his great basilica near the Forum, the last pagan Roman basilica and the only one to break with tradition by being built in vaulted concrete. But the *frigidarium* was also the point of intersection of the two main axes of the building, down which the eye could travel, following a dramatic alternation of light and shadow and conveying a lively sense of the significance of this central hall within the larger complex. The same may be said of the great circular, domed *caldarium* of the Baths of Caracalla. Here the central oculus of the Pantheon has already given way to four large windows in the upper part of the drum, thereby losing the uncanny sense of concentration conferred by the single source of light, but gaining not only in convenience but also in the feeling of participation with the world outside.

Another effective device for the diversification of that most basic of all centralizing types, the domed circular hall, was the piercing of the perimeter wall so as to form a series of apsidal lobes, which might in turn open outward through a curvilinear columnar screen. The germs of these ideas (as indeed of so many later innovations) can be seen in Hadrian's Villa at Tivoli—in the vestibule of the Piazza

380. *Rome, church of Santa Maria degli Angeli, which incorporates the* frigidarium *of the Baths of Diocletian. The structure of the building, including the vaults, is Roman*

381. *Rome, Basilica of Maxentius, coffered vaulting*

382. *Rome, Basilica of Maxentius. The central hall originally had coffered vaulting* ▷

383. *Rome, plans of the pavilion (the so-called Temple of Minerva Medica) in the Licinian Gardens around A.D. 300 (a) and around A.D. 320 (b)*

384, 385. *Rome, pavilion in the Licinian Gardens*

386. *Rome, pavilion in the Licinian Gardens, interior showing the brick ribbing of the vaulting and, below it, traces of the marble facing* ▷

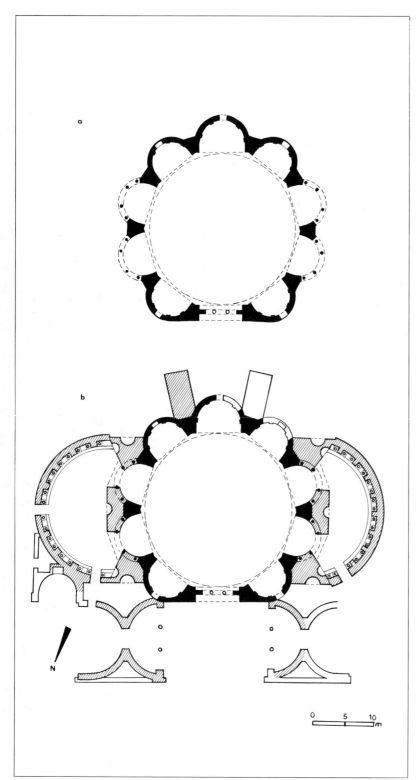

387. *Rome, Markets of Trajan, semidomes (originally faced externally with concrete, later covered with tiles)*

389. *Leptis Magna (Tripolitania, Libya), Hunting Baths, restored axonometric view and plan*

388. *Rome, the Curia Julia as restored by Diocletian*

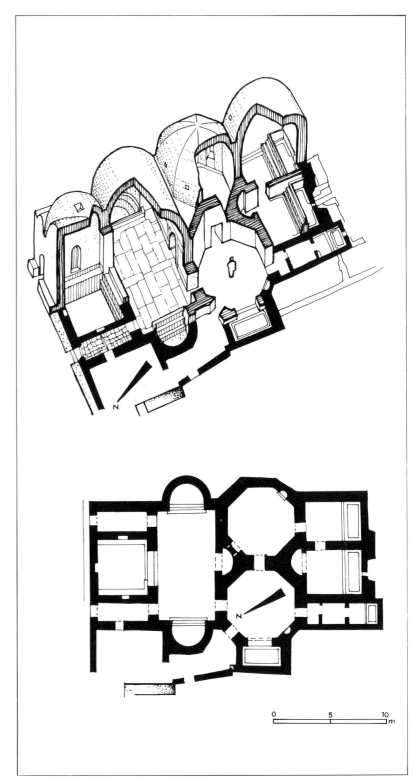

391. *Rome, plan of the Mausoleum of Constantina (today the church of Santa Costanza)*

392. *Rome, Mausoleum of Constantina, interior*

393. *Split (Dalmatia, Yugoslavia), detail of the facade of the fortified residence of Diocletian, from an engraving by Robert Adam (1754)* ▷

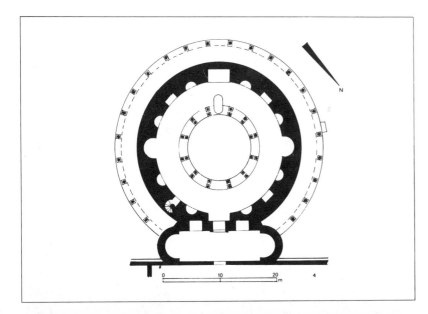

d'Oro *(Plates 183–186)* and in some of the living rooms of the so-called "libraries." By the third and fourth centuries lobed centralizing plans had become a commonplace. A building such as the so-called Temple of Minerva Medica (in reality a pavilion in the Licinian Gardens) anticipated some of the most effective ideas of early Byzantine architecture *(Plates 383–386)*.

The problem of creating a significant new exterior architecture could only be tackled seriously in situations where the established conventions of the classical orders were no longer felt to have an overriding claim. Consequently, it is in commercial and domestic architecture, at Ostia and in buildings such as the Markets of Trajan, that we can first detect the emergence of new models in which, instead of columns and entablature, doors, windows, and balconies are used to create patterned alternations of solids and voids *(Plates 144, 216)*. Once again bath architecture *(Plates 395–398)*—ubiquitous, monumental (but less hampered by tradition than other monumental types), and above all functional—had a very important part to play in the new architectural scene. The plans might be symmetrical, as in the Baths of Trajan and Caracalla, where the massive bulk of the main *caldarium* was framed between the twin ranges of large arcaded windows which constituted the main south facade; or they might be asymmetrical, as in the Forum Baths at Ostia, with the windows incorporated in a progressively developing series of projecting, curvilinear *caldaria*. In either case there is a strong probability that the exteriors of the domes were allowed to stand free, as was certainly true of the semidomes of the Markets of Trajan *(Plate 387)*—which admittedly were not visible from the front—or of the domes and barrel vaults of the Hunting Baths at Leptis Magna *(Plates 389, 390)* and of innumerable small bath buildings throughout the Roman world. These were a new and exciting feature of the Rome skyline, and after the initial shock to conventional taste they must have done a great deal to condition contemporary sensibilities to the shape of things to come.

As always it was the long-established types of building which were the last to yield. As one sees it today, Diocletian's rebuilding of the Curia Julia in the Forum Romanum is a remarkably austere edifice, its brick facade relieved only by the door and three large windows *(Plate 388)*. Close inspection, however, shows that not only was the entablature stuccoed, but the whole facade carried a scheme of imitation drafted masonry, this too in stucco *(Plate 394)*. Ultra-conservative survivals of this sort are not to be confused with such deliberately archaizing revivals as the use of a classical order framing an arcade in the precinct of the Mausoleum of Maxentius on the Via Appia, in the facade of Diocletian's palace at Split (Spalato; *Plate 393)*, and in the

Porta Nigra at Trier *(Plates 403–405)*. Contemporary architectural thinking is better represented by the blind arcading used so effectively in the Constantinian Audience Hall *(Plates 409, 411)* and in the warehouses of the last-named city. Visually such rhythmical arcading fulfilled much the same function as the exterior order of a Greek temple, articulating the masonry mass into a harmonious pattern of light and shade, solid and void. But whereas, for all its sophistication of detail, the Greek order was a direct response to the structural requirements of a timber-roofed, columnar building, the sort of late Roman solution which we see at Trier or in the imperial mausoleums or the gates of the Aurelianic Walls *(Plates 399, 400)* represents a hard-won compromise, whereby the structural logic of an inward-facing, concrete-vaulted architecture was made to yield the elements of an effective and visually satisfying external system. Roman architects never achieved the sort of integration of exterior and interior which characterizes a Gothic cathedral, but one has only to compare the exterior of the Audience Hall at Trier with such Early Christian basilicas as San Simpliciano in Milan and Santa Sabina in Rome to appreciate how much they did accomplish.

Although with the passage of time it becomes increasingly hard to distinguish survivals from revivals, the classical orders did continue to be widely used in the interiors of buildings right down to Christian times. As constructional elements they were an echo from the past: if it had not been for the abundant supplies of marble that were available for use, or re-use, they might well have disappeared altogether, replaced by the more logical device of arcading carried on piers of masonry of the sort already current in second-century Ostia *(Plates 209, 210)*. As it was, they continued to serve a useful purpose in the open, columnar screen walls which played a large part in later Imperial architecture, although more often than not the traditional flat architraves were replaced by arches. The elimination of the flat entablature created certain structural problems. The wall above was normally wider than the column and its capital, and one of the functions of the old cornice element had been to provide a transition to this extra width. One solution was that adopted by the architects of the mausoleum of Constantine's daughter, now the church of Santa Costanza, where the columns were used in pairs *(Plates 391, 392)*. An alternative device, preferred by most Early Christian architects, was to interpose an elongated block of stone or marble *(impost block)* between capital and superstructure. But it was left to Justinian's architects, in sixth-century Constantinople, to carry things to their logical conclusion by creating schemes in which structure and ornament merged to form organically new systems which were virtually independent of their classical antecedents.

397. *Rome, Baths of Diocletian, one of the exedras of the facade of the* frigidarium. *The recesses were framed by columnar aediculae*

398. *Rome, Baths of Diocletian, facade of the* frigidarium *overlooking the swimming pool* (natatio). *Engraving by Piranesi*

399. *Rome, reconstruction drawing of the Porta Appia (today the Porta San Sebastiano), as built by Aurelian around* A.D. *275*

400. *Rome, the Porta Appia (today the Porta San Sebastiano) after its remodeling around* A.D. *400*

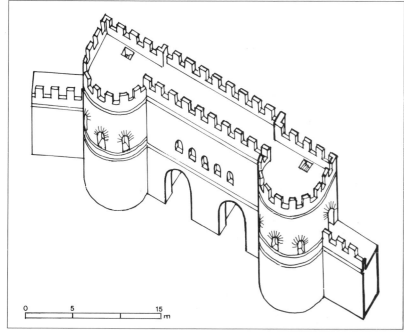

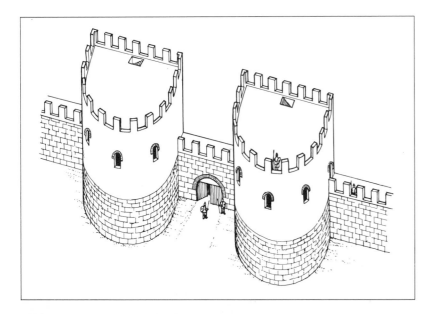

of the Pantheon—the distinction is of limited architectural significance. It comes as no surprise to find that it was in the decoration of vaults and domes (which was often reflected also in the design of pavements) that one can most readily trace the emergence of consistent and structurally meaningful new systems of ornament.

While in Rome itself architects were slowly but steadily consolidating and developing the legacy of architectural ideas bequeathed to them by the authors of the Roman Architectural Revolution, in other parts of the Empire the patterns of civilized life were changing rapidly and dramatically. During the third century barbarian hordes had crossed the frontiers of the Rhine and the Danube, destroying all before them; in A.D. 253 the Parthian armies occupied Antioch; and in 267 Athens was sacked by the Heruli. Rome itself received a grim reminder of the changing times when Aurelian found it necessary to enclose the main inhabited area within the defensive circuit of walls which bears his name. In their original form (*Plate 399*; compare *Plate 400*) the walls and the gates show how little Roman military architecture had changed, or had felt any need to change, during the last three hundred years; but their presence was an ominous sign of the times. The frontiers of the Empire had returned to Italy *(Plate 401)*.

To meet this new situation, the emperor Diocletian (284–305) devised the system known as the Tetrarchy, a college of two senior and two junior emperors, each responsible for the administration and defense of one quarter of the Roman world; and although Rome remained the ceremonial capital, the effective seats of day-to-day government moved to a series of new regional capitals established nearer to the armies and to the sources of danger, along the Empire's northern and eastern frontiers—Trier, Milan, Sirmium (Mitrovica, in northern Yugoslavia), Thessalonica (Salonica), Nicomedia (Izmit, on the Sea of Marmara), Antioch on the Orontes, and—last and greatest—Constantinople. North Africa too had its problems, but not of a magnitude to provoke similar reactions, and from what we know of cities such as Carthage, Leptis Magna, and Alexandria, and of innumerable others in less exposed parts of the Empire, there were a great many places where the patterns which we have described in the two previous chapters continued to operate. Things were changing everywhere, but slowly. In the new capitals, on the other hand, the Tetrarchy established a radically new architectural situation, somewhat akin to that of Leptis Magna a century earlier, though more firmly rooted in current needs—a situation based on imperial patronage, involving massive official building programs and, because these cities were imperial residences, shaped by an all-pervading awareness of what was happening elsewhere, both at the center and at the pe-

One other continuing use of the classical orders deserves mention, namely their survival as part of the standard repertory of conventional motifs suitable for the decoration of the interior surfaces of buildings in the form of marble veneer, stucco, or mosaic (*Plate 412*). Here again it becomes increasingly difficult to distinguish between survival and revival; and since the decorative systems used on wall surfaces had long ago ceased to bear any clear functional relationship to the underlying structure—witness the upper order of the interior

403. *Augusta Treverorum (Trier, Germany), plans of the Porta Nigra at ground level (left) and at the first floor (right). The apse is a medieval addition*

404. *Augusta Treverorum (Trier, Germany), Porta Nigra, detail of the exterior showing unfinished masonry*

405. *Augusta Treverorum (Trier, Germany), Porta Nigra, exterior*

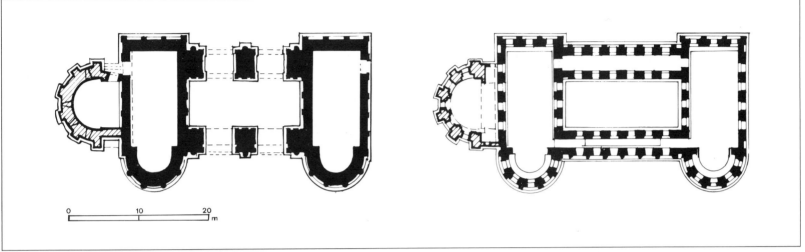

406. *Augusta Treverorum (Trier, Germany), Baths of Constantine (Kaiserthermen), plan*

408. *Augusta Treverorum (Trier, Germany), Baths of Constantine (Kaiserthermen)* ▷

407. *Augusta Treverorum (Trier, Germany), Baths of Constantine (Kaiserthermen), reconstructed view of the east end*

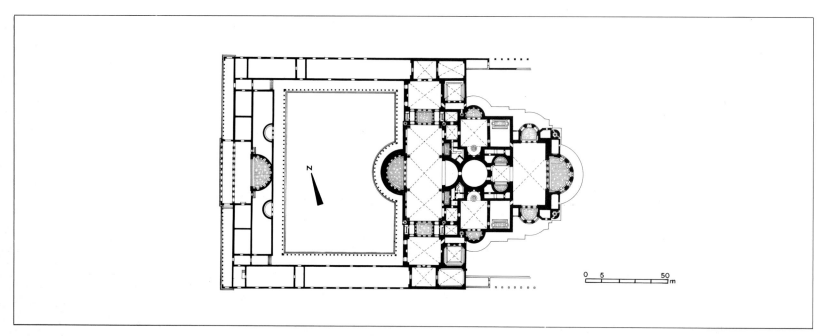

409. *Augusta Treverorum (Trier, Germany), basilica of the Palace (Audience Hall)*

riphery of the Empire. Constantine had spent part of his boyhood at Nicomedia; as a young man he ruled from Trier; for a time, after A.D. 312, he was established in Rome; in 320 he founded, and ultimately in 330 transferred his official residence to, Constantinople. Small wonder, then, if in the seats of authority ideas traveled faster and more freely than ever before.

Virtually nothing has survived of Nicomedia and Antioch, although we have a valuable description of the palace at Antioch by the fourth-century writer Libanius. At Milan we have some remains of the circus which adjoined the palace; at Sirmium excavation is beginning to yield elements of a palace complex, including a circus and an Imperial-type bath building; and at Thessalonica the circular, domed church of St. George is now known to have been built to serve as the Mausoleum of Galerius (293–311), linked architecturally to the site of the palace, which in turn overlooked the circus (hippodrome). At Trier, which was successively the capital of Constantius (293–306) and of his son Constantine, we have not only the substantial remains of the palace, including the great Audience Hall (Plates 409, 411), but also of two huge Imperial-type bath complexes—one of them of earlier date, the other Constantinian (Plates 406–408); a grandiloquent city gate, the Porta Nigra, set at one end of an axial colonnaded street; a large official warehouse; and the inevitable circus. To these we may add the fortified residence which Diocletian built at Split for his own retirement in A.D. 305, a palace in all but name, which included an octagonal, domed mausoleum, now the cathedral; and the residential complex which Maxentius had built for himself beside the Via Appia in Rome between 306 and 312, again incorporating a family mausoleum (in this case circular and with a projecting pedimental porch, on the model of the Pantheon) and a circus (Plates 375, 376).

Even from so bald a summary it will be evident how much the new capitals of the Tetrarchy had in common with each other. Each in its own way had to serve as a kind of miniature Rome in the provinces, with its own local equivalent of the Flavian Palace on the Palatine, overlooking the Circus Maximus, just as in Constantine's "New Rome" on the Bosporus the Great Palace was to overlook the hippodrome. In most cases our knowledge of the individual buildings is fragmentary, but such as it is it indicates that here too there was a broad unity of intention. At Milan, for example, Ausonius, writing around A.D. 388, describes a theater, a circus, two circuits of walls, temples, a palace, a mint, and a bath building erected by Maximian, of which all that survives today is a tower of the outer defenses, added by Maximian to enclose the circus and the palace quarter. The requirements were much the same in each case: defenses, a palace with an adjoining circus, lodging and services for the members of the court and the imperial bodyguard, bath buildings, a treasury and a mint, and possibly the equivalent of a palace chapel and a tomb building.

Many of the models were metropolitan Roman, but not all. The centrally planned mausoleums at Thessalonica and Split stem from the same Roman sources as the mausoleums of Tor de' Schiavi on the Via Praenestina, of Maxentius along the Via Appia, and of the empress Helena along the Via Casilina (Tor Pignattara). The colonnaded street at Trier was, on the other hand, an intruder from the East, of which the only known earlier example in the West is, significantly enough, that of Severan Leptis Magna.

Much the same picture emerges from a study of the detailed treatment and building techniques of the individual monuments. For the most part these were, as one would expect, based on current local use. At Thessalonica, for example, it was local workmen who built the walls of the mausoleum in concreted rubble alternating with courses of brick, and who vaulted it in brick. The Palace of Diocletian at Split, on the other hand, bears evidence of being the work of craftsmen assembled from many parts of the Empire. Although the dressed stone masonry represents a long-established local tradition, it was one that would have been congenial to workmen from many parts of Syria or Asia Minor, areas to which one must look for the sources of such features as the arcading of the central ceremonial courtyard or the extensive use of brick vaulting, or again for such tricks of detail as the open relieving arches over the lintels or the bracketed, arcaded order which decorated the main landward gate, the Porta Aurea (Plate 410). Against these eastern features must be set the arches of the Palace's sea-front gallery (Plate 393), framed between the half-columns of a decorative order—an archaizing westernism for which the contemporary parallels are the courtyard of the Mausoleum of Maxentius in Rome and the Porta Nigra at Trier.

An even more striking example of the free flow of ideas and techniques is that afforded by the Audience Hall at Trier. At first glance one would take this for an up-to-date but otherwise ultra-typical example of contemporary metropolitan, brick-faced concrete masonry. In reality it is built of solid brick, like the Kizil Avlu at Pergamon, and it is thus a seemingly unique example in the West of a method of construction which at this date we find only in Asia Minor. Whatever the weight of conservative architectural tradition in the average provincial city, here in the capitals of the Tetrarchy things were fast moving toward an architecture that was ecumenical in its range, transcending the barriers between one region and another and the even more formidable barrier that still separated East from West.

410. *Split (Dalmatia, Yugoslavia), Porta Aurea of Diocletian's residence*
411. *Augusta Treverorum (Trier, Germany), basilica of the Palace (Audience Hall), interior, view toward the apse* ▷
412. *Rome, church of Santa Maria Maggiore, interior* ▷

In the end, however, things did not work out this way. Under the strong hand of Diocletian the Tetrarchy did its work of re-establishing order and a measure of external security within the Roman world. But as a system the Tetrarchy was foredoomed to failure by the ambitions and dynastic rivalries of the individual co-emperors. One by one Constantine eliminated all his colleagues, and after the defeat of Licinius in A.D. 323 he was left master of an Empire that was once more for a time reunited under a single ruler. But Constantine was a realist, and he understood very well the administrative advantages of the sort of decentralization which the Tetrarchy had represented. When he first planned Constantinople, he almost certainly meant it to be no more than another of the new regional capitals, replacing the less strategically situated Nicomedia and Thessalonica. It was the stubborn opposition of the old pagan aristocracy in Rome which made him decide in 330 to transfer his court (and with it the effective seat of government) to Constantinople. On the death of Theodosius in 395 the briefly won unity was dissolved and the Empire was finally and irrevocably divided into its two constituent parts: the Eastern, or Byzantine, Empire centered upon Constantinople, and the Western Empire, with Rome as its nominal capital but effectively governed from the residences of the imperial court in North Italy, at Milan and later at Ravenna.

It is one of the ironies of architectural history that when Constantine moved his capital to the Bosporus, the city of Rome—which had pioneered the new architecture that was to be the Roman Empire's most important artistic legacy to European civilization—became almost overnight a backwater, a center of traditionalism and, in due course, a mine of inspiration for the propagation of precisely those classical values which the architects of the Roman Architectural Revolution had worked so hard to supersede. In Constantinople the roles were reversed: by history and geography the natural heir to the lively but fundamentally conservative traditions of Romano-Hellenistic classicism of which western Asia Minor had been the natural center, it found itself taking up, developing, and ultimately transmitting to posterity the lessons of the new Roman architecture at the point where they had been broken off in Rome itself. It is not possible to follow up this story in detail. Nevertheless, it will greatly help our understanding of the historical significance of Roman architecture to ask one final question: why did this happen, and what were the political, social, and practical mechanisms which shaped so extraordinary a change of fortune?

It is easy enough to see how the transfer of power and patronage to Constantinople stripped Rome of its position as a creative center of

319

416. *Constantinople (Istanbul, Turkey), church of Hagia Sophia*

the arts. Inevitably it was the new capital which attracted the best architects and gave them scope for their talents, whereas—except for the buildings needed to house the new state religion—Rome had all it could do to keep the monuments of the past in good repair. When in A.D. 357 Constantius II visited Rome for the first and only time, he did so very much in the spirit in which nineteenth-century tourists, comfortably assured of the enduring verities of humanistic culture and art, visited the historical monuments of Renaissance Rome and Florence.

But the move to Constantinople is only a partial answer. One has merely to look at the architecture of the last twenty years of pagan Rome—buildings such as the Basilica of Maxentius, the so-called Temple of Romulus, the Baths of Constantine, the so-called Temple of Minerva Medica, the church of Santa Costanza—to be conscious that, after a period of relative stagnation, the architecture of the capital was again about to embark on a fresh period of exploration and adventure. We are confronted here by another of the might-have-beens of architectural history. Instead, it became a question of establishing centers of worship for the newly enfranchised Christian religion; and whoever was responsible for determining the form of such buildings as the cathedral church of St. John Lateran and the great martyr shrines chose as his model an architectural type—the timber-roofed, columnar basilica—which was already virtually obsolete. Why?

The question has been endlessly and inconclusively debated. Among the answers that have a ring of truth (and it would surely be mistaken to expect any single, all-embracing answer) are the fact that the basilica was untainted by any prior religious associations; that throughout the western world and in many parts of the East the basilica was the familiar, all-purpose building type for housing any large assembly of persons; that in palaces and in the private houses of the great it had ceremonial connotations which suited it well for the public rituals of what had hitherto been a very intimate religion; and, on a more practical note, that it could be built so easily and decorously with materials that were almost everywhere already available. We shall never know which of these reasons, or what others, constituted the decisive factor, but the result was that in Rome and in many other parts of the Roman world the major building activity of the fourth and fifth centuries was directed toward a building type, the basilica, which had taken shape when the concrete-vaulted architecture of Rome was still in its infancy. Much of the history of ecclesiastical architecture in early medieval Europe (and most monumental build-ing of the period was religious) is the history of the slow, laborious recovery of the ground thus lost.

In the region where Constantinople now held political and cultural supremacy the prevailing architectural tradition at the time of its foundation was still by metropolitan Roman standards markedly old-fashioned. It is true that the Tetrarchy had begun to introduce many changes, of which the surviving remains at Thessalonica afford a tantalizing glimpse. But it had been, and it remained, the great strength of the architecture of western Asia Minor and the northern Aegean that it kept alive a vigorous tradition of Romano-Hellenistic taste and practice, and this it was able to transmit to the architects and artists of the new capital, where it became one of the essential strands in the fabric of the emerging Byzantine culture. But to accept this is not to deny that there had also been a steady infiltration of western building types, coupled with a successful search for local equivalents of western building techniques; we saw something of this process in the last chapter. When, for example, Galerius wished to create for himself at Thessalonica a domed rotunda in the western manner, he found the tools ready to hand. So too now Constantine, setting out to build his "New Rome" on the Bosporus, was able to take with him whatever he wished of the accumulated store of old Roman architectural wisdom, secure in the knowledge that it could be interpreted by local builders working in materials and with building practices which they had already made their own.

So it was that, with the exception of North Italy, where buildings such as the church of San Lorenzo in Milan *(Plate 413)* and later (under strong Byzantine influence) San Vitale at Ravenna *(Plates 414, 415)* attest a continuing Roman tradition, the center of architectural activity and experiment moved eastward. It is to Constantinople—in the churches, the palaces, the bath buildings, and the residences of the wealthy court officials—that we must look for what Rome had lost. Here the threads of the Imperial past were picked up and woven into new patterns. The new city was no slavish imitation of the old Rome: from the outset there were features derived from Asia Minor and from Syria. But although that supreme achievement of early Byzantine architecture, Justinian's great church of Hagia Sophia *(Plate 416)*, contained many features that did not derive from Rome, the very idea of such a building would have been impossible without the contribution which Roman architects had already made to the sum of architectural experience. It is not altogether misleading to describe Hagia Sophia as the last great monument of the Roman Imperial architectural tradition.

ROMAN HISTORY	ARCHITECTURE IN ROME AND OSTIA	ITALY AND THE WESTERN PROVINCES	GREECE AND THE EASTERN PROVINCES
c. 850 B.C. Iron Age village established on the Palatine 753 (traditionally) Foundation of Rome Sixth century Rome under Etruscan domination			
	c. 575 B.C. Draining of the Forum valley to serve as a common meeting place 509 Temple of Jupiter Optimus Maximus, Juno, and Minerva dedicated on the Capitoline		
509 (traditionally) Expulsion of the Tarquins Fifth century Period of internal adjustment and gradual absorption of Rome's nearest neighbors			509 B.C. Expulsion of the Peisistratids from Athens
	484 Temple of Castor and Pollux Fifth century First temples in the Forum Boarium-Forum Holitorium area		
		480 B.C. Syracusans defeat Carthaginians at Himera 474 Battle of Cumae. Syracusans destroy Etruscan sea power	480 Athenians defeat Persians at Salamis
			447–430 Athens, the Parthenon
	429 First Temple of Apollo in Circo		
406–396 War against Veii. Beginning of the gradual conquest of Etruria		400 Celtic tribes (Gauls) invade North Italy 396 Capture and destruction of Veii by Rome	
	392 Temple of Juno Regina		
387 Sack of Rome by the Gauls			

ROMAN HISTORY	ARCHITECTURE IN ROME AND OSTIA	ITALY AND THE WESTERN PROVINCES	GREECE AND THE EASTERN PROVINCES	
	367 Temple of Concord c. 350 Sacred precinct of the Largo Argentina established (first Temple C)			
348 Roman treaty with Carthage				
343–341 First Samnite War				
340–338 Defeat of the Latin League at Antium (338) assures Roman supremacy in Latium		338 Colony at Antium		
335–334 Alliance with Capua and other Campanian towns		334 Colony at Cales (Calvi) in Campania	334 Alexander of Molossus, king of Epirus, intervenes in South Italy on behalf of the Tarentines	
		329 Colony at Tarracina (Terracina) 328 Colony at Fregellae (near Ceprano)		
326–304 Second Samnite War			323 Death of Alexander the Great. Emergence of the Hellenistic kingdoms of Macedonia, Egypt, Syria, and (263) Pergamon	
		314 Colony at Luceria (Lucera) in northern Apulia		
	312 Via Appia (Rome to Capua) and Aqua Appia, the first Roman aqueduct			
306 Roman treaty with Carthage				
		303 Colony at Alba Fucens c. 300 Colony at Ostia 299 Colony at Narnia (Narni)		
298–291 Third Samnite War				

ROMAN HISTORY	ARCHITECTURE IN ROME AND OSTIA	ITALY AND THE WESTERN PROVINCES	GREECE AND THE EASTERN PROVINCES
	296 Temple of Bellona near the Circus Flaminius		
295 Defeat of Samnites, Gauls, and Umbrians at Sentinum assures Roman supremacy south of the Apennines			
	291 Temple of Aesculapius on the Insula Tiberina		
		289–283 Colony at Sena Gallica (Senigallia) on the Adriatic coast	
		281–275 Pyrrhus campaigning in South Italy. Defeated at Beneventum (Benevento)	**281–275** Pyrrhus, king of Epirus, allied to the Tarentines. Campaigns in Italy
		273 Colonies at Cosa and Poseidonia (Paestum)	
	272 Aqua Anio Vetus	**272** Surrender of Tarentum (Taranto)	
		268 Colony at Ariminum (Rimini)	
264–241 First Punic War, fought mainly at sea and in Sicily	**260** Columna Rostrata of Duilius in the Forum Romanum, recording naval victory at Mylae		
241 Sicily becomes a Roman province	**241** Temple of Vesta rebuilt in stone	**241** Destruction of Falerii Veteres and foundation of Falerii Novi (Santa Maria di Falleri)	
238 Sardinia and Corsica annexed and created a province (227)	**238** First paved street in Rome		
229–228 First Illyrian War			**229–228** Roman armies operating for the first time east of the Adriatic
	221 Circus Flaminius		**221–205** Ptolemy IV, state barge
	220 Via Flaminia (Rome to Rimini) and first Pons Mulvius		

ROMAN HISTORY	ARCHITECTURE IN ROME AND OSTIA	ITALY AND THE WESTERN PROVINCES	GREECE AND THE EASTERN PROVINCES
218–202 Second Punic War. Hannibal invades Italy, inflicting crushing defeats at Trebia (218), Trasimene (217), and Cannae (216). Withdraws to Africa in 205	**204** Temple of Cybele (Magna Mater) on the Palatine	**218** Colonies at Placentia (Piacenza), Cremona, and Mutina (Modena) **212** Capture and sack of Syracuse **209** Capture and sack of Tarentum	**215–205** First Macedonian War **202–197** Second Macedonian War. Defeat of Philip V at Cynoscephalae. Greek cities declared independent
206 Scipio Africanus drives Carthaginians from Spain, invades Africa, and wins battle of Zama (202)			**197–159** Athens, Stoa of Eumenes of Pergamon
197 Two provinces of Spain established			
	193 Porticus Aemilia, original building **192** Temple of Veiovis on the Capitoline		**192** Antiochus III of Syria invades Greece. Defeated and driven out by Romans. Peace of Apamea (188)
		189 Colony at Bononia (Bologna) **187** Via Aemilia (Rimini to Piacenza)	
	187 Temple of Hercules Musarum **184** Basilica Porcia (demolished by Caesar)		
		181 Colony at Aquileia	
	179 Basilica Fulvia (later the Basilica Aemilia). Pons Aemilius (piers) **174** Porticus Aemilia rebuilt in concrete		**174** Antiochus IV commissions a Roman architect, M. Cossutius, to build the Temple of Zeus Olympios at Athens **171–168** Third Macedonian War
	170 Basilica Sempronia (demolished by Caesar)		

ROMAN HISTORY	ARCHITECTURE IN ROME AND OSTIA	ITALY AND THE WESTERN PROVINCES	GREECE AND THE EASTERN PROVINCES
			166 Delos declared a free port Before 150 Miletus, Bouleuterion 159–138 Athens, Stoa of Attalos of Pergamon
		c. 150 Sanctuary at Gabii c. 150–125 Cosa, basilica	
149–146 Third Punic War 146 Destruction of Carthage	149 Pons Aemilius (stone arches) After 146 Porticus Metelli and temples of Jupiter Stator and Juno Regina, the first Roman buildings in marble Hermodorus of Salamis working in Rome 144–140 Aqua Marcia, the first high-level aqueduct, carried partly on arches		149 Revolt of Macedonia 146 Destruction of Corinth. Creation of provinces of Macedonia and Achaea
133 Reforms of Tiberius Gracchus and of Caius Gracchus (123–122) initiate a century of constitutional and class unrest, leading to civil war and dictatorship		143 Revolt in Spain, finally suppressed by the capture of Numantia (133)	133 Attalus IV bequeaths kingdom of Pergamon to Rome. Province of Asia constituted in 130
	127 Aqua Tepula		
		c. 125–100 Pompeii, basilica 125–121 Subjugation of Mediterranean Gaul. Military base established at Aquae Sextiae (Aix-en-Provence) 118 Colony at Narbo Martius (Narbonne), the first colony outside Italy 111–105 War against Numidians under Jugurtha. Defeated by Marius 113–102/1 Cimbri and Teutones, migrant Germanic tribes, invade South Gaul, Spain, and North Italy	
107 Gaius Marius becomes consul for first time. Roman army reformed 104–101 Marius is reelected consul each year	109 Pons Mulvius rebuilt in stone	102 Marius routs the Teutones near Aquae Sextiae	

ROMAN HISTORY	ARCHITECTURE IN ROME AND OSTIA	ITALY AND THE WESTERN PROVINCES	GREECE AND THE EASTERN PROVINCES
		101 Marius and Catulus rout the Cimbri in North Italy	
	100 Temple of Honos and Virtus built by Roman architect, Caius Mucius	c. 100 Ardea, basilica c. 100(?) Sanctuary of Fortuna Primigenia at Praeneste (Palestrina); Round Temple at Tibur (Tivoli)	96 Cyrenaica bequeathed to Rome, but its cities allowed to remain free
91–88 Social War against Italian allies, who in 89 are awarded Roman citizenship	c. 100–80 Round Temple in the Forum Boarium	89 Extensive building activity, particularly in North Italy, following the Social War	88 Mithridates of Pontus invades the provinces of Asia and Greece, destroying Delos. Defeated by Sulla, he retires to Pontus
88–82 Civil War between Sulla and Marius (d. 86) and his supporters	83 Temple of Jupiter Optimus Maximus destroyed by fire	82 Sack of Praeneste by Sulla	86 Sack of Athens by Sulla
82 Battle of the Colline Gate. Victory of Sulla		c. 80 Sanctuary of Fortuna Primigenia at Praeneste enlarged	
82–79 Sulla is dictator		80 Colony at Pompeii. Capitolium, amphitheater and covered theater built soon afterward, and Stabian Baths modernized	
		c. 80 Ponte di Nona on the Via Praenestina	
		c. 80 Temple of Jupiter Anxur at Tarracina rebuilt	
	78 Basilica Fulvia modernized (renamed Basilica Aemilia). Q. Lutatius Catulus orders construction of the Tabularium (Lucius Cornelius, architect)	c. 80 Temple of Hercules at Cori	
			74 Cyrenaica is constituted a province, to which Crete is added in 67. Bithynia is bequeathed to Rome, provoking Second Mithridatic War
70 Pompey and Crassus are consuls		70 Verres, governor of Sicily in 73, prosecuted by Cicero for pillage of the province	
	69 Rededication of the Temple of Jupiter Optimus Maximus		69 Lucullus inconclusively invades Armenia. First direct contact with Parthia

ROMAN HISTORY	ARCHITECTURE IN ROME AND OSTIA	ITALY AND THE WESTERN PROVINCES	GREECE AND THE EASTERN PROVINCES
67–62 Pompey is commander in the East	**c. 70–60(?)** Rectangular Temple in the Forum Boarium		**67–62** Pompey defeats Cilician pirates (67), defeats Mithridates and annexes western part of Pontus (66). Annexation of Syria and settlement in Judaea
63 Cicero is consul			
	62 Pons Fabricius		
61 Asiatic triumph of Pompey			
60 First Triumvirate (Pompey, Caesar, and Crassus)	**c. 60** Pons Cestius		
59 Caesar is consul			
58–57 Caesar's Gallic command		**58–51** Conquest of the Three Gauls	
55 Pompey and Crassus are consuls	**55** Pompey begins first permanent theater in Rome and Temple of Venus Victrix		
	54 Caesar plans Forum Julium. Basilica Aemilia restored by L. Aemilius Lepidus		
	53 Caesar plans to rebuild the Saepta in marble		**53** Defeat and death of Crassus at Carrhae in Mesopotamia
52 Pompey is sole consul	**52** Curia destroyed by fire		
	c. 50 Caesar plans a theater in the Circus Flaminius		**50–40** Athens, Tower of the Winds
49 Caesar crosses the Rubicon and marches on Rome. Pompey flees to Macedonia. Roman citizenship extended to the whole of North Italy		**After 49** Verona laid out afresh on level ground. First Porta dei Leoni	
			48 Caesar defeats Pompey at Pharsalus. Death of Pompey
	48–44 Extensive rebuilding in the Forum Romanum. Probable opening of the marble quarries at Luni (Carrara)		**48–46** Alexandria, Kaisareion **48–46** Antioch on the Orontes, Kaisareion

ROMAN HISTORY	ARCHITECTURE IN ROME AND OSTIA	ITALY AND THE WESTERN PROVINCES	GREECE AND THE EASTERN PROVINCES
		47–45 Defeat of Pompeians in Africa and Spain	
46 Caesar is named dictator for ten years	46 Dedication of the Temple of Venus Genetrix	46 Colonies at Arelate (Arles) and other sites in Provence 46 Carthage resettled	
45 Triumph of Caesar 44 Assassination of Caesar (March 15th) 43 Second Triumvirate (Marcus Antonius, M. Aemilius Lepidus, and Caesar's nephew and heir, Octavianus). Vitruvius serves as military engineer under Octavianus		44 Colony at Augusta Raurica (Augst) 43 Colony at Lugdunum (Lyon)	c. 45 Eleusis, Inner (Lesser) Propylaea 44 Corinth refounded
		42 Cisalpine Gaul becomes part of metropolitan Italy	42 Battle of Philippi. Brutus and Cassius commit suicide
40 Pact of Brindisi. Marcus Antonius receives command in the East, Octavianus in the West	After 39 Atrium Libertatis built by C. Asinius Pollio to house Rome's first public library	40–31 Series of inconclusive victories in Dalmatia, Illyricum, and Spain, the spoils of which in many cases went to finance public works in Rome	40 Parthians invade Syria
36 Defeat of Sextus Pompeius, son of Pompey, by Agrippa, who thereby secures command of the sea	36 Regia rebuilt by Cnaeus Domitius Calvinus. (first building in Rome known to have been built of Carrara marble) 33 Aqua Julia built by Agrippa as part of an extensive program of public works (roads, water supply, flood control, drainage) After 33 Temple of Diana on the Aventine restored by Lucius Cornificius		37–35 Marcus Antonius campaigns unsuccessfully against the Parthians. Marries Cleopatra, queen of Egypt
31 Battle of Actium and death of Marcus Antonius and Cleopatra 31–23 Octavianus is consul continuously	30 First stone amphitheater in Rome, built by Statilius Taurus c. 30 Porticus Philippi and Temple of Hercules Musarum restored	c. 30–20 Glanum (Saint-Rémy-de-Provence), Monument of the Julii	30 Annexation of Egypt

ROMAN HISTORY	ARCHITECTURE IN ROME AND OSTIA	ITALY AND THE WESTERN PROVINCES	GREECE AND THE EASTERN PROVINCES
27 Octavianus receives proconsular power for ten years and the title of Augustus in January. Effective establishment of the principate	29 Dedication of Temple of Divus Julius. Dedication of Curia Julia. Arch of Augustus in the Forum Romanum, in its original form (Arcus Actiacus) 28 Dedication of Temple of Apollo Palatinus c. 28 Mausoleum of Augustus begun	27–19 Subjugation of the Cantabrians in northwestern Spain	25 Annexation of Galatia
	Soon after 27 Vitruvius completes his treatise on architecture	27 Arch at Ariminum (Rimini)	
	25 Dedication of Agrippa's Pantheon c. 25 Restoration of Temple of Saturn by C. Munatius Plancus	c. 26 Colony at Augusta Taurinorum (Turin) 25 Colony at Augusta Emerita (Merida) in Spain	
23 Augustus receives the *imperium maius* (a controlling authority in all provinces) and tribunician power. Death of Marcellus, nephew and prospective heir of Augustus		24 Colony at Augusta Praetoria (Aosta), permitting control of the St. Bernard passes	
21 Marriage of Agrippa and Julia, daughter of Augustus		c. 21–20 L. Cornelius Balbus campaigns in southern Libya c. 20–16 Augustus and Agrippa active in Gaul	22 Province of Cyprus created 20 Peace with Parthia. The standards captured at Carrhae restored. Establishment of a system of small client kingdoms around the province of Syria. Palmyra comes within the Roman orbit
	19 Arch in the Forum Romanum enlarged in honor of the Parthian settlement (Arcus Parthicus). Aqua Virgo completed. Baths of Agrippa, first public baths in Rome		

ROMAN HISTORY	ARCHITECTURE IN ROME AND OSTIA	ITALY AND THE WESTERN PROVINCES	GREECE AND THE EASTERN PROVINCES
		16 Gates at Augustodunum (Autun)	
		16 Refoundation of Nemausus (Nîmes): the Porte d'Auguste, followed by the Pont du Gard, and (c. A.D. 2–6) the Maison Carrée	16 Colony at Heliopolis (Baalbek). The rebuilding of the sanctuary, begun probably under Augustus, continues until the early third century A.D.
15 Adoption of Drusus and Tiberius, stepsons of Augustus	Before 12 Ostia, theater and Piazzale of the Corporations built; forum extended	Pacification of the central Alpine tribes; creation of the province of Rhaetia 15 Annexation of the kingdom of Noricum in the eastern Alps	c. 15 Athens, Odeion of Agrippa
	13 Ara Pacis decreed. Theater of Lucius Cornelius Balbus, the last major monument in Rome to be dedicated by a private individual	15–9 Conquest of Pannonians and Dalmatians and creation of the province of Illyricum. Roman frontiers advance to the middle Danube	13–12 Philae (Egypt), Temple of Augustus
12 Death of Agrippa	12 Pyramid of Cestius 12–11 Completion of the theater projected by Caesar, dedicated in the name of Marcellus	12–9 Drusus campaigns beyond the Rhine in Germany	12–2 Athens, Forum of Caesar and Augustus
9 Death of Drusus	9 Ara Pacis dedicated	9 Gate at Fanum Fortunae (Fano) 9–7 Tiberius campaigns in Germany 8 Market and earliest buildings in the Old Forum (Forum Vetus) at Leptis Magna 8 Arch at Segusio (Susa)	
	7 Completion of the Diribitorium, begun by Agrippa, with the widest span of timber roofing yet achieved		
6 B.C. Tiberius withdraws to Rhodes		6 B.C. Victory monument at La Turbie (above Monte Carlo)	c. 6 Annexation of Pisidia. Foundation of military colonies, including Antioch
	5 Aqua Marcia restored. Porta Tiburtina		
			4 Death of Herod the Great 4–3 Ephesus, archway of Mazaeus and Mithridates at entrance to agora
	2 B.C. Temple of Mars Ultor dedicated (Forum Augustum still incomplete). Aqua Alsietina built		

ROMAN HISTORY	ARCHITECTURE IN ROME AND OSTIA	ITALY AND THE WESTERN PROVINCES	GREECE AND THE EASTERN PROVINCES
		A.D. 1 Theater at Leptis Magna	c. 30 B.C.–A.D. 14 Corinth, agora, basilica, south stoa, and temples
		c. 2–6 Roman military control established along the lower Danube (future province of Moesia)	
A.D 2 Death of Lucius Caesar, grandson and adopted son of Augustus		c. 2–6 Maison Carrée at Nemausus (Nimes)	
		2–14 Temple of Rome and Augustus at Pola, in Istria	Between 4 and 14 Ephesus, aqueduct of C. Sextilius Pollio
4 Death of Gaius Caesar, grandson and adopted son of Augustus. Tiberius recalled and adopted as heir and successor to Augustus		6–9 Revolt in Pannonia, quelled by Tiberius. Province of Pannonia established	6 Annexation of Judaea
	A.D. 6 Rededication of Temple of Castor and Pollux, rebuilt by Tiberius	9 Defeat of P. Quinctilius Varus and annihilation of three legions in Germany. Frontier stabilized along the Rhine	
	10 Rededication of Temple of Concord, rebuilt by Tiberius		
JULIO-CLAUDIAN DYNASTY (14–68) 14 Death of Augustus. Succeeded by Tiberius (14–37), whose heirs are his son, Drusus, and his nephew and adopted son, Germanicus	After 14 Temple of Divus Augustus. Domus Tiberiana, the first of a number of enlargements of the imperial residence on the Palatine. Temple of Rome and Augustus at Ostia. Villas on Capri 16 Arch in the Forum Romanum	14–17 Germanicus campaigns in Germany 14–19 Arch at Mediolanum Santonum (Saintes) 14–19 Temple of Rome and Augustus at Leptis Magna 15 Creation of united provinces of Moesia, Macedonia, and Achaea 17–24 Revolt of Tacfarinas in Africa	15 Temple of Jupiter at Damascus already well advanced 17 Severe earthquake in province of Asia. Cities given assistance by Tiberius 17–18 Germanicus in the East. Cappadocia and Commagene annexed
19 Death of Germanicus. Ascendancy of the Praetorian praefect, Sejanus	19 Arches of Germanicus and Drusus in the Forum Augustum 21–23 Castra Praetoria built. For the first time troops are stationed in the capital 22 Ara Pietatis Augustae decreed	After 21 Arch at Arausio (Orange)	

ROMAN HISTORY	ARCHITECTURE IN ROME AND OSTIA	ITALY AND THE WESTERN PROVINCES	GREECE AND THE EASTERN PROVINCES
23 Death of Drusus			
26–37 Tiberius withdraws to Capri	**26–37** Virtual cessation of public building in the capital		
31 Conspiracy and death of Sejanus			
			32 Temple of Bel at Palmyra dedicated
37–41 Gaius Caligula is emperor	**37–41** Domus Tiberiana extended. Much domestic building on recently annexed imperial estates. Iseum established in the Campus Martius **38** Aqua Claudia begun		
41–54 Claudius is emperor	**41–54** Artificial harbor at Portus. Granaries at Ostia. Draining of the Lago Fucino	**41–43** Annexation of Mauretania and creation of provinces of Caesariensis and Tingitana	**41–54** Miletus, Baths of Capito Corinth, Julian and south basilicas, colonnaded street Perge, *palaestra*
	43 Ara Pietatis Augustae dedicated	**43** Invasion of Britain	
		44 Province of Britain established **c. 45** Virunum becomes capital of Noricum. Temple of Claudius on the Magdalensberg left unfinished **46** Annexation of Thrace	
	50–60 Underground Basilica outside the Porta Maggiore **51** Arch along the Via Flaminia, commemorating British victories **52** Aqua Claudia completed. Porta Maggiore	**50** Colonia Agrippensis (Cologne) founded on site of former legionary camp	
		53 Old Forum (Forum Vetus) at Leptis Magna completed	

ROMAN HISTORY	ARCHITECTURE IN ROME AND OSTIA	ITALY AND THE WESTERN PROVINCES	GREECE AND THE EASTERN PROVINCES
54–68 Nero is emperor	**54–c. 60** Nero's family villa at Anzio modernized. Villa at Subiaco **59** Macellum Magnum on the Caelian hill **c. 60–64** Domus Transitoria **62** Severe earthquake at Pompeii **62–64** Baths and *gymnasium* of Nero **64** Great Fire of Rome **64–68** Domus Aurea (architects Severus and Celer)	**60** Revolt of Queen Boudicca in Britain	**54–68** Restoration of Theater of Dionysus at Athens. Construction of stage of theater at Ephesus **63** War in Armenia against the Parthians. Armenia established (66) as a client kingdom
68–69 Year of the Four Emperors. Military revolts in Spain, Africa, Gaul, and Germany. Suicide of Nero. Civil War, from which Vespasian, military governor of Judaea, emerges victorious			**66** Revolt in Judaea
FLAVIAN DYNASTY (69–96) **69–79** Vespasian is emperor	**69** Temple of Jupiter Optimus Maximus burned **69–79** Temple of Divus Claudius (Claudianum) completed. Templum Pacis. Colosseum **75** Rededication of Temple of Jupiter Optimus Maximus	**70–80** Amphitheater at Puteoli (Pozzuoli) begun **70–80** Forum at Verulamium (St. Albans) **73** Capitolium at Brixia (Brescia) **73–74** Agri Decumates between upper Rhine and Danube annexed, bringing the northern frontier of the Empire to its definitive form **77–84** Agricola's Scottish campaigns	**70** Capture and destruction of Jerusalem by Titus. Spoils dedicated in the Templum Pacis in Rome
77 Publication of Pliny the Elder's *Natural History* **79–81** Titus is emperor	**79–81** Temple of Divus Vespasianus begun **80** Inauguration of Colosseum while still incomplete. Baths of Titus. Fire again destroys Temple of Jupiter Optimus Maximus, as well as many historic buildings erected in the Campus Martius	**79** Destruction of Pompeii and Herculaneum **79–81** Completion of amphitheater at Pola Other notable Flavian monuments: Verona, Porta dei Borsari, second Porta dei Leoni, Amphitheater(?); Nemausus (Nîmes), amphitheater; Arelate (Arles), amphitheater	

ROMAN HISTORY	ARCHITECTURE IN ROME AND OSTIA	ITALY AND THE WESTERN PROVINCES	GREECE AND THE EASTERN PROVINCES
81–96 Domitian is emperor	**81–96** The architect Rabirius is active. Temple of Jupiter Optimus Maximus on the Capitoline restored. Temple of Divus Vespasianus completed. Arch of Titus. Porticus Divorum built, and many older buildings rebuilt in the Campus Martius. Forum Transitorium and Temple of Minerva (dedicated by Nerva). Domus Augustana (architect Rabirius; in use by 92). Villa at Albanum (Albano)	**81–96** Headquarters of the African legion advances to Lambaesis (Algeria) **85–89** Fighting on the lower Danube. Legionary fortress established at Aquincum (Budapest)	
96 Domitian assassinated. End of the Flavian dynasty	**92–96** Stadium of Domitian (Piazza Navona). Ostia, beginning of major redevelopment		c. 90 Gerasa (Jordan), South Theater **96** Ephesus, Temple of Domitian
DYNASTY BY ADOPTION (96–193), THE LATER MEMBERS OF WHICH WERE KNOWN AS THE ANTONINES **96–January 98** Nerva is emperor	**96–97** Dedication of Forum Transitorium **97** Frontinus, water commissioner (*Curator Aquarum*), writes treatise on the aqueducts of Rome	**96** Military colony at Cuicul (Djemila, Algeria)	
98–117 Trajan is emperor. The first non-Italian emperor, born at Italica in southern Spain	**98–117** The architect Apollodorus of Damascus is active. Ostia, aqueduct, basilica and curia, warehouses. Huge inner basin added to the Claudian harbor at Portus	**98** Legionary fortress established at Vindobona (Vienna) **100** Military colony at Thamugadi (Timgad, Algeria) **101–102** First Dacian War **105** Bridge of Apollodorus over the Danube **105–107** Second Dacian War. Dacia annexed and province of Dacia established, with Sarmizegetusa as capital	**98–117** Ephesus, Nymphaeum in honor of Trajan's father; Humeitepe Baths. Pergamon, Trajaneum c. 100 "Kiosk" at Philae (Egypt)
101–102, 106–107 Trajan campaigns on the Danube frontier		**106** Bridge over the Tagus at Alcántara	**106** Annexation of Arabia, including Petra, and creation of province of Arabia, with capital at Bostra. Bostra laid out with colonnaded streets

ROMAN HISTORY	ARCHITECTURE IN ROME AND OSTIA	ITALY AND THE WESTERN PROVINCES	GREECE AND THE EASTERN PROVINCES
	109 Baths of Trajan inaugurated (architect Apollodorus) 112–113 Dedication of Forum and Column of Trajan (architect Apollodorus) 113 Rededication of (restored) Temple of Venus Genetrix	109 Victory monument (Tropaeum Traiani) at Adamklissi in the Dobrudja (Rumania)	111–113 Pliny the Younger is governor of Bithynia. Letters to Trajan concerning local architectural problems
114–117 Trajan campaigns in the East 117 Death of Trajan in Cilicia 117–138 Hadrian is emperor 120 (or 121)–123 Hadrian in Gaul, the Germanies, Britain, and Spain 123–127 Hadrian in Asia Minor (123–125) and Greece (125–127) 127–128 Hadrian in Rome except for a short visit to Africa 128–131 Hadrian in Athens, southern Asia Minor, Syria (129), and Egypt (130) 138–161 Antoninus Pius is emperor. Adopts M. Aurelius and L. Verus (138)	117–138 Large parts of Ostia rebuilt, including Capitolium (117–127) and whole quarter between forum and river; quarter to the east of the theater, including Baths of Neptune and barracks of the Vigiles (before 137); House of the Triple Windows and Baths of the Seven Sages. Mausoleum of Hadrian and Pons Aelius built c. 118 Temple of Divus Traianus begun. Pantheon begun 118–138 Villa near Tibur (Tivoli) 125–128 Pantheon completed 135 Temple of Venus and Rome consecrated 139 Mausoleum of Hadrian completed 141 Temple of Faustina begun (rededicated to Antoninus and Faustina in 161) 145 Temple of Divus Hadrianus (Hadrianeum) completed	114 Arch at Beneventum (Benevento) 115 Arch at Ancona 116 Arch and new forum at Mactar (Tunisia) 122–130 Hadrian's Wall in Britain 123 Hadrianic Baths at Leptis Magna Some early second-century buildings: Autun, Temple of Janus; Périgueux, Temple of Vesunna; Segovia, aqueduct; Nîmes, Temple of Diana; Lambaesis, Praetorium Some notable mid-second century buildings: Carthage, Antonine Baths (143–162); Cuicul, Market of Cosinius; Sufetula, forum and basilica; Leptis Magna, Arch of Antoninus Pius; Bagacum (Bavai), forum; Nicopolis-ad-Istrum (Bulgaria), forum	114–117 Invasion of Parthia. Armenia (114) and Mesopotamia (116) are annexed as provinces 115 North Gate at Gerasa 115–118 Revolt of Jews in Cyrenaica, spreading to Egypt, Cyprus, and Palestine 117 Abandonment of Trajan's policy of expansion. Frontiers re-established on approximately the same lines as before 114 Some notable Hadrianic buildings: Athens, Arch, Library, completion of the Olympieion; Aezani (Phrygia), temple; Cyzicus, Temple of Hadrian; Ephesus, Temple of Hadrian (c. 117–120), Library of Celsus (completed c. 135); Aphrodisias, baths; Attaleia (Antalya), city gate; Perge, colonnaded street and nymphaea; Side, temples; Palmyra, the earliest colonnaded streets, agora, theater; Gerasa, South Gate; Luxor, Temple of Serapis (126) 130 Colony of Aelia Capitolina founded on site of Jerusalem. Resulting revolt suppressed and Judaea becomes province of Syria Palaestina 130 Foundation of Antinoöpolis (Egypt) Some notable mid-second century buildings: Pergamon, Asklepieion; Smyrna, agora; Sardis, baths; Ephesus, Baths of Vedius; Perge, theater; Palmyra, Temple of Ba'alshamin (begun in 131)

ROMAN HISTORY

161–180
Marcus Aurelius is emperor. Lucius Verus is co-emperor until his death in 169

168–180
M. Aurelius almost continuously occupied with warfare along the Danube frontier

175–176
M. Aurelius briefly in Syria

180–192
Commodus, son of M. Aurelius, is emperor (co-emperor since 177)

192
Commodus assassinated (December 31st). Brief period of civil war

SEVERAN DYNASTY (193–235)

193–211
Septimius Severus, native of Leptis Magna, is emperor. Marries Julia Domna, daughter of the hereditary high priest of Emesa in Syria

197
Septimius Severus campaigns against the Parthians

211–217
Caracalla is emperor

214–215
Warfare along the Danube frontier

217–222
Elagabalus is emperor

222–235
Severus Alexander is emperor

ARCHITECTURE IN ROME AND OSTIA

161–162
Column of Antoninus Pius

176
Panels of a triumphal arch, now in the Museo Capitolino

180
Panels of a triumphal arch, used on the Arch of Constantine

180–193
Column of M. Aurelius

After 193
Extensive additions to the Domus Augustana; Porticus Octaviae rebuilt (203); Septizodium (203); Camp of the Equites Singulares (193–197); Camp of the Legio II Parthica at Albanum (Albano)

203
Arch in the Forum Romanum

204
Arch of the Argentarii

c. 205–208
Marble plan of Rome

211–217
Temple of Serapis on the Quirinal

212–216
Baths of Caracalla

217–222
Temple of Sol Invictus Elagabalus (god of Emesa) on the Palatine; Amphitheatrum Castrense

217–235
Iseum Campense restored

222
Temple of Elagabalus rededicated to Jupiter Ultor

227
Aqua Alexandriana, the last new aqueduct; restoration (or rebuilding) of Baths of Nero

ITALY AND THE WESTERN PROVINCES

Some notable buildings of the later second century:

Timgad, Capitolium; "Arch of Trajan"; Cuicul, theater (161), Imperial baths (183); Thugga, Capitolium (166–167); Thuburbo Maius, Capitolium (168); Leptis Magna, Arch of M. Aurelius (also many earlier buildings—temples, theater, baths—restored in marble); Sabratha, theater, temples; Oea (Tripoli), arch (163); Vesontio (Besançon), Porta Nigra (c. 167); Odessos (Varna, Bulgaria), baths

Some notable Severan buildings: Leptis Magna, arch, basilica, forum, colonnaded street, new harbor; Thamugadi, North Baths, Market of Sertius; Cuicul, new forum, arch (216), and temple of Severan family (229); Mactar, baths; Theveste, Arch of Caracalla and temple

GREECE AND THE EASTERN PROVINCES

162–166
Renewed trouble with the Parthians. Mesopotamia becomes a Roman protectorate

Some notable buildings of the later second century:
Ephesus, Serapaeum (?); Aspendos, theater; Athens, Odeion of Herodes Atticus (160–74)
Gerasa, Temple of Zeus (163), Temple of Artemis, North Theater (161–166), West Baths, *gymnasium*
Palmyra, colonnaded streets

c. 200
Garrison established at Dura-Europos. Palace of the area commander (*Dux Ripae*). Synagogue and Christian church (before c. 256)

Some notable Severan buildings: Ancyra, Baths of Caracalla; Ephesus, baths by Magnesia Gate, upper order of stage building; Sardis, entrance to Antonine bath building remodeled ("Marble Court"); Pergamon, Kizil Avlu (or later); Baalbek, Round Temple (?); Palmyra, triple arch and adjoining colonnaded street

c. 226
Parthians in Persia replaced by new dynasty, the Sassanians. Ardashir invades Mesopotamia and Cappadocia (230) and threatens Antioch

ROMAN HISTORY	ARCHITECTURE IN ROME AND OSTIA	ITALY AND THE WESTERN PROVINCES	GREECE AND THE EASTERN PROVINCES
235–275 Years of Imperial crisis. Succession of short-lived emperors, nominated by the armies, coupled with devastating barbarian invasions from across the Rhine and Danube, reaching far into Gaul, North Italy, the Danubian countries, Greece, and Asia Minor. The emperors include: Maximinus (235–238), the first of a number of soldier-emperors from the Balkan provinces; Gordian III (238–244); Philippus (244–249), an Arabian; Gallienus (253–268), sole emperor from 260 to 268; Claudius Gothicus (268–270); Aurelianus (270–275)	**235–271** No significant public building in Rome Arch of Gallienus (an Augustan monument rededicated) Licinian Gardens (pavilion is later)	**235–275** Almost continuous incursions by barbarian tribes. Precarious maintenance of Roman authority except in Gaul, where Postumus (260–268) and Tetricus (270–274) establish an independent Gallic Empire. In 251 the Goths defeat and kill the emperor Decius; in 254 they reach Thessalonica, and in 256–257 they devastate western Asia Minor. In 267 the Heruli sack Athens. In 275 northern Gaul is devastated **274** Roman garrison withdraws from Dacia **276** Aurelian and Probus re-establish Roman authority Towns throughout Gaul, North Italy, and the Balkan Peninsula throw up hasty defenses, but otherwise no significant public building in the European provinces Some building in Africa, on a limited scale: **238–244(?)** Amphitheater at Thysdrus (El-Djem, Tunisia) **253–268** Licinian Baths at Thugga (Dougga, Tunisia)	**235** Persian aggression temporarily halted by Philippus (244–249) **250–260** Shapur I of Persia destroys Dura (c. 256) and captures Roman emperor Valerian (260) **260–273** Eastern frontier effectively held against Persians by Odaenathus (d. 267) and Zenobia of Palmyra, who extend rule over Asia Minor and Egypt. In 271 Zenobia declares independence, but is defeated and captured by Aurelian, who reestablishes central Roman authority Very little public building:
	271 Walls of Rome begun **274** Temple of Sol Invictus **283** Curia destroyed by fire		**244–249** Philippus lays out new town of Philippopolis (Shēhba) in Arabia **258–269** Walls of Nicaea (Iznik)
DIOCLETIAN AND THE TETRARCHY **284–305** Diocletian, a Dalmatian, is emperor **285** Maximian is nominated *Caesar* and in 286 co-emperor (*Augustus*) **293** Establishment of the Tetrarchy. Diocletian and Maximian are *Augusti*, Galerius and Constantius Chlorus are *Caesares* **303** Diocletian visits Rome		Maximian's principal residence at Milan Constantius is resident at Trier: Audience Hall of palace; Imperial baths (Kaiserthermen); Porta Nigra Imperial residence at Sirmium **287** Britain independent under Carausius	Diocletian's principal residence at Nicomedia (Izmit); also Antioch Galerius is resident at Thessalonica: Mausoleum; remains of palace and hippodrome
	298–306 Baths of Diocletian **303** Restored Curia rededicated. Arcus Novus in the Via Lata		**286** Philae (Egypt), arch

ROMAN HISTORY	ARCHITECTURE IN ROME AND OSTIA	ITALY AND THE WESTERN PROVINCES	GREECE AND THE EASTERN PROVINCES
	c. 300 Pavilion in Licinian Gardens (Temple of Minerva Medica; remodeled c. 320)		
305 Diocletian and Maximian abdicate. A contested succession leaves Maxentius (son of Maximian, but a usurper) in control of Rome and Italy, Constantius of Gaul and Britain, and Galerius and Maximinus Daia of the East	After 300 Series of wealthy private houses at Ostia (of Cupid, of Fortuna Annonaria, etc.)	305 Diocletian retires to palace at Split (Spalato) in Dalmatia	
306 Death of Constantius, who is succeeded by his son Constantine (the Great)	307 Fire, after which Temple of Venus and Rome is rebuilt, Basilica Nova and Temple of Romulus are begun; completed by Constantine	306 Britain reconquered by Constantius	
310 Death of Maximian	306–312 Circus and Mausoleum of Maxentius		
311 Death of Galerius			
312 Constantine defeats and kills Maxentius at the Battle of Pons Mulvius			
313 Edict of Milan. Empire divided between Constantine in the West and Licinius (Augustus since 308) in the East. Christianity legalized	315 Arch of Constantine completed c. 315 Baths of Constantine After 313 Work begun on cathedral church of St. John Lateran and on principal martyr shrines (St. Peter's Basilica Apostolorum, first basilica of San Lorenzo, etc.) c. 320 Mausoleum of Helena	c. 320(?) Villa at Piazza Armerina	
324 Defeat and death of Licinius. Constantine becomes sole emperor. Imperial residence transferred to Constantinople	325–350 Mausoleum of Constantina		324 Foundation of Constantinople 325 Council of Nicaea 330 Formal dedication of Constantinople as the "New Rome"
	331 Basilica of Junius Bassus		

SELECTED BIBLIOGRAPHY

GENERAL WORKS

BIANCHI BANDINELLI, R., *Rome, the Centre of Power: Roman Art to A.D. 200,* London, 1970.

———, *Rome, the Late Empire,* London, 1971.

BOËTHIUS, A., and WARD-PERKINS, J. B., *Etruscan and Roman Architecture,* Harmondsworth, 1970.

BROWN, F. E., *Roman Architecture,* New York, 1961.

CREMA, L., *L'architettura romana,* Turin, 1959.

DEICHMANN, F. W., *Studien zur Architektur Konstantinopels im 5. und 6. Jahrhundert nach Christus,* Baden-Baden, 1956.

Enciclopedia dell'arte antica classica e orientale, 7 vols., Rome, 1958–66 (Supplement, 1971).

HEILMEYER, W.-D., *Korinthische Normalkapitelle: Studien zur Geschichte der römischen Architektur-dekoration,* Heidelberg, 1960.

KRAUTHEIMER, R., *Early Christian and Byzantine Architecture,* Harmondsworth, 1965.

LUGLI, G., "Architettura Italica," in *Memorie dell'Accademia Nazionale dei Lincei,* II, 1949.

MARTIN, R., "Architettura greca," in *Architettura Mediterranea Preromana,* Milan, 1972.

RAKOB, F., "Römische Architektur," in *Das römische Weltreich* (*Propyläen Kunstgeschichte,* II, T. Kraus, ed.), Berlin, 1967.

RIVOIRA, G. T., *Roman Architecture,* Oxford, 1925.

SCHMIEDT, G., *Atlante Aerofotografico delle Sedi Umane in Italia,* Florence, 1970.

VITRUVIUS, *De architectura* (English translation, F. Granger, Loeb ed.), 2 vols., London, 1929, 1934.

VOLBACH, W. F., and HIRMER, M., *Early Christian Art,* London, 1961.

WHEELER, R. E. M., *Roman Art and Architecture,* London, 1964.

TOWN PLANNING

CASTAGNOLI, F., *Orthogonal Planning in Antiquity,* Cambridge (Mass.), 1972.

MANSUELLI, G. A., *Architettura e città,* Bologna, 1970.

TACITUS, *Annales,* XV, 43 (for Nero's town-planning regulations).

WARD-PERKINS, J. B., *Cities of Ancient Greece and Italy: Planning in Classical Antiquity,* New York, 1974.

BUILDING MATERIALS AND CONSTRUCTION TECHNIQUES

BLAKE, M. E., *Ancient Roman Construction in Italy from the Prehistoric Period to Augustus,* Washington, D.C., 1947.

———, *Roman Construction in Italy from Tiberius through the Flavians,* Washington, D. C., 1959.

———, and TAYLOR BISHOP, D., *Roman Construction in Italy from Nerva through the Antonines,* Philadelphia, 1973.

BLOCH, H., *I bolli laterizi e la storia dell'edilizia romana,* Rome, 1947.

BRUZZA, L., "Iscrizioni dei marmi grezzi," in *Annali dell' Istituto di Corrispondenza Archeologica,* XLII, 1870.

CHOISY, A., *L'Art de bâtir chez les romains,* Paris, 1873.

COZZO, G., *Ingegneria romana,* Rome, 1928 (reprint, 1970).

FRANK, T., *Roman Buildings of the Republic: an attempt to date them from their materials,* American Academy in Rome, 1924.

GNOLI, R., *Marmora Romana,* Rome, 1971.

LUGLI, G., *La tecnica edilizia romana con particolare riguardo a Roma e Lazio,* 2 vols., Rome, 1957.

WARD-PERKINS, J. B., "Tripolitania and the Marble Trade," in *Journal of Roman Studies,* XLI, 1951.

———, "Notes on the Structure and Building Methods of Early Byzantine Architecture," in D. Talbot-Rice (ed.), *The Great Palace of the Byzantine Emperors,* II, Edinburgh, 1958.

———, "Marmo: uso e commercio in Roma," in *Enciclopedia dell'arte antica...,* IV, Rome, 1961.

BUILDING TYPES

DE FRANCISCIS, A., and PANE, R., *Mausolei romani in Campania,* Naples, 1957.

FRONTINUS, *De aquaeductis urbis Romae* (English translation, C. E. Bennett, Loeb ed.), London, 1950.

GAZZOLA, P., *Ponti romani,* Florence, 1963.

GRIMAL, P., *Les jardins romains,* Paris, 1943.

KÄHLER, H., "Triumphbogen (Ehrenbogen)," in Pauly-Wissowa, *Real-Enzyklopädie,* 2, VII, A. I., 1939.

———, "Die römischen Torburgen der frühen Kaiserzeit," in *Jahrbuch des deutschen Archäologischen Instituts,* 57, 1942.

———, *Der römische Tempel,* Berlin, 1970.

NEUERBERG, N., *L'Architettura delle fontane e dei ninfei nell'Italia antica,* Naples, 1965.

RICKMAN, G. E., *Roman Granaries and Store Buildings,* Cambridge (Eng.), 1971.

TAMM, B., *Auditorium and Palatium,* Stockholm, 1963.

For articles on individual building types, with detailed bibliographies and in many cases lists of known examples, see also *Enciclopedia dell'arte antica...* under the following headings: *anfiteatro* (G. Forni, I, 1958); *arco onorario e trionfale* (M. Pallottino, I, 1958); *basilica* (G. Carettoni, II, 1959); *biblioteca* (H. Kähler, II, 1959), *circo e ippodromo* (G. Forni, II, 1959); *magazzino* (*horreum*) (R. Staccioli, IV, 1961); *mercato* (*macellum, emporium*) (R. Staccioli, IV, 1961); *monumento funerario* (G. A. Mansuelli, V, 1963); *ponte* (J. Briegleb, VI, 1965); *teatro* (G. Forni, Suppl., 1971); *terme* (*thermae, balnea*) (H. Kähler, VII, 1966).

ROME: GENERAL WORKS

ASHBY, T., *The Aqueducts of Ancient Rome,* Oxford, 1935.

———, and PLATNER, S. B., *A Topographical Dictionary of Ancient Rome,* Oxford, 1929.

BRIZZI, M., *Roma: i monumenti antichi,* Rome, 1973.

CARETTONI, G., COLINI, A. M., COZZA, L., and GATTI, G., *La pianta marmorea di Roma antica,* Rome, 1960.

COARELLI, F., "L'ara di Domizio Enobarbo e la cultura artistica in Roma nel II sec. a. C.," in *Dialoghi di Archeologia,* II, 1968.

———, *Roma,* Milan, 1971.

DEICHMANN, F. W., "Untersuchungen an spätrömischen Rundbauten in Rom," in *Archäologischer Anzeiger,* 1941.

GROS, P., "Hermodorus et Vitruve," in *Mélanges de l'Ecole Française de Rome,* LXXXV, 1973.

LUGLI, G., *Roma antica: il centro monumentale,* Rome, 1946.

MACDONALD, W. L., *The Architecture of the Roman Empire,* I, New Haven, 1965.

NASH, E., *Pictorial Dictionary of Ancient Rome* (rev. ed.), London, 1968.

SHIPLEY, F. W., "The Building Activities of the Viri Triumphales from 44 B.C. to 14 A.D.," in *Memoirs of the American Academy in Rome,* IX, 1931.

———, *Agrippa's Building Activities in Rome,* St. Louis, 1933.

STRONG, D. E., "Late Hadrianic Architectural Ornament in Rome," in *Papers of the British School at Rome,* XXI, 1953.

ROME: INDIVIDUAL BUILDINGS

BARTOLI, A., *Curia Senatus: lo scavo e il restauro,* Florence, 1963.

BOËTHIUS, A., *The Golden House of Nero,* University of Michigan, 1960.

BRILLIANT, R., "The Arch of Septimius Severus in the Forum Romanum," in *Memoirs of the American Academy in Rome,* XXIX, Rome, 1967.

COLINI, A. M., *Stadium Domitiani,* Istituto di Studi Romani, 1943.

DE FINE LICHT, K., *The Rotunda in Rome: a Study of Hadrian's Pantheon,* Copenhagen, 1966.

GIULIANO, A., *Arco di Costantino,* Milan, 1955.

GRANT, M., *The Roman Forum,* London, 1970.

LEON, C., *Die Bauenornamentik des Trajansforums,* Vienna-Cologne, 1971.

MINOPRIO, A., "A Restoration of the Basilica of Constantine," in *Papers of the British School at Rome,* XII, 1932.

MORETTI, G., *Ara Pacis Augustae,* Rome, 1948.

RAKOB, F., and HEILMEYER, W.-D., *Der Rundtempel am Tiber in Rom,* Mainz, 1973.

RICHMOND, I. A., *The City Wall of Imperial Rome,* Oxford, 1930.

SIMON, E., *Ara Pacis Augustae,* Tübingen, 1967.

WATAGHIN CANTINO, G., *La Domus Augustana,* Turin, 1966.

ZANKER, P., *Forum Augustum,* Tübingen, 1958.

———, "Das Trajansforum in Rom," in *Archäologischer Anzeiger,* 1970.

———, *Forum Romanum. Die Neugestaltung durch Augustus,* Tübingen, 1972.

CENTRAL AND SOUTHERN ITALY

The Sanctuaries of Republican Latium

DELBRUECK, R., *Hellenistische Bauten in Latium,* 2 vols., Strassburg, 1907–12.

FASOLO, F., and GULLINI, G., *Il Santuario di Fortuna Primigenia a Palestrina,* Rome, 1953.

GIULIANI, C. F., *Tibur* (*Forma Italiae,* I,7), Rome, 1970.

Ostia

BECATTI, G., "Case Ostiensi del Tardo Impero," in *Bollettino d'Arte,* XXXIII, 1948.

CALZA, G., "Topografia generale," in *Scavi di Ostia,* I, Rome, 1953.

CALZA, R., and NASH, E., *Ostia,* Florence, 1959.

MEIGGS, R., *Roman Ostia,* Oxford, 1960.

Hadrian's Villa

AURIGEMMA, S., *Villa Adriana,* Rome, 1962.

KÄHLER, H., *Hadrian und seine Villa bei Tivoli,* Berlin, 1950.

Pompeii and Herculaneum

For comprehensive bibliographies of these two sites, see A. MAIURI, "Ercolano" and "Pompei" in *Enciclopedia dell' arte antica…,* III, 1960, and VI, 1965.

MAIURI, A., *La Villa dei Misteri,* Rome, 1931.

———, *Ercolano: i nuovi scavi (1927–1958),* Rome, 1958.

MAU, A., *Pompeji in Leben und Kunst,* Leipzig, 1908.

SPINAZZOLA, V., *Pompei alla luce degli scavi di Via dell'Abbondanza,* Rome, 1953.

Other Central and South Italian Sites

BROWN, F. E., "Cosa 1" and "Cosa 2," in *Memoirs of the American Academy in Rome,* XX, 1950, and XXVI, 1960.

MERTENS, J., *Alba Fucens,* vols. 1 and 2, Institut Historique Belge de Rome, 1969.

———, *Ordona,* vols. 1 and 3, Institut Historique Belge de Rome, 1965 and 1971.

ROTILI, M., *L'Arco di Traiano a Benevento,* Rome, 1972.

NORTH ITALY AND THE WESTERN PROVINCES

General

WARD-PERKINS, J. B., "From Republic to Empire: reflections on the early provincial architecture of the Roman West," in *Journal of Roman Studies,* LX, 1970.

North Italy

BAROCELLI, P., *Aosta,* Ivrea, 1936.

BESCHI, L., *Verona romana: i monumenti in Verona e il suo territorio,* Istituto per gli Studi Storici Veronesi, I, 1960.

CALDERINI, A., "Milano romana fino al trionfo del Cristianesimo" and "Milano durante il Basso Impero," in *Storia di Milano,* Milan, 1953.

———, CHIERICI, G., and CECCHELLI, C., *La Basilica di S. Lorenzo Maggiore in Milano,* Milan, 1951.

FOGOLARI, G., "Verona: il restauro della Porta dei Leoni," in *Notizie degli Scavi* (Supplemento), 1965.

KÄHLER, H., "Die römische Stadttore von Verona," in *Jahrbuch des Deutschen Archäologischen Instituts,* L, 1935.

MIRABELLA ROBERTI, M., in *Storia di Brescia,* I, Brescia, 1963.

RICHMOND, I. A., "Augustan Gates at Torino and Spello," in *Papers of the British School at Rome,* XVI, 1932.

ZORZI, F., *et al., Verona e il suo territorio,* I, Verona, 1961.

The European Provinces

AMY, R., *et al.,* "L'Arc d'Orange" (Supplement XV to *Gallia*), Paris, 1962.

BOON, G. C., *Silchester: the Roman Town of Calleva,* Taunton, 1974.

FOUET, G., *La Villa Gallo-Romaine de Montmaurin* (Supplement XX to *Gallia*), Paris, 1969.

FRERE, S. S., *Britannia,* London, 1967.

GARCÍA Y BELLIDO, A., *Arte romano* (2nd ed.), Madrid, 1972.

GOSE, E., *Die Porta Nigra in Trier,* 2 vols., Berlin, 1969.

———, *Der gallo-römische Tempelbezirk in Altbachtal,* Mainz, 1972.

GRENIER, A., *Manuel d'archéologie gallo-romaine,* III: *L'Architecture* (Paris, 1958), and IV: *Les Monuments des eaux* (Paris, 1960).

KRENCKER, D., and KRÜGER, E., *Die Trierer Kaiserthermen,* Augsburg, 1929.

LAUR-BELART, R., *Führer durch Augusta Raurica,* Basel, 1948.

MANSUELLI, G. A., *Il monumento augusteo del 27 a. C.: nuove ricerche sull'Arco di Rimini,* republished from *Arte Antica e Moderna,* nos. 8 and 9, Bologna, 1960.

MARASOVIĆ, J. and T., *Diocletian Palace,* Zagreb, 1970.

RIVET, A. L. F., *The Roman Villa in Britain,* London, 1969.

ROLLAND, H., *Fouilles de Glanum* (Supplement I to *Gallia*), Paris, 1946.

———, *Le Mausolée de Glanum* (Supplement XXXI to *Gallia*), Paris, 1969.

RUESCH, W., "Die spätantike Kaiser-residenzen Trier in Lichte neuer Ausgrabungen," in *Archäologischer Anzeiger,* 1962.

Sirmium, vols. I and II, Belgrade, 1971.

North Africa

BALLU, A., *Les Ruines de Timgad (antique Thamugadi),* Paris, 1897.

———, *Les Ruines de Timgad: sept années de découvertes,* Paris, 1911.

BIANCHI BANDINELLI, R., ed., *Leptis Magna,* Rome, 1963.

COURTOIS, C., *Timgad: Antique Thamugadi,* Algiers, 1951.

GSELL, S., *Monuments antiques de l'Algérie,* 2 vols., Paris, 1901.

LESCHI, L., *Djemila: antique Cuicul,* Algiers, 1953.

LÉZINE, A., *Architecture romaine d'Afrique,* Tunis, n.d. (c. 1961).

PICARD, G.-C., *La Civilisation de l'Afrique romaine,* Paris, 1959.

REBUFFAT, R., "Maisons à peristyle de l'Afrique du Nord," in *Mélanges de l'Ecole Française de Rome,* 81, 1969.

ROMANELLI, P., *Topografia e Archeologia dell'Africa Romana,* Turin, 1970.

SQUARCIAPINO FLORIANI, M., *Leptis Magna,* Basel, 1966.

TOYNBEE, J. M. C., and WARD-PERKINS, J. B., "The Hunting Baths at Leptis Magna," in *Archaeologia,* XCIII, 1949.

WARD-PERKINS, J. B., "The Art of the Severan Age in the Light of Tripolitanian Discoveries," in *Proceedings of the British Academy,* XXXVII, 1951.

THE EASTERN PROVINCES

Greece

Ancient Corinth: a Guide to the Excavations (6th ed.), American School of Classical Studies at Athens, 1954.

Corinth: Results of the Excavations Conducted by the American School of Classical Studies at Athens, 16 vols., 1932–67.

GIULIANO, A., *La cultura artistica delle province della Grecia in età romana,* Rome, 1965.

HÖRMANN, H., *Die inneren Propyläen von Eleusis,* Berlin-Leipzig, 1932.

ROBINSON, H. S., "The Tower of the Winds and the Roman market place," in *American Journal of Archaeology,* XLVII, 1943.

THOMPSON, H. A., "The Odeion in the Athenian Agora," in *Hesperia,* XIX, 1950.

TRAVLOS, J., *Bildlexikon zur Topographie des antiken Athen*, Tübingen, 1971.

Asia Minor: Ephesus, Miletus, Pergamon

Altertümer von Pergamon, 11 vols., Berlin, 1912–68.
BOEHRINGER, E., *Pergamon*, in *Neue deutsche Ausgrabungen im Mittelmeergebiet und im Vorderen Orient*, Berlin, 1959.
Forschungen in Ephesos veröffentlicht vom Österreichischen Archäologischen Institut in Wien, 7 vols., 1906–71.
GERKAN, A. von, and KRIESCHEN, F., *Thermen und Palästren* (*Milet*, I, 8), Berlin, 1925.
KEIL, J., *Führer durch Ephesos* (5th ed.), Vienna, 1964.
KLEINER, G., *Die Ruinen von Milet*, Berlin, 1968.
ZIEGENAUS, O., "Die Ausgrabungen zu Pergamon in Asklepieion," in *Archäologischer Anzeiger*, 1970.

Other Sites in Asia Minor

AKURGAL, E., *Ancient Civilizations and Ruins of Turkey*, Istanbul, 1970.
BEAN, G. E., *Aegean Turkey: an Archaeological Guide*, London, 1966.
————, *Turkey's Southern Shore: an Archaeological Guide*, London, 1968.

————, *Turkey beyond the Maeander: an Archaeological Guide*, London, 1971.
KRENCKER, D. M., and SCHEDE, M., *Der Tempel in Ankara*, Berlin-Leipzig, 1936.
LANCKORONSKI, K., *Städte Pamphyliens und Pisidiens*, 2 vols., Vienna, 1892.
MANSEL, A. M., *Die Ruinen von Side*, Berlin, 1963.
NAUMANN, R., and KANTAR, S., "Die Agora von Smyrna," in *Kleinasien und Byzanz* (*Istanbuler-Forschungen*, 17), Berlin, 1950.
ROBINSON, D. M., "A preliminary report on the excavations at Pisidian Antioch and at Sizma," in *American Journal of Archaeology*, XXVIII, 1924.

Syria

Annales Archéologiques de Syrie (since XVI, called *Annales Archéologiques Arabes Syrienne*), I, 1951; in progress.
BUTLER, H. C., *Publication of an American Archaeological Expedition to Syria in 1899–1901*, II: *Architecture and Other Arts*, New York, 1903.
————, *Princeton University Archaeological Expeditions to Syria in 1904–5 and 1909* (parts A and B), Leiden, 1906–20.
KRENCKER, D. M., and ZSCHIETZSCHMANN, W., *Römische Tempel in Syrien*, Berlin, 1938.

Syria, I, 1920; in progress.
WARD-PERKINS, J. B., "The Roman West and the Parthian East," in *Proceedings of the British Academy*, II, 1965.

Baalbek

COLLART, P., and COUPEL, J., *L'Autel monumental de Baalbek*, Beirut, 1951.
WIEGAND, T., ed., *Baalbek*, 2 vols., Berlin-Leipzig, 1921–23.

Other Sites in the East

BROWNING, I., *Petra*, London, 1973.
COUPEL, P., and FREZOULS, E., *Le Théâtre de Philippopolis en Arabie*, Paris, 1956.
The Excavations at Dura-Europos, Preliminary Reports: First Season (1927–28) to Ninth Season (1935–36), New Haven, 1929–52.
KRAELING, C. H., *Gerasa, City of the Decapolis*, New Haven, 1938.
TCHALENKO, G., *Villages antiques de la Syrie du nord*, 3 vols., Paris, 1953.
WIEGAND, T., ed., *Palmyra: Ergebnisse der Expeditionen von 1902 und 1917*, 2 vols., Berlin, 1932.

LIST OF PLATES

LIST OF PHOTOGRAPHIC CREDITS